*Laughing
on the Outside,
Crying
on the Inside*

Laughing on the Outside, Crying on the Inside

The Bittersweet Saga of the Sock-It-to-Me Girl

Judy Carne
with Bob Merrill

Rawson Associates : New York

Library of Congress Cataloging in Publication Data

Carne, Judy.
  Laughing on the outside, crying on the inside.

  1. Carne, Judy. 2. Actors—Great Britain—Biography.
3. Television personalities—United States—Biography.
I. Merrill, Bob, 1958–   . II. Title.
PN2598.C239A35 1985   792'.028'0924 [B]   84-42539
ISBN 0-89256-271-4

Packaged by Rapid Transcript, a division of March Tenth, Inc.
Composition by Folio Graphics Company, Inc.
Manufactured by Fairfield Graphics, Fairfield, Pennsylvania
Designed by Jacques Chazaud
Published simultaneously in Canada by Collier Macmillan Canada, Inc.
Second Printing November 1985

For my dad,
who lives again in the pages of this book.

Contents

Foreword

by Henry Gibson

Perched high upon drenched tufts of straw
The sparrow leaned to sing.
"This storm shall pass," she bravely trilled,
Then slipped and broke her wing.

Now limp and damp and out of breath,
Her wingtip ripped and sore,
This haywire, highwire Ariel
Climbed back. Then fell once more.

In tearful agony she chirped,
"But I exist to fly:
Up there I never feel the pain.
Oh please! Just one more try!"

Yes, the storm passed. Yes, the sun shone.
And once again she flew.
A bruised bird's song has sweeter notes
Than other sparrows' do.

Acknowledgments

I give my heartfelt thanks to Lois and Henry Gibson for being one of the few certainties in my life; to Annie Lomax for her friendship and inspiration when I needed it the most; to Mitch Douglas, my literary agent; and to Francesco Scavullo for contributing the beautiful cover photograph.

Thanks to Paul Micou, a wonderful writer and invaluable help to the book, for transcribing my rambling and seemingly endless journals, from which I have included excerpts; to Henry Jaglom for inspiring me to start writing them; and to Suzan Kroul, who stored them in her basement for so many years.

Much gratitude to Billy Barnes, Ruth Buzzi, Bob Crewe, Frank De Sal, Ed Friendly, Dean Goodhill, Frank Halatek, Arte Johnson, Paul Kimm, Lorne Michaels, Richard Malmed, Allan Manings, Stirling Moss, Gary Owens, Philip Pitzer, Barry Took, and Jo Anne Worley for taking time out to reminisce with me.

Still more thanks for their help and guidance to James Brady, John Carmen, Colin Clayson, Jim Collins, Brad Collins, Vic and Kath Hancock, Billy Heller, Minnie Hickman, Janiz Minshew, Lynne Morrison, Maura Moynihan, Susan Mulcahy, Claire O'Connor, Mary Ann Payne, and my manager, Jo Peters.

This book is published with the kind permission of a permissive society.

Judy Carne
Carne Lodge
Northampton, England
April 1985

Laughing
on the Outside,
Crying
on the Inside

1. Caged In

I awoke from a nightmare. It was quiet and dark, and I felt a tightness around my skull. I was in a hospital, and while my night nurse had gone to get a cup of tea, I had fallen asleep. As I slept, it had all come flooding back to me in the form of a nightmare: I remembered the accident.

I needed to tell someone quickly, in case my amnesia returned. I had to explain that it hadn't happened the way Bergmann claimed it had. I could see it all clearly now, where before I only remembered getting into his car and starting off. . . . My memory was a blank from that point on. I had to tell someone the whole story immediately.

When I moved my head I felt pain and heard a terrible scraping sound. When I moved my feet there was a rattling noise. As my eyes adjusted to the darkness, I saw what had happened: During my nightmare I had thrashed about and was now trapped diagonally in my bed. My feet were stuck in the venetian blinds of the window by the bed, and my head—with an antenna-like brace that was screwed into my skull and attached to a body cast—was stuck in the drawer of the bedside table.

I couldn't reach the call button for my nurse, or even the light switch, so I felt around for the *0* on the telephone, and dialed it.

"Hello, operator? This is going to sound strange, but . . . my name is Judy Carne, and I'm here in the hospital, and—"

"Oh, honey, I *heard*! What a horror story! Are you *okay*?"

Even in my predicament I couldn't help but smile.

"Actually, no. You see, I'm sort of . . . *stuck* here. If you'd kindly call the hospital back and tell them I need help getting *unstuck,* I'd be extremely grateful. It's rather an emergency."

"Aw, sure, honey. You just sit tight."

Moments later the nurse rushed into my room and untangled me. Seeing that I was near hysteria, she called the doctor, who quickly arrived to give me a shot. I begged him to wait, terrified that if they put me under, I might forget again.

The only account of the accident had been supplied by my ex-husband, Robert Bergmann. He'd been driving, and was uninjured. I had a broken neck.

He told the police and the doctors that I'd grabbed at the steering wheel, forcing our car off the road and down an embankment. In my vulnerable condition he even had me believing that we were *still* married. He claimed that no divorce papers existed in Los Angeles, and that we were married in the eyes of the law. As a result the authorities were treating him as next-of-kin, and not doubting his version of the accident.

But now I remembered everything very clearly, so before allowing the doctor to give me that shot, I told him *exactly* what I remembered.

It happened only six days after I was acquitted in Cincinnati. That was the reason we went to Bucks County, Pennsylvania: to relax after that horrific trial, in a little cottage hidden away in the country, belonging to Bergmann's mother. We stopped for dinner at a nearby restaurant to celebrate the verdict.

During the meal I noticed Bergmann's speech seemed slurred. I began to worry if he'd be able to make the drive to the cottage, even though it was only a few miles away.

After finishing dinner at about 9:30 P.M., we went out to the car and I listened to him rant and rave about how he was perfectly capable of driving. I'd only had some wine with dinner, so I pleaded with him to let me drive. He wouldn't hear of it and told me to get in the car or he'd leave without me. I said a prayer, got in the car, and off we went.

He started driving erratically—quickly accelerating, swerving from side to side, then braking suddenly. It was like a scene from a bad suspense thriller: dark, winding roads, driver out of control, scared female passenger trying to step on the brakes.

Whenever I went for the wheel, a slap across the face sent me slamming into the passenger door. This fighting, speeding, and swerving went on for a couple of miles on the narrow country road. When he had accelerated to a particularly dangerous speed on a straightaway, I tried for the brakes one last time, but again he knocked me back. I looked up through the windshield and saw a turn coming. It was a sharp bend, and I knew we weren't going to make it—we were going much too fast.

I considered opening my door and jumping for it, but in that split second it seemed safer to simply hang on through what was certain to be at least a bad spin.

Bergmann tried to brake, but it was too late. We skidded, crashed through the guardrail, and plunged down the steep hill. He was thrown clear from the car and out of danger. I was alone in a tumbling automobile, heading down toward the trees.

I curled up into a ball as the car plummeted. It wrapped around a telephone pole at the bottom, and I was propelled with my head between my knees, smashing into the windshield with the base of my neck.

I was in and out of consciousness for the longest time. When I touched my head, I felt broken glass caught in my hair. I remember the wail of machinery and the sound of a blowtorch. I could hear voices discussing what was wrong with me, and soon found myself in the ambulance on the "rack"—named after the famous medieval torture device—with clamps on my skull attached to sandbags, keeping my neck stretched to prevent further injury. There were needles and tubes in almost every available orifice, and I could see Bergmann hovering around, uninjured, fading in and out of my vision.

Photographers were already on the scene for my arrival at the hospital. Sensing the commotion, I begged the paramedics who had just saved my life to please cover me with a sheet as they took me on the stretcher from the ambulance into the emergency ward. This resulted in a rather macabre picture in the next day's newspapers of what appeared to be a corpse being delivered to the morgue, with the caption "Judy Carne being admitted after crash. . . ."

I struggled to hear the mumbling voices as they took me into intensive care. "It's bad, Doctor, she's broken her neck. . . ."

Upon hearing this, I felt an adrenal surge. I opened my eyes.

"I guess this is the *ultimate* 'Sock it to me,'" I said with a weak smile, as the doctors looked at me in amazement.

But it was not a laughing matter. When I asked them to tell me what my chances were, they were evasive and tried to be as reassuring as possible. But I insisted on knowing the truth.

"Please, I can take it," I begged them. "I *need* to know."

After they'd stabilized me in the intensive care unit, a doctor spoke up. "Well, Judy, in these cases the survival rate is about fifty/fifty." He explained that my chances of walking again were uncertain, because I had broken my C-2 vertebra, the one that snaps when people are hanged. They said it was a miracle that I survived at all.

Once I knew this, I felt I had a choice between life and death. It was the turning point, the key to my recovery. I refused to give in, and mined the depths of my willpower.

As I struggled for life, meaningful faces and moments from my past flashed before my eyes. One face stood out—for some reason I felt I had to hear from my first husband. Each day I asked the nurses the same question: "Has there been any word from Burt Reynolds?"

"Not yet, Miss Carne," they answered cheerfully, "but there have been hundreds of letters from all over the world."

Every twenty minutes the nurses had to check for signs of creeping paralysis; they stuck pins in me to test for numbness. Each time I was grateful to feel the pain of those pins.

"Identify this object," a nurse would say, brushing a handkerchief or a feather on my leg. "Hold this object and tell us what it is," was another way of checking for paralysis. Each time, I was able to tell them exactly what it was.

After these encouraging signs, the doctors put me into a "halo": a contraption of steel rods, attached to a plaster body cast, that rose up and literally *screwed* into my skull to align my neck and my hips. I would remain a prisoner in this stainless steel cage for months, looking like the Bride of Frankenstein.

Caged In

I had broken my neck near one of the best orthopedic hospitals in the United States—Temple University Hospital in Philadelphia. Because the paramedics handled me with such delicate care, I am alive and walking today.

That is how I found myself: waking from the dream that brought back my memory of the accident, my life barely saved and my career ruined unless yet another miracle permitted a full recovery.

Believing he was my husband, the doctors had told Bergmann to notify my parents at their home in Northampton, England. He never did. My mum and dad heard about the accident from my cousin, who rushed into their fruit and vegetable shop with the news.

"I don't know if there are *two* Judy Carnes," she told my dad, "but I just heard on the news that she's had an accident in America."

My dad raced home and started placing calls to both the British and U.S. embassies. He reached the head of the neurosurgery department at Temple University Hospital, Dr. William Buchheit, who told him what had happened and assured him I was in good hands. He said there was no sense flying in from England while I was heavily sedated and in intensive care, so my father organized his business affairs and arrived a few days later.

I wept for joy when I saw my dad there to rescue me. His first move was to clear up the whole divorce matter, assuring everyone—including *me*—that my divorce from Bergmann six years earlier was perfectly legal. When Dr. Buchheit heard this, he barred Bergmann from the hospital.

With my dad around, some stability returned to my life. I could forget about Bergmann and know that someone I loved and trusted would take care of me. I counted my blessings: I hadn't been killed in the car crash, and I hadn't been paralyzed.

After only one week I was taking a few halting steps by myself—progress the doctors never dreamed I would make so rapidly. I felt in control of my recovery, determined to overcome my injury. It was clear that the best thing for me was to return to England, to recover at home with my parents in a truly secure environment.

A press conference was held on the day of my release, in a room crowded with camera crews and reporters from all over the country. Dr. Buchheit walked in abruptly to make a statement: "I've read

7

some erroneous reports in the newspapers which I think should be clarified. When Miss Carne was admitted into my care after the crash, there were no traces of drugs or alcohol in her body."

My eyes teared up. Thank God someone had set the record straight.

I was taken to the airport and carefully seated in the Concorde for my flight home. As we arrived at Heathrow Airport, the English press were there in full force, and the newspapers ran pictures of me in my halo, with headlines proclaiming BRAVE JUDY RETURNS HOME AFTER ACCIDENT. I felt the warmth and support of the entire country. It was a wonderful feeling to have the love and security of my family—a supportive structure I'd never known in the seventeen years I lived in America.

Caged in by my steel halo for almost five months, I tried to come up with some answers to the nagging questions I had avoided for so long. How did I get to such a low point after such success? What turned my confidence into desperation and self-destruction? Why did I feel like a clown, laughing on the outside, crying on the inside?

2. Joyce

Northamptonshire is an English county in the Midlands north of London that consists of rural farmland, much of it belonging to the current Royal Father-in-Law, Earl Spencer. Within it lies Northampton, primarily a shoe manufacturing town, with a brewery to boot. It was there that my grandfather opened his fruit and vegetable shop at the turn of the century, Frank Botterill and Sons.

The younger of his two sons was Harold, my father, who proudly bought the business from the old man in 1938 and celebrated his independence by marrying my mother, Kathleen Campbell. His freedom was short-lived, however, because four months after my entrance into the world as Joyce Botterill on April 27, 1939, Great Britain was at war with Hitler's Germany. My dad was sent to fight for our country, and my mum went to work at a ball-bearing factory. They put their flourishing business back in the care of my grandfather, and their newborn daughter in the care of my grandmother.

The fruit and vegetable business had brought my grandfather considerable wealth, causing my grandmother—"Nan" to me—to become quite extravagant. She was fond of pouring champagne into her tub for decidedly decadent bubble baths. She took me to my first dance lesson when I was three years old. Lessons were a privilege during the war years, but since my aunt ran a dance school, it was easily arranged.

Nan was an expert seamstress. She loved to spoil me with pretty clothes she'd made, especially dance costumes. This, too, was a privilege, because cloth was hard to come by during the war. I'd stare up at her in wonderment as she worked the pedals of her sewing machine, pleading, "Please, Nan, give me lots of petticoats so that when I turn, they'll all swing 'round!"

Nan did a great job of shielding me from much of the war's terror. The German Luftwaffe often raided military targets in the provinces, such as the munitions factory in Northampton, where my mother worked. Whenever an air-raid warning sounded, we were supposed to go to the shelters, but Nan refused, insisting that they weren't going to bomb *her* house. Instead, we gathered under the staircase and I sang and practiced my tap dancing while she played the piano. Blackouts were imposed during the air raids to confuse the German pilots, so we covered our windows with black shades and burned a small candle on the piano. To me it was *fun,* but then I barely knew there was a war on. When I saw the burned-out houses the day after a bombing, my nan told me they were tearing them down on purpose.

"They're probably putting up some ghastly new buildin', Joyce," she said. "It's a disgrace what they're doin' to the neighborhood!"

The schools were very crowded during the war, and Nan knew that I wouldn't be missed if she kept me with her for the day. It was her way of keeping me apart from what she called the "riff-raff," so I spent most of my time with adults. Nan told me I didn't have anything in common with other children, and as an only child I had every reason to believe her.

I saw my dad infrequently during the first six years of my life. He was a sergeant in the army, a member of an ambulance corps that brought the injured back from the front. He was a loyal soldier who always held on to the wallet of a fellow soldier who had been killed, making sure it safely reached the man's family in England.

My uncle Stan first met my mother working in the town bakery, and often took her on double dates with my dad and his then-fiancée, a hoity-toity girl refined enough to gain my nan's approval.

Kathleen, however, was fun and down to earth, half Maltese and possessing Latin good looks. She was passionate and emotional, yet respectful and chaste—a good Catholic girl. She captured my dad's fancy, so when he later discovered his fiancée in bed with another bloke one day, that was the end of that: Kath was the new object of his affection.

Nan, somewhat of a snob, naturally thought she wasn't good enough for her son, but my father cared more about true love than he did about her dowry, and they were married a few months later.

Mum was an avid moviegoer. She took me to my very first film—*The Snake Pit,* starring Olivia de Havilland as a woman struggling with the torment of life in an insane asylum. I thought it was just great.

I was fascinated by my mum's lovely singing voice and I copied her as we sang along with the radio. She knew an endless number of songs and I learned every one she taught me by heart, building up confidence in my own voice, as well as an impressive repertoire.

When I was six years old, I begged Dad to let me perform at a town concert in Northampton. I got up on the stage in an outfit my nan had made, petticoats and all, and sang "Maybe It's Because I'm a Londoner," adding a few dance steps I'd learned. The crowd loved this Cockney Shirley Temple, and my dad beamed with pride. From that moment on he was my biggest fan, believing in me completely, giving me support, confidence, and inspiration. "Joyce, there's nothing you can't do—no role you can't play, no song you can't sing, and no dance you can't dance—if you're willin' to *work* for it."

After the war my mother's work at the ball-bearing factory ended and my father returned with the rest of Britain's soldiers. Settling down into civilian life, he faced the task of rebuilding his fruit business, and my mum became an integral part of that process, as manageress. I pitched in by helping out whenever possible—a wonderfully grown-up thing to do, I thought. My nan saw it in a different light.

"What the bloddy 'ell 'ave you got her workin' behind the counter for?" she protested when she saw me in the shop. "You don't want people thinkin' you got your bleedin' daughter *workin'* for you!"

Nan preferred to take me along to cocktail parties where the rich ladies in fox furs, pearls, and veiled hats played cards while I learned the proper etiquette for serving tea.

Despite Nan's objections, I continued to help out, especially on the Saturday open markets in Northampton town square. While my mother minded the store, my father and his assistants operated a fruit stall in the square, sending their lorry back and forth for supplies. Business was brisk all day, so Dad put me to work.

"All right, pull your whack, Joyce," he'd tell me. "You've got to learn somethin' about arithmetic." He promised me a small percentage of the day's gross, which I eagerly calculated and presented for his approval at the end of the day.

Being under four feet tall, I stood on an apple crate to serve the customers, and loved barking out the various sales pitches.

"Roll up! Roll up! Tuppence a pound apples! Tuppence a pound apples! Got a loverly bunch of 'em!" I shouted, imitating the rhythms of the vendors. I dressed like them, wearing a smock my mum altered and a pearl-button cap. I resembled an urchin from a Dickens novel—a true Cockney "born within the sound of Bow Bells."

My uncle Ron had his own fruit stall nearby. He worked only three days a week, preferring to play the horses on his days off. He could afford to sell his fruit for less since he didn't have the overhead of a shop, like my dad, who supplied him.

"Cheapest on the market!" was my uncle Ron's pitch. A crowd was always gathered around his stall, because he had the biggest mouth on the market. People bought their fruit from him just to get insulted and have a laugh. "No use feelin' up those cucumbers, miss, they won't get any harder!" he'd crack, getting a rise out of the crowd and attracting even more customers.

The open market had a wonderful carnival-like atmosphere. I loved to wander around the square, visiting friends of my dad's and performing for them whenever possible.

"How are ya doin' in school, then, Joyce?" they'd ask.

"Oh, very well, thank you. Would you like to 'ear me do my song?" Before they could say no, I'd burst into "On the Sunny Side of the Street," tap dancing my heart out on the cobblestones. I took these opportunities to practice my routines because it was no fun doing them alone. When favorable reports reached my dad about these small performances, it filled him with pride.

After I had spent a few years at my aunt's modest dancing school, my parents decided I was ready to attend the best dance school in

12

Joyce

Northampton—the Pitt-Draffen Academy of Dance. I worshipped Denise Pitt-Draffen, a graceful woman in her mid-thirties to whom I went for training each day after school.

Life went on in this way: school in the mornings, dance lessons in the afternoons, and Saturdays spent helping out at the bustling open market. My father's business flourished again as life in England slowly returned to normal after the war. One summer afternoon my dad proudly drove home in a beautiful burgundy 1948 Jaguar, a symbol of his financial recovery.

Shortly after my ninth birthday, Denise Pitt-Draffen called my father in for a little chat about my progress.

"Mr. Botterill, your daughter has learned everything we have to teach her. We feel that she deserves to have a more intense kind of professional training. My suggestion is a theatrical boarding school. Now, I know you may not want to be apart from Joyce, but it may be the best thing for her. . . ."

She recommended the Bush-Davies Theatrical School for Girls in East Grinstead, Sussex, forty miles south of London. In the days before motorways, it was a four-hour drive from Northampton—a major expedition for most English people, who think a day's car ride could only result in falling off the edge of the earth.

Nevertheless we made the trip, and I sat anxiously in the back seat of my dad's Jag, wearing my best Sunday dress. The winding Sussex road through the forest was eerie and magical. As we entered the front gate of the school, a gap in a seemingly endless stone wall through the woods, I peered through the car window at a large, austere Gothic house crowned with turrets and surrounded by enormous, ancient trees. This was Charters Towers, its name emblazoned on a carved wooden crest above the huge oak doors to the building.

We were greeted by a staff member and ushered into the front hall with its beautifully polished parquet floor and high ceiling. Portraits of Margot Fonteyn and Alicia Markova adorned the walls, and we climbed a majestic staircase that led to the headmistress's office and living quarters.

Her office overflowed with dance memorabilia. There were photographs, paintings, and etchings, all of them dominated by the centerpiece of the collection—a beautiful bronze statue of perfect ballet feet on pointe.

A short, powerful-looking woman entered and sat down behind her desk, her stern demeanor immediately evident as she glared at me during the introductions. This was Noreen Bush—owner, head-mistress, and principal ballet instructor of the school.

I was seated near her desk, mesmerized by the perfection of the bronze ballet feet. "Do you like that statue, Joyce?" she asked me, noticing my wonderment. "That is your *name,* isn't it? Joyce?"

"Yes, madam," I said, snapping to attention.

"Would you like to be able to do that?"

"Yes I would, madam."

"Well then, walk over there, face my desk, stand in first position, and point your foot as hard as you can."

I did as she said and arched my foot in imitation of the statue. She gasped and half stood to get a better look. It was as though she had waited all her life to have a young girl walk into her office and point her foot in just this way.

"Victor? Victor! Come in here and look at this child's feet!" she shouted excitedly. "Bring the others!"

Miss Bush came around from behind the desk as her husband, Victor, entered with assorted staff members behind him. She gestured at my still-pointed foot. "Do you *see* that?" she said. "Do you *see?*"

"Try an arabesque," she ordered. I gently raised my arms and leg into position, but she was still in awe of my feet. The high arch needed for an aesthetic toe point is something only nature can provide, and Miss Bush saw her chance to develop a promising ballerina.

"What is it you want to do?" she asked me.

"I want to be a ballerina," I said proudly.

"*Just* a ballerina?"

"Well, I love singin' and dancin' too. . . ."

Noreen Bush had by now noticed my strong Midlands accent, not quite Cockney but similar in that I swallowed my *H*'s, sounding decidedly "lower class."

"Do you know what an *H* is, Joyce?" she asked me.

"A letter of the alphabet?"

"That's right, now can you *say* one?"

"Aytch."

"Correct. Now repeat after me: 'Oh, Horace, aren't you horrid.'"

"Oh, 'orace, aren't you 'orrid," I said meekly.

"But where is the *H,* my dear girl? We're going to have to speak properly, aren't we now?" she said, turning to address my parents, who sat staring in disbelief at this humiliating interrogation.

"Well, Mr. and Mrs. Botterill, I think your daughter has the potential to flourish here at Bush-Davies. If you so desire, she may enroll for the forthcoming school year."

Dad thanked her, but said we'd think about it and let her know our decision. Everything had happened so quickly; we left her office dazed.

Bush-Davies seemed like an exciting place. I wanted to go there more than anything, but first there were some things to be considered.

It was expensive—twenty-five pounds a week, which was a lot of money in 1948. My parents would have to make many sacrifices. They also had mixed feelings about sending me away; my mother was in tears at the thought. "But 'arold," she sobbed, "she's our only *one.*"

"We gotta think what's best for 'er, Kath," my dad consoled her.

I kept imagining those bronze feet on Noreen Bush's desk and the beautiful Sussex countryside. By the time we reached Northampton, it was settled—I would start Bush-Davies in the fall.

My mother was still upset by Noreen correcting my accent so harshly, but my dad saw the other side of the coin: "Where she's goin', Kath, she'll *need* a proper accent!"

Mum and Dad gave up a lot to put me through Bush-Davies. They did without a staff at the shop and worked the long hours themselves. Their six-day work week included trips to Covent Garden every Tuesday and Thursday morning at 4:30 A.M. to bring fresh fruit back in time for the shop's opening. In the evenings my dad did his bookkeeping, plus the books for other small businesses to earn extra money.

When the autumn of 1948 arrived, I was brimming with excitement about the adventure ahead, and made the long journey to Sussex, this time to stay.

Bush-Davies was like a convent; we were the nuns and our god was Art. Our unspoken vow was to work hard and devote ourselves to all aspects of the theater, accepting the isolation from our families. East Grinstead, near the south coast of England, was a peaceful place where the seventy-five Bush-Davies girls, from ages eight to sixteen, could be assured of few distractions from the task at hand.

I was miserable during my first term because it was hard for me to make friends with the other girls. Many of my schoolmates were well-bred doctors' and lawyers' daughters who were there to be turned into "ladies" before being put up for marriage. I was the only one whose parents had to struggle to pay the tuition.

My accent compounded the problem. The other girls taunted me about my lower-class *H*'s so much that I tried to change my accent to sound like them. In my zeal, I put *H*'s in all the wrong places, making the girls laugh harder and embarrassing myself even more.

It was all so confusing; my nan had instilled in me the belief that I was better than other girls, yet the girls at Bush-Davies made me feel inferior to *them,* boasting about their horses and the many presents their mummies and daddies bought them.

The older girls had elaborate initiation rituals for the new arrivals. The most traumatic involved getting tied to a tree during dinner and sworn to one's honor not to divulge the real reason for missing the meal. If the victim dared reveal the truth of her absence, she was likely to find spiders in her bed or her ballet shoes slashed by a razor.

I became the frequent target of cruel and humiliating pranks, such as being locked out of Charters Towers in the rain. I was left, soaking wet and petrified, the sound of my screams and pounding on the door drowned out by the driving rain.

Not surprisingly, I tried to run away twice during those early days at Bush-Davies. The first time I was missed immediately, and the matron retrieved me as I waited, penniless, at the train station.

Determined to make it to London, I brought more money on the second occasion and actually boarded the train. I could only afford a ticket to the neighboring town, however, and when I got off there, the sight of a small girl in full school uniform alerted the authorities. After only minutes of freedom I was on my way back to face the wrath of Miss Bush.

Noreen Bush was from the Russian school of ballet instructors, demanding perfection at all costs. She was five feet tall, with a long nose and straight black hair tied back in a bun. She had long, bright-red fingernails, and was never without her cane, which she used to tap out the beats as we danced. She chain-smoked, inhaling long drags of her cigarette and letting the smoke seep out of her nostrils and mouth as she counted out loud during our practice.

Her very presence made us gulp with fear. We gathered outside the room for our classes, trembling at the sound of her footsteps coming down the long staircase.

We feared Miss Bush's harsh methods of punishment. One step out of place and we'd feel the familiar sting of her cane against our feet, one arm in the wrong position and we'd feel the painful grip of her sharp red fingernails digging into our skin. As a promising student much was demanded of me, and I received harsher treatment than the other girls. My feet and ankles were always bound to cover the marks and heal the blisters on my toes.

The scene was something out of *Jane Eyre,* but that was simply the way in which one of the most well-respected theatrical schools in England was run.

From my initial interview as a skinny little girl with bright brown eyes, a wide smile, and natural ballet feet, Noreen Bush took a special interest in me and insisted on calling me "Judy"—explaining that "Joyce" didn't suit me.

We developed a profound love/hate relationship. She was obsessed with developing my talent and potential, but determined to break my stubborn and precocious nature. She wouldn't tolerate back talk, least of all from the student she thought most likely to succeed.

"Everyone gather round and watch this," she'd call out to the girls if I had done something correctly. She rarely complimented me to my face. After I demonstrated for the others, she simply said, "*This* you can do well—but everything *else* needs a lot of work."

I gradually realized that her toughness was somehow necessary if I was to succeed. When I was ten years old she had me on ballet pointe, two years before the age when that is considered healthy for a young girl's feet. I wore bandages for extra support.

My parents were allowed to visit me four times a year. On the first of those occasions they were worried when they saw my feet.

"Come on, Joyce, what are those bandages, then?" Mum asked.

I tried to explain that it was all part of ballet training to have your legs bound, but my mother didn't believe me, and unwrapped them to see for herself. She nearly fainted at the sight of my blistered feet and bruised ankles. I admitted to her that the marks were from Noreen Bush's cane during ballet class.

My parents stormed into her office and demanded an explanation. Were they paying twenty-five pounds a week to have their only child beaten every day? I sat outside her office while they talked with Miss Bush, expecting to hear shouting and maybe find myself on my way back home, but to my surprise the three of them emerged smiling and chatting amicably. My parents later told me what Miss Bush had said.

"Mr. and Mrs. Botterill, you have an extremely talented daughter, *but* . . . she's very stubborn. She has to be broken. I'm trying my best to do what you are paying me to do, to turn her into the best performer and dancer she can be. If you question my methods or motives in this matter, I suggest that this isn't the right school for your child." This made sense to my parents. They wanted me to get the best training available.

"I know that as her parents you are upset by seeing her sore toes, but it's not possible to dance on one's toes every day without getting them—it is how the feet become tough. Where you see sores, I see toes that will one day be perfect for ballet. You must trust me to do this the best way I know."

My parents came out of that meeting saying, "What's a little caning? We've got to think of her future. The woman knows what she's doing." And so I stayed.

Although I idolized Margot Fonteyn and wanted to be like Moira Shearer in *The Red Shoes,* I soon realized that I didn't want to be *just* a ballerina. Tap dancing, singing, and acting had also captured my imagination. As my personality grew, I trained for other types of performance at Bush-Davies while maintaining the fundamental discipline of ballet.

Our daily schedule was grueling. We woke up, ate breakfast, and spent the morning in our academic classes—arithmetic, English, history, and other basics. The afternoon was devoted to our theatrical training, which consisted of ballet, tap, and modern dance, followed by piano, singing, and acting lessons.

In academics I was virtually useless, but my teachers were understanding. They had to be, because I was always being yanked out of classes early to participate in the various productions, which we rehearsed and performed every few months in Charters Towers Hall.

We were required to attend church twice every Sunday, at 8 A.M. and 12 noon. We walked the mile to East Grinstead in our gray and burgundy school uniforms, with skirts, knee socks, blazers, and boater hats, and with our school badge prominently displayed.

On one of those Sundays my rebellious nature reared its mischievous head. I tagged along at the back of the line and bolted for freedom when the matron wasn't looking, gleefully removing my tie and hat for a wonderful walk through the countryside.

The matron discovered my absence upon counting heads at the church, so when I returned, Miss Bush was waiting for me, one hand on her hip and the other holding her cane, poised for punishment. In addition to caning, I was stripped of all privileges, including the right to eat with the rest of the girls. For one week I had to wait at mealtimes in my room until the rest of the girls were fed; only then was I allowed to get my plate and eat alone in silence, humiliated in front of the entire school.

On my first holiday home, my parents noticed that my speech was starting to sound "upper crust," like the other girls.

"Mummy, my hair looks horrid," I said, leaning on my *H*'s.

"Well, get *you*!" my mum said, nudging my dad.

"Ya see, Kath? The school's payin' off!"

When I visited Denise Pitt-Draffen, she was pleased to see the progress I'd made. I practiced at her studio, and at her suggestion I entered the All-England Dance Competitions which were held at King George's Hall, on Tottenham Court Road in London.

Three of us represented the Pitt-Draffen Academy in these contests, as opposed to the forty or fifty girls sent from larger schools in other regions. To Miss Pitt-Draffen's delight all three of us were successful. I placed first in the song and dance category for two consecutive years, 1949 and 1950.

During the summer of 1950 my dad bought the first TV set in the town of Northampton, an event that made the local papers. We all sat around excitedly, as the first program came on at eight o'clock.

"Someday you'll be on that box, Joyce," he said, pointing at the tiny black-and-white image flickering in its huge wooden casing.

* * *

Isolated as we were at Bush-Davies, I developed close, intense feelings for other girls. We shared everything, even our baths to conserve water. In the middle of the night we crawled into bed with one another, muffling our giggles and cuddling until we fell asleep.

I had a crush on Jane Taylor, an older girl who was beautiful, talented, and fun to be with, all the things I longed to be. I spent my pocket money on gifts for her and kept her picture under my pillow. I'm sure I would have been as passionate anywhere else, but at boarding school we couldn't go home each night for love and affection. We only had each other to turn to.

Boys were strictly forbidden under any circumstances, even on Saturday afternoons in the village. If anyone was caught even talking to them, the strictest punishment was applied. Being somewhat of a ringleader, I was determined to find a way around this most frustrating of all rules. I didn't have to look far.

Noreen Bush had a son named Paul. He was in college when I was in my early teens, and on his visits home he was quite a celebrity. He was, after all, the only male specimen we ever saw.

I had just turned fourteen before one of his visits, and I made a point of attracting his attention one day when I saw him on the grounds. I contrived a way to bump into him, talk to him, and make him laugh. Eventually I asked him to show me his cottage.

"If I snuck out at night, Paul, could I come and see you . . . here?"

"Well, all right, but only if you are very careful."

He was as terrified of his mother as I was, so our first rendezvous required careful planning. At night the prefects went around making sure the windows were closed and everything and everybody were in their proper places. I stuffed a pillow in my bed to replace my body and my friend Jeanette Bishop distracted the prefect with a question of some sort. This was my cue to make a dash for the window before they locked it. I scampered across the lawn down the path toward Paul's cottage, wrapped in layer upon layer of clothing over a bra stuffed with tissues.

I was convinced I would be executed if caught. It was bad enough sneaking out at night to see a boy, but of all boys, this was Noreen Bush's own son. Though she considered me destined for stardom, that didn't mean I could have a moonlight escapade with *her* son.

Joyce

I tapped on Paul's window, trembling. When he saw my face pressed against the glass, he quietly let me in. Soft classical music purred in the background, and there I sat with my fair-haired hero.

The danger of the situation contributed to my excitement, but I was disappointed to see him cringing in fear when I moved closer to him on the divan. I was determined to make the first move if necessary, but when I'd practically pressed my body against his, he slithered away from me onto the floor, nervously trying to keep the conversation going. I had visualized a sophisticated, romantic scene from the movies—the cigarette holder, the silk ascot, the champagne and caviar, the deep stirring kisses—but this fantasy was dispelled as I watched my knight in shining armor cowering on the floor.

I put my hand on his shoulder and he froze. I had a good grip on him, though, and after executing several awkward and ill-timed kisses, he could bear no more and pushed me away to catch his breath. I realized then that I'd risked expulsion for nothing, that my midnight tryst had failed miserably.

"I've got to go now, Paul," I announced, deciding to forgo the good-night kiss. I turned and sped out the door.

Darting back across the lawn toward Charters Towers, I started to invent the story I would tell the other girls, knowing that they lay anxiously in their beds, waiting to hear the intimate details of my daring romantic adventure. I would tell of the champagne, the candlelight, the low music, the advances I fended off with all my might before finally giving in. . . .

Unfortunately, one of the older girls—a prefect—had seen me running across the lawn from her window. Upon waking the next morning, I was bluntly told by the matron to report immediately to Miss Bush's office, where she solemnly confronted me with the prefect's testimony. Once again I was stripped of all privileges.

This punishment could not have been more ill-timed, as my parents were due for a visit the following weekend. Miss Bush informed me that I would not be allowed to see them.

I was confined to an attic with a direct view of the driveway, and I sobbed uncontrollably when my folks arrived. They were greeted by Miss Bush, who informed them that their daughter was being disciplined and therefore unavailable for visitation.

"But we've come all this way to see her," my mum pleaded.

"I am sorry about that, Mrs. Botterill," she said firmly, "but your daughter has been caught sneaking out at night, and she must be punished. I'm sure you understand the seriousness of this offense."

Mum only understood that the long drive had been for nothing, but Dad, with his army training, saw the sense in this treatment and gave Miss Bush his vote of confidence.

I watched from the window as they got back in their car. "Mum, Dad, please, don't leave me!" I cried out to them in vain, inaudible from the Charters Towers attic. As their car drove away, my screams turned into sobs, and I sat there, devastated and heartbroken.

After this experience I vowed never to suffer such trauma again, and tried to become a model student: My bed was made with hospital corners, my clothes were perfectly folded, and my language was always ladylike. I never again so much as considered disobeying Miss Bush or the matron, and my visit to Paul was the last time I consciously ventured into the night. Unconsciously, however, my nocturnal activities increased: I started to wander around in my sleep.

On the night before a big dance exam at the London Academy of Music and Dramatic Arts, I was found doing my ballet exercises while fast asleep. I clearly remember waking up with my foot on the railing overlooking the great hall, regaining consciousness only to see Noreen Bush's eyes glaring down at me. I screamed, expecting to be slapped, but instead she displayed rare understanding and gently put me back to bed.

Miss Bush did not want her prize pupil dissipating her energy pirouetting through the night, so she decided that I needed sleep medication. Each night before lights out, I reported to the matron for my tablespoon.

There were other abnormalities about my physical development: Unlike the other girls, I wasn't making much progress toward womanhood. At fifteen my breasts resembled bee stings, and there was no sign of my period. All my friends had already had theirs, so I thought perhaps it had something to do with class distinction, a product of their breeding—maybe greengrocers' daughters had to wait until last.

When I turned sixteen, Miss Bush began to orchestrate my formal entrance into the world of professional theater. I was ready to go to auditions in London. She helped me assemble a resumé and placed me with a noted theatrical agent. This was one of the benefits of attending a theatrical school with a fine reputation.

There was one matter that had to be settled—"Joyce Botterill" was not a very practical stage name. On one of my parents' visits, Miss Bush asked to see the three of us in her office.

"Now that your daughter is embarking on her career, Mr. and Mrs. Botterill, we have to discuss what her professional name should be."

"What's wrong with 'Joyce Botterill'?" my dad asked defensively.

"I don't see her as a 'Joyce.' It's too harsh. I've always called her 'Judy,' and 'Botterill' is not quite right for the theater. It's hard to pronounce and doesn't fit well on the marquee. We'll have to do some thinking and come up with a simpler surname, preferably four or five letters."

Noreen left us to ponder the question, but my father's only comment was, "It's been a perfectly good name for *me* all my life, Joyce—but it's up to you."

Some weeks later we presented a play called *Sister Bonaventure.* I played an evil murderess named Sarah Carne. As soon as I saw the name, I thought, would Carne go with Judy? Why not? Judy . . . Carne!

I started writing it out on scraps of paper, in block capitals, in script, and as an autograph. I wrote it on a piece of paper with a fake *Playbill* heading and printed famous names around it. I brought it straight to Miss Bush, who took one look at it and smiled.

"Judy Carne. Right. Just what I asked for. Four and five letters—perfect for the marquee!"

In late February my London agent—a kindly and proper gray-haired lady named Dorothy McAusland—sent me on my first audition in London. It was for a television musical called "The First Day of Spring," to be aired, appropriately enough, on March twenty-first.

Thanks to the preparation provided by Bush-Davies, I went into that first audition with all the confidence in the world. My parents drove me to a theater in London, and when I saw the other girls, I was surprised to see them dressed in their dowdy rehearsal gear. I wore white lace baby-doll pajamas covered with little red hearts, my hair bunched at the sides with bright red ribbons.

As I waited anxiously in the wings with my parents, I could see the stone-faced men who would decide my fate sitting out front, clipboards in hand. Behind the piano sat the composer of the show, Ronnie Cass, playing accompaniment for the girl ahead of me. Suddenly the music stopped, as the girl burst into tears and ran off the stage.

"Why is she crying, Dad?" I asked.

"'Cause she knows *you're* comin' on next—now go on!"

Before they could finish announcing my name, I ran out and placed a prop chair in the center of the stage. My audition number was carefully planned: I sang "My Heart Belongs to Daddy" with modern dance steps, then sat on the chair in mid-song to quick-change into my shiny red tap shoes for the big finish. I bowed and curtsied, acknowledging the imaginary conductor and blowing kisses to the empty balcony.

"Thank you very much, Miss Carne, we'll let you know," the director said.

I ran off into the waiting arms of my parents and asked, "Did I get the part, Dad? Did I get it?"

"They're going to let us know."

"'Let us know'? You mean they're not going to tell me *now*?"

I was ready to go on that very night, if necessary, but the answer didn't come until the following week, when Miss McAusland called to tell me that I'd been chosen for the part.

There was no graduation from Bush-Davies—you left when you were ready, and with my first audition a success, I was given a grand send-off when Mum and Dad collected me for the trip to London.

Stepping into the car I heard cries of "Good luck, Judy!" from above, and I looked over my shoulder to see all the girls leaning from the windows of Charters Towers, waving good-bye.

Noreen Bush stood alone in front of the oak doors, waving along with the others but, as always, standing apart. As we pulled away, I waved back and noticed a look of pride on her face that I'd never seen before. I stared, spellbound, from the back window of the car as she grew smaller and smaller, vanishing from view as we drove through the gates.

3. London

We drove straight into London, to a flat that Miss McAusland had found, where someone would always be on hand to keep an eye on me. It was a one-room bed-sitter on Gloucester Place, owned by a gentle, understanding widow named Mrs. Horsley, whose son John was already an established legitimate actor. Mrs. Horsley loved the theater and was always willing to help young people who were starting their careers.

My parents always made it clear to me that I'd be on my own once my Bush-Davies training was completed, but now that the moment had arrived, they were nervous about leaving me alone in London. Mrs. Horsley served us tea and assured them I would be safe in her care.

My room was right next to Mrs. Horsley's, not lavish, but comfortable. I had a hot plate to cook on, a wash basin if I didn't want to trudge out to the family bathroom, and a gas heater that ran on shillings inserted every couple of hours. I soon learned to keep a pocketful of coins on hand for those chilly March nights in London.

Rehearsals began immediately for "The First Day of Spring." Ronnie Cass, our dry-witted musical director, took me under his wing. Unaware of his reputation as a practical joker, I was convinced there was an Equity rule requiring the youngest member of the cast to make the tea and clean up after the others. I'd struggle in each day with tea for thirty people, thinking this was my duty, at the same time desperately trying to remember my lines.

It was quite some time before I pursued a nightlife of any kind. After rehearsals I'd head straight home to my room, where Mrs. Horsley had preheated my bed with a hot water bottle.

I played the sister of the lead in "The First Day of Spring," with a solo number that gave my parents a thrill when we watched it at home in Northampton. "You see, Joyce," my dad said, "I *said* you'd be on that box." He was so proud, he didn't even mind the credits reading "Judy Carne"—all of Northampton knew it was his daughter.

Ronnie Cass suggested I might be right for an "intimate revue" called *For Amusement Only,* by a brilliant young writer named Peter Myers, with Ronnie composing the music. The intimate revue was a sophisticated form of theater consisting of comedy sketches, singing, and dancing, as well as political satire and parodies of all kinds. This would also be a fabulous opportunity to do a West End show.

Myers and Cass knew I could sing and dance, but they wanted me to read a few lines to see how I handled the sexual double entendres and other material that might have been over my head at sixteen. The reading went well, and they hired me on the spot. Rehearsals began in April, and by May we started tryouts in the provinces.

We stayed in "digs"—the homes of people to whom we paid a small fee. Away from the watchful eye of Mrs. Horsley, I took the opportunity to get rid of my ignorance of sexual matters, since neither my parents nor my teachers at Bush-Davies had clued me in. Each assumed the other had taken care of the matter.

"Oh, don't bother with any of that, Joyce, it's vile," my mother said. "You're better off dancing!" I was sophisticated about certain things, with the attitude of someone who *must* have known all about sex. In fact I knew nothing.

I was infatuated with an older man in the cast, and after two weeks of determined aggression on my part he gave in and consented to relieve me of my innocence. I expected fireworks, trumpets, and earthquakes. What I got was a quick roll in a field, with few words spoken and many tears shed. I thought perhaps I had done something wrong, and was miserably disappointed.

26

London

This unfortunate interlude was all the more upsetting because I had to play opposite the man each night. But the show must go on, and we returned to London for the opening of *For Amusement Only* at the Apollo Theater near Piccadilly Circus.

As if my ill-fated sexual initiation hadn't been confusing enough, I was shocked by the steamy neighborhood through which I walked to work. I was routinely flashed in broad daylight, accosted by street toughs, and fondled on the Underground. Hardly a day would go by without a cry of "'Ello darlin', 'ow much do you cost, then?"

This was the West End, the hub of London's theater world, the place I had spent my life dreaming about. Part of the fantasy lived up to my expectations when *For Amusement Only* opened to rave reviews. We took dozens of curtain calls and I received my first bouquet of flowers. I couldn't have had a more exhilarating start to my career. The critical acclaim assured us a long run, and being involved in a hit show meant getting my name in lights and instant acceptance from people in show business whom I had respected and admired from afar.

A lot of theater people congregated after work at Isow's, a restaurant in Soho. There I was lucky enough to strike up a friendship with Lionel Blair and his sister Joyce.

Lionel was an experienced choreographer and performer, and he became a big brother to me. He gave me the kind of advice a novice needs, from details like how much to tip your dresser to valuable stage hints about riding out laughter and how to handle applause.

"*Never* be caught on stage after the applause has died," I remember him telling me. More than anything, Lionel encouraged me to develop a style of my own.

Joyce Blair was like a sister to me. She was a wonderful mentor who taught me everything from how to dress and make up properly to defending myself against the street life around Piccadilly Circus.

A close friend from Bush-Davies, Jeanette Bishop, got in touch to say she was moving to London to work as a model. She was stunning, with a Grace Kelly look, and certain to succeed in the big city. I was itching to move into a place of my own, so we decided to be roommates.

I promptly found a cozy furnished flat in a recently converted Georgian house in Bryanston Square. We took the basement, which had been the servant's quarters. It was extremely modern by 1956 standards, with an "All-Mod-Con" kitchen (all modern conveniences), a bath *with* a shower (I'd never had one), and a large Murphy bed that we shared. It took the two of us to pull it down out of the wall each night.

For the first time, I was independent, cut off from parents, teachers, and chaperones. On weekends I returned home to my parents in Northampton, but in London, my life took on new dimensions.

I acquired a Yorkshire terrier, named Kilty, who went everywhere with me. I also started to date more often. Still disillusioned from my first sexual encounter, I made sure to end the evenings with nothing more than long and passionate good-night kisses on the old-fashioned love seat in the hall. Then I found out I was pregnant.

When I first missed my period, I panicked and went to Joyce Blair, telling her of my one sexual experience. She said that pregnancy rarely resulted from the first time, but she took me to a distinguished Harley Street doctor, who confirmed the worst: I was two months pregnant.

I was destroyed by this miserable luck, but I had no one to blame more than myself. The physician felt sorry for me and performed the abortion for free. He did it early in the morning, so I'd have time to recover for my evening show. During the operation he was even kind enough to fit me with an IUD, the new, sophisticated method of contraception at that time. I walked out of that office assured of never making the same mistake again.

I threw myself into my work after this unsettling experience, performing with the Lionel Blair dancers whenever it didn't interfere with my *For Amusement Only* schedule. Lionel loved the fact that I could act as well as dance, and hired me for a series of appearances on "The Dave King Show," a popular television variety program. One week I was featured in a song and dance number with a young actor named Roger Moore, years before he gained fame as "The Saint" and 007.

Another guest on the show was a talented young pop singer named Glen Mason, to whom I was instantly attracted. The feeling was mutual, and we began to see a lot of each other—my first steady relationship. I loved hanging around the recording studio and was fascinated by the process of making records.

One of Glen's best friends was another future James Bond, Sean Connery, who was then a struggling Shakespearean actor. Glen and Sean were part of a celebrity soccer team that also included Tommy Steele and Adam Faith. Every Sunday they played matches for charity and afterward gathered at Glen's flat to feast on my shepherd's pie. Sean was most appreciative. "I'm tired of sausages and beer," he'd say. "This is my only home-cooked meal of the week!"

For Amusement Only continued to play to packed houses. It had become *the* show to see in London, and people kept coming back for more, since the sketches and songs were kept up to date with the current social and political trends.

Many in the cast were destined for greatness. Ron Moody later immortalized himself as Fagan in *Oliver!,* and Barry Took went on to become one of Britain's top comedy writers, a guiding force behind the comedy of Marty Feldman and "Monty Python's Flying Circus."

F.A.O. gained enormous popularity with visiting Americans. During a matinee one afternoon, a man sitting in the stalls roared uncontrollably throughout the entire show. He had such a loud and penetrating laugh that we were convinced someone had planted this fellow as a joke, to distract us. Afterward he came backstage and introduced himself. It was Jack Benny.

We all knew him to be one of America's foremost comedians and it was flattering to see him brimming with such enthusiasm about the show. He loved our Shakespearean send-up, "Wherefore Art Thou Juliet?," a brilliant role reversal pitting an effeminate Romeo against a Brunhildesque Juliet. But his favorite sketch was "The Vagabond Student," an uproarious parody of amateur theater groups, in which everyone played parts contrary to their own ages. Thelma Ruby, a large woman in her fifties, played the young princess while I, the youngest in the cast at seventeen years old, played an elderly duchess, complete with an ill-fitting gray wig and heavy wrinkle lines sloppily drawn in with makeup. With Ron Moody as the hilarious young prince traipsing around in tights, the sketch never failed to stop the show. Jack Benny said he wanted to arrange an appearance on "The Ed Sullivan Show" in New York City.

That appearance never came about, but Jack Benny spread the word, and a steady stream of American show biz folk came in to see the show. I recall wonderful backstage visits by the movie mogul Sam Goldwyn, an impeccably handsome Tyrone Power, and Van Johnson, who was then charming all of London in *The Music Man.*

In the summer of 1958 my roommate Jeanette moved out of Bryanston Square to live with her boyfriend, but I'd met another actress my age named Janet Rowsell, who was looking for a roommate.

Janet and I had a lot in common: She was pixieish, exactly my height, and had a well-developed sense of humor. We got along famously and even made our film debut together in a musical called *Jazzboat.* The movie was filmed entirely on a cruise ship, and I appeared as a Lionel Blair dancer, while Janet had a small speaking part. Starring in the picture were Lionel Jeffries, Joyce Blair, Roy Castle (the world's fastest tap dancer at 1440 taps per minute), and a talented young man named Anthony Newley, who had written some of the songs.

We often set sail for days at a time, so the girls had to double up in some of the bunk rooms. One night Tony Newley turned up in our cabin, dressed in full admiral's uniform and demanding to see our passports. It was all great fun, and since we weren't on English soil, we didn't miss an opportunity to raise hell, blaring our swinging prerecorded soundtrack through the ship's speakers all day and all night.

I got to know Tony quite well during the filming of *Jazzboat.* He had just been through a divorce and was under contract as an actor to film producer Cubby Broccoli (who'd just obtained the movie rights for an Ian Fleming spy thriller, *Dr. No*). Tony's pet project at the time was a musical he was writing, with an unusual title: *Stop the World, I Want to Get Off.* "I'm writing it about myself," he told me. "One of the songs is 'What Kind of Fool Am I?,' 'cause that's exactly what I am!"

He often sang little bits of the songs from his show at gatherings, to get people's reactions, sometimes even playing us a tape that he'd made with his collaborator, Leslie Bricusse.

We began to see a lot of each other after *Jazzboat.* His flat in London had a special cleaning lady who came every day: his mother.

"Leave the door open a bit," he said when we were in his bedroom.

"But your mother's in the other room—she'll hear us."

"I know, it's more exciting this way!"

His devilish sense of humor was just like mine. He loved schoolgirl outfits, so I dug out my old Bush-Davies uniform and surprised him on a dinner date. When he saw me, he flipped.

"I'll *never* forget you for this," he said, laughing, as the other people in the restaurant looked at him like some kind of pervert.

When *Stop the World* became a smash hit in London, Tony was the boy wonder of show biz. He'd grown from playing the original Artful Dodger as a kid to being a handsome young writer/composer/performer with a hit show. In his unmarried state, the women lined up for miles.

Janet and I decided to surprise him one night backstage by turning up in identical schoolgirl outfits, licking lollipops. We knocked and entered his dressing room to find Tony sitting there with a new admirer: Joan Collins, who had been in to see the show that night. As he awkwardly made the introductions, she glared at us disapprovingly, already looking like the venomous Alexis Carrington. It was a rough moment for poor Tony, so Janet and I got the picture and politely excused ourselves. "It's okay, Tone, we just wanted to give you a flash," I said as we beat a hasty retreat.

I'll never forget the look of pure shock on Joan Collins's face, and Tony, trying to suppress his laughter. We didn't see much of Tony after Joan stepped into the picture; they soon married and settled down to have children.

In the spring of 1958 *For Amusement Only* closed after a two-year run. I remember seeing the great Charles Laughton in tears at the closing night cast party, lamenting the loss of such a fine revue.

That summer, I was cast for a guest shot on "Danger Man," starring Patrick McGoohan (the show was later distributed in America under the title "Secret Agent"). I played a nightclub singer who somehow gets tangled up in a murder plot, and not surprisingly, I developed a deep crush on Patrick. In his early thirties, he was lean and handsome, with a wry sense of humor. Undoubtedly noticing my wide-eyed infatuation, he gently made a point of telling me about his wife and children and stressing how happily *married* he was.

The part was an excellent break for me—in addition to it being my first speaking part on film, I also recorded two songs from the episode for MGM Records.

At that time there was a lot of talk about a new London hairdresser named Vidal Sassoon, who had been operating out of a tiny salon on Bond Street. He had built up quite a reputation for his revolutionary ideas about hair design, and he was just opening a huge salon on New Bond Street in Mayfair. Janet and I went to find out what all the excitement was about.

We arrived to find a whirl of activity. Cool jazz music emanated from hidden speakers in the walls, and we sat with dozens of women, all waiting to be coiffed by one of the select hairdressers. Every now and then a handsome, impeccably dressed man with a confident smile strolled through the bustling salon, consulting with customers and saying something special to each one that made them smile.

"That's Vidal," Janet told me as we watched him make his rounds. At one end of his salon was an area where certain elegant ladies received the special benefits of Vidal's individual attention.

Vidal's creations lived up to their reputation. We were given the "geometric cut," a whole new concept in hairdressing, an angular, space-age design that was so distinctive, people everywhere could be heard to whisper, "Oh, look—she's got a Sassoon cut. . . ."

My recent forays into movies, television, and recording had gone beyond the scope of Miss McAusland's theatrical representation, so at summer's end I signed with the MCA agency, which was able to represent me on all levels. I won a part in a West End musical, *Chrysanthemum,* a pastiche set in Victorian England.

The show lasted only three months, but during the run I began to frequent The White Elephant, a chic private club and restaurant on Curzon Street. It was there that I finally met and began a special friendship with Vidal Sassoon, the boy wonder of New Bond Street.

Vidal was then developing the regimen that's helped him stay so youthful. His obsession with finding the healthiest life-style was ahead of its time—he was jogging before they knew what to call it. I learned about proper skin care and diet from Vidal, and he gave me a special boyish cut that he designed for me. He helped me form my own look and develop a personal sense of style and fashion.

Vidal was self-educated, a barber's apprentice from the East End of London. He always sought out people who could expand his horizons and brought them into his group of friends, which was an exciting cross section of talented people. Vidal, with his boundless energy and genius, brought new meaning to the word *hairdresser.*

Many of his friends were startled by the bold concept of interior design in his sumptuous, modern penthouse on Curzon Place. The living room was a wash of whites, beiges, and browns, with luxurious sofas and cushions on a plush shag carpet. The subtle lighting consisted of directional pin spots: Everyone looked alluring in it. The modern decor was warmed by exquisite sculptures and paintings. His glamorous bathroom was a dream of marble, mirrors, and stainless steel.

Our friendship slowly grew in a sincere and lovely way. He invited me to dinner parties at his flat, and we spent time together going to the movies and escaping to the country on Sundays, where he pursued his passion for water skiing. He made me aware of some of the problems that can accompany even the most well-deserved success.

Vidal described his devastating divorce of the previous year. He blamed himself, admitting that he'd poured so much of his time into his work that he'd neglected his marriage. He said the trauma of that breakup had left him unable to relate to women physically, even though he was surrounded daily by the most beautiful women in the world.

Vidal felt totally free of pretense with me. He loved to joke and impersonate the Cockney accent he grew up with, not having to worry about raising the eyebrows of people who wouldn't understand his sense of humor.

After one dinner party at his penthouse, when the guests had all gone home, I stayed to help him with the post-party clean-up. He was especially warm and affectionate. He sat me down, took me by the hand, told me how much he cherished our friendship, and invited me to stay the night if I wanted to.

I was happy to be his friend on any level, so more out of affection than passion, I spent the night. We talked and cuddled in the dark until we fell asleep. I spent a few nights with him in this innocent way. Then one evening after a party, he gave me an unusually serious look.

"Hey, stay tonight," he said. "I'd really love it if you would. . . ." He'd never said it quite that way before.

Later, in bed, he held me close. We kissed, but suddenly he pulled away. I sensed how critical a moment this was, and went for the joke.

"Well, what the 'ell have I come up here for, mate?"

He gaped as I continued my Cockney tirade: "You've been leadin' me on all this bleedin' time, and I got *nothin'* to show for it! That's it, I'm leavin'," I said, gathering my things.

Vidal burst out laughing, and then I felt his touch on my arm. He pulled me back onto the bed, his inhibitions forgotten.

Later, as we recovered from a breathtaking exchange, he got out of bed and paced around the room excitedly. He was beaming.

"I can't believe it . . . that was wonderful!"

"Yes, Vidal, you *shall* go to the ball!" And indeed he did.

The White Elephant reached a special level of excitement when Sammy Davis, Jr., came to town, usually to headline at the Palladium. He was crazy about London and thrived on hanging out with the show folk, who were equally crazy about him.

Each night the maitre d' reserved the largest table in the house for him, and during the evening a constant flow of interesting people dropped by. Sammy sat at the head of the table holding court, enrapt in conversation. Lionel and Joyce Blair were very close to him, and on a given evening, Tony Newley, Peter Finch, Terry Stamp, Shirley Bassey, Albert Finney, Alma Cogan, and others would stop in, all drawn by Sammy's charismatic presence. He delighted in picking up the tab and made it impossible for anyone to pay. Buying *him* a drink required careful scheming with the waiters.

Sammy offered me a lot of encouragement. "Hang in there, Judes," he said. "With your personality, there's no way you're not going to make it." He told me to learn from watching my peers, and with the group Sammy attracted at those social gatherings, all I had to do was open my eyes and absorb it all.

One evening at the White Elephant, Janet and I were sitting with a group of people when I heard a loud and infectious laugh coming from several boisterous Americans at the table next to ours. Never the shy type, I leaned over and interjected, "Could you keep it *down*? We're trying to do some serious drinking over here!"

They looked at me in shock, and then laughed. A man at the table came over and introduced himself as James Harris. He was attractive, with a warm smile and a slick American sense of humor. He mentioned that he was in town scouting locations for a film version of Nabokov's *Lolita,* which he was producing, and which would be directed by Stanley Kubrick. By the end of the evening we got along so well that I'd agreed to go out with him the next night.

Jimmy and I became inseparable during his stay in London. He'd become a hero of The White Elephant crowd for bringing from America a very precious commodity—Lenny Bruce records. Lenny endeared himself to our crowd with his immortal routine about the Las Vegas nightclub comic who bombs in front of an audience at the London Palladium. It was the "in" thing to play Lenny's records at parties, and likewise, we all went mad for Shelley Berman, Mort Sahl, and the button-down mind of Bob Newhart.

When Jimmy returned to America to tell Kubrick of his progress, he wrote to me from Hollywood, keeping me abreast of *Lolita*'s developments. I was knocked out to hear that he'd signed one of my idols for the film—Peter Sellers.

Jimmy asked if I knew of any available flats in London for when he came back to shoot the film. When I lined up a place, he was so delighted, he asked if I could do the same for Kubrick, who needed a larger place for his wife and children. Again, it was no problem. Kubrick was grateful when he arrived, since he was a devoted family man who needed a comfortable home to retreat to after his long hours of filming.

In the spring I was chosen as a panelist for the English TV show "Juke Box Jury," hosted by David Jacobs, a popular disc jockey. Other panel members included premier warblers Petula Clark and Cleo Laine, the huggable Richard ("Dickie") Dawson, and his then-wife Diana Dors, who made sparks fly on every show.

We voted whether the current pop records would be a "Hit" or a "Miss." I represented the voice of "teenage Britain" but rarely agreed with the other panelists, almost always voting for the new American rock 'n' roll songs, like Bill Haley's "Rock Around the Clock."

Meanwhile, Lenny Bruce records weren't the only counterculture novelty around London—the evil weed was catching fire. My initiation came when Lionel Blair escorted me to a party at Shirley Bassey's house in Belgravia, the most desirable area in Mayfair. Shirley already had a number of hit records and frequently hosted impromptu gatherings for her many friends. On this night we dropped in to find Lionel Bart, who wrote *Oliver!,* and Georgia Brown, who had been Bart's inspiration for the part of Nancy—a gutsy, brassy lady who was somewhat of a den mother to the theater crowd. I noticed someone rolling a dainty little cigarette that emitted a curious, pungent smell when it was lit. It was passed around, and when it came to me, I felt honored to have my first encounter with a "reefer" among people I so respected and admired. Lionel Blair was concerned, however. He'd brought me to the party and felt a twinge of paternal responsibility.

"Judy's never had it before," he said protectively.

"Oh, for God's sake, Lionel, it's just a bleedin' plant," the others said. I took a few puffs and spent the evening finding the silly side of everything and giggling. Even the Lenny Bruce records had never sounded quite so funny.

That autumn I was cast in the Richmond Repertory Theater's production of *The Boy Friend.* I played Polly, the part Julie Andrews had made famous in the West End hit. Since it was repertory, the show was only scheduled to run for a month, but as my first starring role it was a big step for me. I was also proud of my very first review, which said that ". . . Judy Carne, with her sweet little face, look of innocence and deadpan style of comedy, is an irresistible Polly, the poor little rich girl who has to invent a boy friend because her papa forbids her to have one. . . ."

The White Elephant continued to be the hub of my social activity. It was there that I met Stirling Moss, Britain's top race-car driver, and somewhat of a national hero. He seemed too warm and gentle a man to be engaged in such a dangerous sport, and surprisingly humble as well. He was interested in my career, going out of his way to see as many of my performances as he could. We started seeing each other regularly and it became a comfortable romance in which I learned something new about the world every time I saw him. That's how he was—tuned in to the latest happenings on *any* subject.

Stirling's eccentric wit is legend. He took his creeping baldness in stride, looking at the positive side: "I tell the barber to take a bit off the sides, polish the top, and I'm out of there for fifty pence!"

Though his house in Shepherd's Market was in the heart of London, it was shielded from the noise. If Vidal Sassoon was ahead of his time in terms of decor, Stirling was equally advanced in the electronic automation of his home. He had a button for everything and electricians on constant call. The panel beside his bed was like the controls of an airplane. One button lowered a television from the ceiling, another controlled the stereo, while yet another could open his garage door. His concern was the efficient use of space, and in that way, he was revolutionary in his concept of interior design.

Stirling was very disciplined. Each day was planned out in advance: He would be up early every morning to exercise, and then push another button which ran a bath at just the desired temperature.

The bathroom was most civilized, with dual "his and hers" facilities for everything. Both bathtubs were sunken and formed in the shape of race cars, the hot and cold faucets controlled by a steering wheel in each tub. The toilet seat was electronically warmed, as were the towel racks, which held luxurious, terry-cloth bathrobes.

Despite his eccentricities, he was wonderfully considerate. Many a night he drove me home from an after-show bite to eat, reminding me, "Judy, tomorrow is Saturday and you've got two shows. I've got a big day, too, so let's be realistic . . . Sunday we'll have all day to do as we please. . . ." There was a relaxed logic about him in everything he did, but he was never boring. We even had pet names for each other: He was "Stan" and I was "Doreen," don't ask me why.

Stirling was fond of my roommate Janet, so when Steve McQueen came to London to pick up pointers on racing from the master, the four of us went out together in the evenings. Like Stirling, he was very humble about his profession, even to the point of insecurity. He seemed unaware of his stature.

Although Janet and I knew next to nothing about racing, we often visited the track to see them in action. We loved to get caught up in the excitement and drama of the pit, proudly wearing our treasured racing jackets—each with our hero's name emblazoned on the back.

In February of 1961 Stirling came up to Scotland to see me in a new intimate revue called *On the Brighter Side,* starring Stanley Baxter. The show was working its way to London for a spring opening.

The press went crackers about Stirling and his "chorus girl." THE SECRET LOVE OF STIRLING MOSS was a typical headline. When photographers swarmed around the stage door as we left one night after the show, Stirling lost his cool and grabbed one of their cameras and smashed it to the ground. The photographer was a huge bloke— about six feet five; Stirling was only five feet nine, but feisty, and he gave this looming photog a pummeling he wasn't likely to forget. The other paparazzi snapped pictures of *that,* which ended up in all the newspapers.

The press made Stirling out to be a notorious womanizer, which made him seem callous. In truth, he is simply a great lover of women. He was particularly drawn to me because I never had designs on him. I wasn't planning on becoming Mrs. Moss (although I did attend the Cordon Bleu cooking school, *just* in case). Like Tony Newley and Vidal, Stirling simply enjoyed having an open, yet meaningful relationship with a female who wouldn't get too possessive. As time went on, he was away racing most of the time and I was usually working, so we rarely got to see each other. Our relationship settled down into a lovely friendship.

My schedule was full: During the day, I filmed a BBC TV series, "The Rag Trade," playing a wisecracking Cockney seamstress with a beehive hairstyle. The show attracted attention for its political overtones and the fact that it was sustained almost exclusively by women: With blind allegiance to a strike-happy shop steward, we made life hell for the boss of a tatty garment factory.

At night I continued to appear in *On the Brighter Side,* which ran for a year. It was a classic intimate revue full of farces, parodies, and sheer lunacy; there was a tribute to frozen vegetables, and a send-up of royalty called "A Plea for the Throne," comparing the seat of royalty with that porcelain seat found in the bathroom.

In the cast was David Kernan, with whom I sang a lovely romantic duet called "Late Last Evening." It was so popular, we recorded it

for Decca Records, which released it with "A Plea for the Throne" on
the flip side. The record briefly found its way into the charts, but
more importantly, it gave my dad an endless amount of pleasure. He
played it so often he wore out the grooves.

The course of my life might have been quite different had a new
and completely unexpected opportunity not come from the other side
of the Atlantic. An American producer named Cy Howard was casting a TV series called "Fair Exchange," and he needed an English
family with a thoroughly modern teenage daughter. Even though I
was twenty-one at the time, I still passed for a teenager, so my agent
sent me over to the Grosvenor House Hotel in Park Lane for an
audition.

A page boy ushered me into Howard's suite. He was sitting with
his feet up on his desk, smoking a pipe, the epitome of a high-
powered Hollywood producer. I tried to break the ice.

"'Allo, guvnor, I 'ear you're lookin' for an English bird to take
back with you to 'ollywood," I said boldly.

"In the first place, don't make with the jokes," he snapped. "In the
second place, put another log on the fire. And in the third place, I
want you to read this script as though you're determined to get the
part, even if it kills you."

I put a log on the fire and nervously began to read. The phone rang
and Cy picked it up and nodded for me to continue, while declaring
into the phone, "Sure, baby, I love ya. What else, baby?"

I finished and he looked at me for a moment before speaking.

"Listen, kid, that wasn't bad, but I want you to act like you're
worried about my reputation. Do it again."

I glared at him, wanting to tell him where he could stick his bloody
reputation. Then I read it again.

"That's much better," he said, "but you know, the girl I'm looking
for is a really zippy type with a ponytail, big smile, shiny teeth, and
all that jazz. I'll let you know, kid. Next, please!"

I was up against two hundred fifty other girls, so when I received a
call back, special measures had to be taken. I dashed to Vidal's
salon, where one of his assistants pinned on a ponytail. Then it was
off to the dentist for a quick tooth polishing. When I showed up at Cy
Howard's suite the next day, he took one look at me and laughed.

"You sure want to get to Hollywood, kid. Go into the other room,

I'll be with you in a minute." I did as he said, and after an anxious hour, he entered, seeming friendlier than before.

"So what do you like to do for fun, Judy?"

"Well, I'm a dancer," I said. "In fact, I'm a wicked twister."

"Can you *really* do the twist?" he said suspiciously.

"Sure, you want to see me?"

"Well, we don't have any music here. . . ."

"That's okay, I don't need any." With that I got up and started to gyrate around the room, à la Chubby Checker. Cy laughed.

"That's great, Judy, just great. Let me ask you something: Would you be able to join us for dinner tonight?"

Naturally I said yes, so we went downstairs to join his colleagues from the American studio that was producing "Fair Exchange," Desilu Productions. By the time the food arrived, I realized I had the part. They explained that the show was a comedy series about an American and an English family that exchange their teenage daughters for a year. I would be flown to Hollywood to film the pilot.

I realized that "Fair Exchange" was going to change the course of my life. In only two weeks, I would be going to America. My mum had the normal reaction of a mother whose daughter is about to move 6000 miles away—she cried her eyes out. But my dad recognized the potential of the opportunity, and he was thrilled for me. It was only a pilot, after all, so it couldn't do any harm. I'd also never been to America before, so who could argue with a free trip?

"She won't be back, you know," my mum told Dad.

"Don't be ridiculous," he said.

"You just watch, 'arold, she'll be coming 'ome one of these days with a wedding veil over 'er eyes and an American boy with a big Stetson hat. . . ."

I was given a huge send-off party at The White Elephant, and everyone gave me advice about what to expect in America. Vidal was convinced this was my big break, and he gave me the names of people to look up in Hollywood if I became lonely. Tony Newley told me not to take people on face value alone, and to be wary of fast talkers.

"Don't worry, Tone, I'm a big girl now," I reassured him.

"I hope so," he said. "Just don't become too jaded. And watch out for yourself—the Americans will eat you up if you're not careful."

London

On the day after Christmas I met the rest of my television "family" at Heathrow Airport for the flight to Hollywood: Victor Maddern and Diana Chesney, who played my parents; and Dennis Waterman, who played my kid brother.

It all began to sink in: I would be in another culture with another currency and another way of life, all so far away from everything and everyone I knew. I was scared to death. I wondered whether I would be able to pull it off. What if the show failed? Would I get another chance? Would the Americans accept me? Would they even *like* me?

These questions floated around in my head during the twelve-hour nonstop flight to Los Angeles. I was fairly certain about only one thing: It would be the greatest adventure of my life.

4. Hollywood

Desilu Studios put us up at the Roosevelt Hotel on Hollywood Boulevard, across the street from Grauman's Chinese Theater, where Dennis Waterman and I immediately rushed to inspect the famous hand- and footprints embedded in the pavement.

It didn't take long for me to put my typically English foot in my mouth. I used the British expression for a wake-up call, asking the bellboy if he could "knock me up" at eight o'clock the next morning. The young man blushed, and was so taken aback that he left without a tip. I apparently had asked him to be the father of my child.

I immediately fell in love with the California life-style. After twenty-three years of damp English weather, it seemed as if the warm climate, palm trees, avocados, and sandy beaches would agree with me.

The pilot for "Fair Exchange" required a full month of rehearsal and filming at the studio, on a huge set that contained not only a New York street, but a London mews, complete with cobblestones, horse carts, and the ever-present fog machines.

Cy Howard's conception of life in England was blatantly stereotypical—we *always* acted in fog. The "London" set was continually doused with rain and blanketed with fog, and the "British" men always wore bowler hats with umbrellas at the ready. Horse and carriage was the preferred mode of transportation.

"This isn't a period piece, Cy," I told him, "this is *now!*"

"This is what Americans want to see," was his stock reply.

I learned that Desilu was an amalgamation of the names Desi Arnaz and Lucille Ball. They weren't just television stars, they were an American institution. Lucy seemed tirelessly energetic, and I occasionally caught a glimpse of her tooling around the lot in her monogrammed golf cart, her bright red hair flashing in the sunlight. She was just beginning work on "The Lucy Show" for CBS, and her schedule allowed little time for anything else. If I happened to see her in the commissary on a lunch break, she was always gracious and showed genuine concern for my morale.

"Now tell me, Judy, how are things going over there? I hope you're not too lonely."

"I'm not, Miss Ball, I just love it here," I said honestly.

She'd leave me with a wink and a friendly "Keep up the good work!"

Even though Desi and Lucy were divorced, they instilled a family feeling at their studio, and this camaraderie served to keep our spirits up, being so far away from home. Everyone treated us like an actual family visiting from England.

There were many indications that "Fair Exchange" would be picked up by a network. Our show had the unique distinction of being the first one-hour sitcom ever attempted, and the pilot's extravagant expense hinted at the studio's inner confidence.

The rest of my TV family returned to England as we waited for word from the network, but I wanted to stay in Hollywood as long as possible, so I moved to Sunset Towers, a new block of apartments for transients. I spent my time constructively, seeking out agents and looking for a more permanent place to live. Desilu saw to it that I wasn't lonely, by arranging for studio personnel to escort me to publicity events connected with their shows.

I adored the people from Desilu but I longed for friends who had nothing to do with my work, to whom I could relate on other levels. At the time, America was positively mad for Chubby Checker; "The

Twist" was not just a hit record and dance, it had become a national pastime. Since it had helped me win my part on "Fair Exchange," I went over to the Peppermint Twist, a dance club on Sunset Boulevard that was sponsoring a twist contest. I was ever so curious to see what went on at these events.

It was a wild scene inside the club: Music blared from gigantic speakers on all sides, and women danced in cages mounted near the stage where the contest was to take place. I thrived on the frenzied atmosphere of hundreds of people my own age gyrating to the music, and I soon struck up a conversation with a group that was rooting for one of the dance competitors, a girl with a banner around her that read SUZY K.

I started talking to a handsome young man named Randy, who explained the intricacies of competitive twisting as we watched his friend Suzy K. go on to win the contest. She joined us afterward and I told them the story of how my twisting abilities had landed me six thousand miles from home.

When she wasn't moonlighting as a twister, Suzy K. was a legal secretary named Suzan Kroul. She was extremely friendly, and concerned that I get acclimated to California living as soon as possible. The next day she gave me a tour of the best places to shop, plus a badly needed driving lesson.

Suzan's friend was Randy Rothstein, a real estate broker "to the stars." He was pure Hollywood, complete with a flashy MG and a gold chain around his neck (very revolutionary for 1962). He helped me find a secondhand car—a monstrous boatlike contraption with large fins on the back. It was totally American, and I loved it.

Since I'd decided to stay in Hollywood as long as I could, affordability was a prime factor in deciding where I should live. Suzan was also looking for a place, so we pooled our resources and rented a place off Sunset Boulevard in close proximity to Desilu as well as the leading twist palaces. On weekends Randy would throw parties in one of the furnished yet unoccupied mansions he was showing to prospective clients. He even let Suzan and me spend weekends in some of them; we swam and took sun, inviting our friends over and pretending we *owned* the luxurious properties.

In late March we got the news that "Fair Exchange" would be on CBS's fall schedule. In June we would start filming the first episode and nearly all of my time would be spoken for, so I took the opportunity to go home to see my parents. Now that "Fair Exchange" was ensured at least a year's run, I could make a triumphant return.

I arrived in London to sobering news. My parents told me that Stirling Moss had been in a severe automobile crash while racing at Goodwood, and that he lay in a coma, near death.

All of England held its breath as Stirling struggled for life in the hospital. The crash had broken almost every bone in his body, and the press kept a daily vigil, reporting on his condition.

Everyone was overjoyed when the news broke that he had come out of his coma. My dad drove me to the hospital, where a close friend of the Moss family warned me to be prepared for the seriousness of Stirling's condition. "Judy, he remembers nothing. He's likely to say the strangest things. . . ."

"What kind of things?" I asked.

"He won't recognize you. He doesn't even recognize his mother."

With this, I entered the room. Stirling lay there, bandaged from head to toe, most of his limbs up in traction. As I drew closer, I saw his eyes bulging through holes in the bandages. I noticed that his hands were perfect, seemingly untouched by the accident.

"Hello, Stirling," I said, gently taking his hand.

He looked at me curiously. "You're very cute. . . . I suppose I know you. Do I?"

"Yes, you do," I said, fighting back tears.

"Well, then . . . we all know what *my* name is, what's yours?"

I smiled with a gulp. "Judy . . . Judy Carne."

"Did I know you very well?"

"Oh, yes, very well . . ."

"What do you do?"

I tried to break the somber mood with humor. "What do I do? What do I *look* like I do? I'm an actress, *that's* what I do. My ego is destroyed that you don't know who I am!"

He laughed out loud, so I continued. "I've known you for three years and we've had a *lot* of laughs!"

"Please, tell me about some of them," he said eagerly.

"I'll never forget the time you came to see me perform in Glasgow. I've still got the pictures taken outside the stage door of you trying to grab that photographer who was twice your bloody size. It was all over the newspapers the next day, and you looked so ridiculous— your fist barely reached his chin!"

"That's right!" he said excitedly.

The nurses in the room gasped; he really *did* seem to remember.

"I wanted to strangle that bloke—my God, I hate that kind of invasion of privacy," he said, starting to sound like his old self again. We talked for a while and then the nurse came. I said good-bye and kissed his hand.

When I saw my dad in the hallway, I hugged him and wept for joy. "Dad, I think he knew me. . . . I think he had a flash in there."

I was in touch with the hospital each day after that. They told me that Stirling was beginning to put together bits and pieces of his life and that the doctors were encouraged. After returning to Hollywood, I still got progress reports. Stirling eventually remembered everything about his life up until the moment he got into his race car on that fateful day at Goodwood. I felt pride at having contributed to his miraculous recovery—through laughter.

When the filming of "Fair Exchange" began, my social life blossomed. As a regular on a TV series I was invited to numerous parties, including one thrown by Desi Arnaz himself.

Desi had a penthouse apartment at the Chateau Marmont, with a dazzling view of L.A. I wasn't yet used to Hollywood parties and I remember wondering who all the buxom, glamorous girls could be. I hadn't seen any of them around the studio.

I took all of this in, mingling with friends and acquaintances as waiters constantly replenished my glass of punch. Before I knew it, I was hopelessly drunk, so I retreated to a bedroom and passed out. I awoke long after the party was over, pulled myself together, and wandered out onto the balcony to get some fresh air. There in the darkness stood Desi, in a bathrobe, surveying the bright lights of Sunset Boulevard. "Are you feeling better?" he asked me.

"Yes, I think so," I said, holding onto the railing, still feeling a little green.

"Why don't you . . . stay awhile?"

"I'm sorry, Mr. Arnaz, I really shouldn't. . . ."

"Please, call me Desi."

I joined him for a cup of coffee, but he soon fell asleep on the couch, so I covered him with a blanket and quietly slipped out to find his driver, who took me home.

A few weeks later Desi invited me to his horse ranch outside L.A., where he spent most of his time, away from the hustle and bustle of the studio. I was flattered by his invitation and enjoyed the luxury of having a chauffeur-driven car take me on the drive to Del Mar, a few hours south of L.A. It was the first time I'd seen a California ranch, with acres of beautiful, rambling country where scores of thoroughbred horses roamed. I was taken to my own suite in the huge, Spanish-style house.

Desi had given his staff instructions to make me comfortable; he even had his housekeeper prepare English tea for me. The bathroom was large and luxurious, and elegant white silk curtains were draped around my bed.

"Mr. Arnaz is downstairs, if you'd like to join him for a drink," the butler announced.

I descended a long staircase to the living room, feeling like Alice in Wonderland among the huge furniture and exquisite art works. Desi appeared from a set of double doors, wearing a ten-gallon hat, ruffled sleeves, and a bright red bandanna cocked off to one side. A slight paunch hung over his belt, and he held a drink in his hand.

"Judy, what a day this is for you to have come," he said, his thick Cuban accent as irresistible as ever. He was excited because it was the day his champion stud horse was to breed. "What a treat you are about to see. Come with me, I will show you something special."

We got into his golf cart and drove to a row of stables. Desi shouted a few commands in Spanish and several ranch hands scampered to their assigned places for "the event."

"You watch, and I will 'splain it all. I will guide you through this magnificent moment."

The mare was led out into an area adjoining the stables and placed into a wooden frame similar to a rodeo stall. The ranch hands tied her up so she was capable of little movement.

"This protects her from injury," Desi whispered.

Out of a gate charged six stallions, who gathered around the mare, teasing her with horse kisses and rearing up, their tails whooshing in the air.

"Isn't that too many horses for her?" I asked Desi naively. "What does she need *all* of them for?"

"They are teasing her, arousing her—you'd be excited too, no?"

I giggled with embarrassment as he 'splained it all to me with great gusto. After a few minutes of teasing by the stallions, the mare was crazed and started to buck wildly around her. The stallions were called away, and Desi's excitement began to grow.

"Here he comes," he cried with a gleam in his eyes. The stud entered, strutting majestically like a toreador, his phallus growing so immense it almost dragged in the dirt. Desi's eyes widened and he nudged me.

"Now is the big moment, Judy," he said as the stall was removed to expose her hind quarters. "Don't look away or you'll miss it. . . ."

The stud slowly approached the trapped mare, and in one swift movement reared up and mounted her. He shook his mane, she let out a series of whinnies, and then it was over.

"You know how much he got for that, Judy?"

"No, how much?"

"Seventy-five thousand dollars."

"For what?"

"For what you just saw!"

"But however do they pay him?"

"No, no, *we*—the ranch—get the money."

The stallion was out of sight when they finally untied the mare. There was much jubilation among the ranch hands, who lifted their beer bottles and drank to the newly conceived animal.

I was overcome by it all and had to go back to my room to pull myself together. The vision of this event, which we'd watched from only a few yards away, was embedded in my mind, and I wondered if perhaps Desi expected me to reenact the scene with him after dinner. As it turned out, I was able to gently avoid his advances with a combination of humor and feigned innocence.

I spent the next day sunning by the pool with some other guests who were visiting that afternoon. When I returned to my room, I noticed a bouquet of roses on the table. On closer inspection I saw that they were wrapped in a gold bracelet with what appeared to be diamonds and emeralds. There was a card with it that simply said: "Roses for an English Rosebud—Love, Desi."

Hollywood

I didn't know what to do. It was a beautiful gesture, but accepting such a valuable gift would have made me feel obligated in some way. I sought out the butler and explained that I didn't want Mr. Arnaz to think me ungrateful, but I couldn't accept it. He gave me a knowing smile and took back the bracelet.

I returned to Hollywood, my mind blown by the whole experience. Desi had been wonderful to me. I realized he was just lonely, as I was, but I didn't want to court disaster—after all, he was my *boss*.

Now that part of their daughter's dream had come true, my parents naturally wanted to see the fruits of their investment. They came to watch me work and find out what Hollywood was *really* like.

I was able to drive my parents straight from the airport to their own private Hollywood home, thanks to Randy, who'd arranged the whole thing. He told me that since the place was empty and not likely to sell in the next two weeks, he hated to see it go to waste. The house was the epitome of Californian comfort—totally modernized, with buttons to control almost everything. My parents were so impressed that it later inspired them to build their own home just like it in Northampton, which they named Carne Lodge.

By this time I'd become part of a British colony of friends in Hollywood, which included England's glamour queen, Diana Dors, and her husband Dickie Dawson, who was just starting out in America as a comedian. They lived with their two children in a Hollywood mini-mansion which my parents found quite breathtaking when I took them there one afternoon.

They were big fans of Diana's so she gave them a personalized tour of the house, which included her luscious bedroom, with its purple velvet drapes and gold trim everywhere. Dickie cooked up some American-style barbecue and we sat by the pool having a good laugh about the many blunders that English people make as they adjust to American living.

My mother recounted her recent experience at a beauty parlor in Beverly Hills. "The hairdresser was called to the phone and he left me with me 'ead in the basin for twenty bleedin' minutes. When he got back, I asked him, 'Where 'ave you been, then, out for coffee and a fag?' He nearly fainted! He didn't know that *fag* is just our word for a cigarette!"

My parents' stay might have been a normal tourist visit to America had international events not conspired to bring the world to the brink of a nuclear exchange—the Cuban missile crisis.

I had long been raving to them about the delights of American television, but when they tuned in for their first glimpse, they were confronted on every station by President Kennedy's ominous speech, preparing us for the worst: the very real possibility of war.

As my parents settled down to sleep that night, they heard a police siren blare outside the house. To English people who lived through World War II, that sound means only one thing: "Get to the bomb shelters." They sat bolt upright in bed.

Had they not just seen the President of the United States on television, solemnly warning that a confrontation of major proportions was taking place? Was this not World War Three?

"It's *war*, Kath!" my father said.

"What are we going to do?"

Dad was already out of bed. "We're goin' home, that's what."

Mum started packing while he called to warn me of the impending doom. I was fast asleep.

"Joyce, it's *war*," he said in a steely tone.

"Dad? What's going on?" I said in a daze.

"No time to talk, Joyce, we're packin' our things, and we're leaving. Are you comin' with us or not?"

He told me about the siren, and I remembered having the same gut reaction, thinking that bombs were falling, only to discover that it was a police car. In England the police used a high-speed bell.

I explained this to him but he was beyond comprehension. He had heard sirens and he wanted to evacuate his family from California.

"What do you hear now, Dad?" I asked.

"Nothing," he admitted. "Maybe it was just a first warning."

"Don't you think *I* would have heard something? Before you call the airport, let's wait fifteen minutes and see what happens."

Fifteen minutes later I called him back. "Hear anything?"

"No. I suppose you're right, Joyce. What the bloody 'ell is Kennedy up to, then?"

I didn't quite know how to answer that, so I just told him to watch television and listen to the radio to make sure we were safe. They weren't really convinced until the next day, when I drove them to lunch and a wailing police car passed us at high speed. My parents were uneasy for the rest of their visit. They always kept their suitcases packed at the ready.

Like father, like daughter: I'd asked a bellhop to impregnate me; my dad had mistaken a police siren for the end of the world.

When it came time to promote "Fair Exchange" before its fall debut, I was sent off on a publicity junket. *Junket* to me had always meant a pudding of some kind, but a Desilu interpreter explained that in America it meant that CBS would be sending stars from their various shows to a desirable location for a few days of promotion—in this case, Miami, Florida.

We were the hopeful prospects for the new television season and the press would be there in droves, ensuring that our arrival on the tube would not go unnoticed; whether the show would be a hit or not was another matter. I'd heard of Florida, of course: sunshine, orange juice, alligators, the Everglades . . . but I hadn't met a Floridian in person. Yet.

5. My Buddy

Traveling *anywhere* in America was a new experience for me, so as we boarded the plane for Miami, I was bubbling with excitement. Settling into my seat, I noticed a man sitting a few rows behind me looking unusually relaxed and not the least bit excited by the journey. He was dark and handsome, but then so were most of the actors on the flight. This man caught my attention because of the bemused smile on his face as he calmly viewed the scene.

I had to sneak little glances behind me to see him, and every time I did he was looking right back at me. When I met his eyes for the third time I stared at him intensely and then broke into a mischievous smile, turning my head back quickly as I imagined the grin that remained on his face.

Once the plane was airborne, drinks were served and people started to mingle, getting to know one another. A network executive went around introducing everyone, and before I knew it, I was standing in front of the man I had noticed from the beginning.

"Judy, this is Burt Reynolds. Burt, this is Judy Carne."

We shook hands and right away I noticed a friendly twinkle in his eye and a readiness to laugh that gave him an irresistible charm.

"Isn't this exciting?" I said to him. "Is this your first trip to Florida *too*?"

"Nope," Burt replied, "I was born there. This is just a free trip home."

That was the first line out of his mouth, and I giggled. It was so contrary to the superficial show biz banter going on around us. He was able to see the humor of the situation, and I felt as though I'd found someone with whom I could relate.

Burt told me he was on a popular western called "Gunsmoke," and I told him all about "Fair Exchange." We spent the entire flight engrossed in conversation, telling our life stories and making each other laugh. We made an instant connection and became unaware of the trip, our work, or our commitments in Florida. Our first meeting was so magical and devastating that if we'd been left more to ourselves, we probably would have ended up ravishing each other in the plane's lavatory. We wouldn't have cared *where* we were: in the aisles, sprawled over the cocktail trolley, or strapped to the wings!

Arriving in Miami Beach, we were fussed over by all kinds of network publicity people and then taken to the swank Fontainebleau Hotel, overlooking the ocean. As I unpacked my bags, the phone rang. I picked it up and heard Burt's cheerful voice.

"Guess who?"

"I give up."

"What are you doing?"

"Unpacking," I told him.

"How about having a drink?"

"Sounds *divine*." He said he'd drop by my room in fifteen minutes and we'd call room service.

I finished unpacking with great enthusiasm, trying to remain calm as I prepared for his arrival. We had spent five hours together on the plane and the magic between us was unmistakable; *now* came the moment of truth. When I heard his knock, I ran and opened the door, and we looked at each other for a moment, with devilish smiles on our faces. When he crossed the threshold, I felt a rush through my body and we fell into each other's arms like long-lost lovers. We began to hug and kiss passionately until our rapture was rudely interrupted by the ring of the hotel phone, with a reminder that I was due downstairs for cocktails in a half an hour.

"We can't get into this right now," said Burt.

"You're right," I said, pulling myself together. "It's show time!"

"Right, we've got to go down there and talk about ourselves!"

The network itinerary required us to attend a cocktail party and dinner and be present for after-dinner drinks, so we arranged to meet as soon as our duties were over.

We were giddy with anticipation during the publicity function, eyeing each other across the room and making faces about what a bore it was compared to what *we* had in mind. Burt passed by me several times and whispered, "Won't be long now . . ."

Finally the moment came—we slipped away gracefully, giggling like little kids as we ran like mad upstairs to bed. Our hotel suites were on the same floor, with identical balconies facing the ocean, so I don't remember whose room we were in that night. I don't think *we* even knew at the time.

We were immediately in love, so we immediately made love. I was engulfed by him, my small body lost in his large frame. He paid scrupulous attention to my sexual desires, sending passionate chills through me. It was a unique encounter for me because we mixed our passion with laughter—an exhilarating combination. With Burt, I felt a freedom in bed that I'd never felt before.

I remember us wandering naked onto the balcony during the night, embracing and watching the moon reflect off the water, and feeling that balmy Florida breeze waft over us. It was such a beautiful moment; I wondered whether I could ever be happier.

So much of our time was spoken for by our itinerary of personal appearances, TV spots, and interviews. It was exciting to know that we could look forward to being together again each night. We crowded our romance in whenever we could.

When they finally gave us a free afternoon to spend as we wished, we rented a car to visit Burt's family in nearby West Palm Beach. He showed me where he was born and raised, and Palm Beach itself, where he dreamed of living one day. Burt, Sr., was the local police chief, and Burt's mother, Fern, was a soft-spoken woman who was half Cherokee Indian. I met his brother Jim, who was a football coach, and his sister Nancy, who was married and had two very sweet children, Richie and little Nancy. It was a wonderful family unit, something I was missing terribly. Burt told me that if his kids turned out like Nancy's, he'd be a very happy man.

Although Burt and I were the products of different cultures, we

My Buddy

shared a certain humbleness of roots and had grown up with the desire to someday make it over to the "right side of the tracks." That we found each other in Showbiz, USA, of all places, was miraculous.

By the time our responsibilities in Miami Beach were completed, we were inseparable and it was time to return to Los Angeles. We took a lot of good-natured kidding from the others on the trip who had witnessed our whirlwind romance and couldn't believe their eyes. But their jokes didn't bother us. We were in love.

As a promising running back on the Florida State college football team, Burt was destined for a professional athletic career until a serious injury in his junior year put an end to those aspirations. He recuperated and entered college in Palm Beach, where he became interested in drama, eventually moving to New York City.

When I met Burt, he'd moved to California and was living in a modest bachelor pad in Hollywood. We worked long hours on our respective shows, but all of our free time was spent together, some nights at his place and others at the apartment I shared with my friend Suzan Kroul. After a few weeks these logistics got to be a bore. We just *had* to live together—so we rented our first home.

We found a lovely, rustic wooden cottage set high above Laurel Canyon, surrounded by greenery on a secluded cul de sac called Hermit's Glen. I contributed some antiques and a lot of imagination, while Burt brought a bed, a few chairs, and an assortment of Early American furnishings, because that was his taste: Frontier Macho. There were guns, rifles, knives, football pictures, and trophies all over the walls. I even recall a saddle or two.

His attire reflected the same taste: He wore only jeans, denim jackets, and cowboy boots that looked as if they came from the "Gunsmoke" costume rack. I was amused by it all, especially the cowboy hats. Whenever Burt wore one I would burst out laughing.

"What's so funny?" he'd ask.

"You . . . wearing those silly hats!"

"They're not silly, they helped *make* this country!"

"But Burt, that was a hundred years ago! You don't have to go around looking like a cowhand."

"Well, you don't have to go around looking like Peter Pan!"

His point was well taken. In those days I was—and still am—

drawn to wearing boyish things. Most of my clothes were from London's Carnaby Street and outrageous by Hollywood standards back then. I wore tailored cotton suits with shirts, waistcoats, and ties, and kept my hair short, which I thought suited me best.

Burt was not fond of the pixie look. The casual Judy had been fine for just messing around, but as soon as we started living together, everything had to be very conventional, and he literally set out to change me.

"You must wear a dress. And a bra. And heels. And grow your hair." I started to grow my hair to please him but I never *did* wear bras—with my boyish figure, I didn't need to.

My influence on him also brought about some changes. Burt was three years older than I. His physique was a bit chunky, a carryover from his football days, and the weight showed in his face, accentuating his resemblance to Marlon Brando. After we'd lived together for a few months, I got him to shed ten pounds, which brought out his cheekbones and diminished his thick, football-player's neck.

The comparison to Brando really bugged him, especially in his early years as a struggling actor in New York, where he shared a flat with Rip Torn and George Maharis. He told me a story once about walking into a neighborhood bar, feeling rather down because he wasn't getting anywhere in his career. As he sat there drinking his beer, a guy at the other end of the bar was very drunk, saying things to Burt like "How ya doin', Marlon baby!" Every time this drunk took a sip, he'd say, "Here's to ya, Marlon! Keep up the good work, Marlon!"

Burt just sat there taking it all until he finally snapped. Racing to the end of the bar, he lifted the heckler and threw him down to the ground, only to see, as he stared down at the floor in horror, that the guy had *no legs*! He lay there like an upturned turtle, unable to get off his back, flailing his arms about and screaming.

"Oh, my God, I'm sorry, I didn't know!" Burt cried, devastated. He helped the guy back to his seat and then ran out of the bar. Apparently the man was a regular whom people had learned to ignore. Unfortunately, Burt didn't know that.

A few years later, while living in Los Angeles shooting his first television series, "Riverboat," he finally had an encounter with

My Buddy

Brando himself. Burt was sitting in a restaurant when a press agent came over to his table, grabbed his arm, and dragged him over to where Brando was sitting.

"Hey, Marlon, whaddya think?" he said in a loud voice, pointing at Burt. "Look at this guy—dig the likeness, man!"

He made a big scene and Burt was *really* embarrassed. Brando just looked up from his plate of food, stared at Burt blankly, and raised a very limp hand, which he dangled in the air like a dead fish. Burt nervously shook it as best he could but was really hurt and put down by the incident. It was crushing to meet an idol of his in such a humiliating way. Years later he was able to laugh about it, but as a struggling actor, he didn't find it very funny.

Another change I helped bring about involved his name. His family and friends did not call him Burt, as I found out on our first visit to his parents home in Florida.

"Hiya, Buddy!" they said, greeting him.

"Who's Buddy?" I whispered to Burt.

"That's me, silly. They call me Buddy because I'm a junior, Burt Reynolds, Jr. If they call me Burt, what'll they call my dad?"

"How about 'Dad'?"

"I call him Pop."

"The English don't say *pop* . . . that's a fizzy drink."

Burt realized that he was getting nowhere with me on this point and gave up. I refused to acknowledge the existence of this nickname, and if friends of Burt's used it around me, I gave them a hard time.

"Hey, Judy, how's Buddy?"

"Who?"

"Buddy!"

"Oh, you must mean Burt. I call him Burt—he's fully grown now, you know!"

Perhaps if I hadn't been so insistent, it would have been: "*Deliverance,* starring Jon Voight and *Buddy* Reynolds"!

I loved to cook for Burt. He took great pride in my abilities as a homemaker. On my first visit to the set of "Gunsmoke," everyone greeted me warmly and told me how much Burt had been raving about my cooking.

"When are we going to be invited to sample some of those great English dishes Burt keeps telling us about?" they wanted to know.

We started inviting people over to dinner more often, friends such as Amanda Blake, Milburn Stone, and Ken Curtis—who were also known as Kitty, Doc, and Festus.

Another frequent dinner guest was one of Burt's closest friends, Hal Needham, a stunt man whom he had worked with on "River-boat" the year before. Burt had tremendous admiration for him. Hal was fearless, which made him one of the busiest stuntmen in the business. He also bred and trained stunt horses at his ranch in the San Fernando Valley, which featured air-conditioned stables.

"I gotta take good care of my horses," Hal would explain. "They're my bread and butter. Nothing's too good for them."

He was right. At that time there was a myriad of westerns on television: "Bonanza," "Rawhide," "Wagon Train," "Laramie," "The Big Valley," and of course "Gunsmoke," to name just the successful ones. As a result, Hal was in constant demand and so were his horses. He would sometimes work many shows in one day— "Bonanza" in the morning, "Gunsmoke" in the afternoon, and maybe a few stunts on a police drama between them.

On weekends we'd often hop into Burt's bright red T-Bird convertible and drive out to Hal's ranch for a visit. He would greet me with "Hiya, Judy!" and in one swift motion lift me up in the air like a small child, and I'd end up perched on his shoulder. He knew that I could handle it because I was a dancer, and I loved it. He'd hold me above his head for a while before I'd say, "Great, Hal, that's really super. You can put me down now!"

"Okay, Judy. Here, Burt . . . *catch!*" I'd fly through the air into Burt's arms, ending up perched on *his* shoulder.

They often worked out and did stunts together. Hal did tricks with his horses that other stunt men wouldn't even consider, and I watched with Hal's wife, Arlene, who was great to talk to.

"Did you see that?" Burt would yell from a heap of horses, his jeans covered in mud and his face blackened from the dust.

"You two weren't gabbing during those horse falls, were you?"

My Buddy

"Oh, no, Burt, it was *great!*" I'd say, whether I'd seen it or not.

Hal had horses specially trained to fall and others that would rear up. Burt loved the horse falls: Hal would give a single command with his foot and his horse would fall and roll over as if it had been shot. He taught Burt how to fall without hurting himself.

Burt was such a superb athlete that with Hal's help, he rarely needed stand-ins, priding himself on the ability to perform most of his stunts. He loved it so much, in fact, that they'd have to discourage him from getting carried away on the set.

"The scene only calls for you to knock the drink over, Burt. You can leave out the back flip," the director would plead.

If a scene called for him merely to be shoved, he'd insist on being punched backward through a window. He would suit up for these stunts at the drop of a cowboy hat, eagerly donning the protective pads on his shoulders, chest, legs, thighs, and behind. Once on a visit, I watched the whole procedure.

"I think I'm protected now," he said, covered from head to toe with thick foam rubber. "What do you think?"

"If they dropped you out of a *plane,* you'd probably bounce back!"

When Burt came home from a day of stunts, he would be charged up, flowing over with the details and wanting to share the adventure of it all with me.

"I did this double roll, see, then I jumped over a horse before crashing through the window."

I would be wide-eyed with amazement. A well-choreographed stunt scene is an exacting mixture of athletics and acting, with little room for error. If Burt did make a mistake, he would shrug off his bruises. I'd see an awful black and blue mark and ask, "Burt, what happened? You must be in a lot of pain!"

"Naw, that's nothing. But I came *this close* to losing an eye!"

He described his near misses so vividly that I became terrified.

"Burt, they're not taking enough precautions."

"Sure they are," he explained. "I didn't say I lost an eye, I just said I came *this close!*"

Years later Hal Needham went on to form the Stuntman's Association, and Burt helped steer him into film directing with *Smokey and the Bandit.* Today they still share a close friendship.

Watching Burt and Hal practice together was my first introduction to stunt work. If only I knew how valuable this knowledge would be years later on "Laugh-In."

A few months after moving into Hermit's Glen, we visited the home of some friends who told us that their basset hound had just given birth to a large litter of puppies, all of whom were in need of homes. The minute we saw these comic little dogs with their sad eyes, big feet, and floppy ears, we were sold. We picked our favorite of the litter and named him Clyde.

We loved Clyde because he was a constant source of laughter. He was a natural comedian, uncoordinated and always falling down. Getting him to do tricks was impossible—he would respond to any command with a blank stare followed by a yawn. He also had the habit of not watching where he was going, and if he heard his name called while on the run, he'd turn his head around and end up slamming into the nearest wall.

Clyde also took the liberty of urinating whenever and wherever he pleased. One favorite place was the drapes. This didn't diminish our love for him, though; we spoiled Clyde rotten, and even fought over who got to feed him.

Clyde was included in everything we did. Burt often took him to the set of "Gunsmoke," and if we were invited out, he was part of the package. After a while, Clyde became so identified with us that he often got more laughs than we did—even our friends who didn't like dogs asked us to bring him over.

This was the case with Clint and Maggie Eastwood. Like Burt, Clint was on a popular western at the time, "Rawhide," playing Rowdy Yates, his first major role. Also like Burt, Clint would one day become one of the biggest movie box-office attractions in the world.

Maggie was blond and slender, with a healthy, natural look. She was reserved but full of warmth and friendliness, which made her a perfect match for Clint. They lived in the hills of nearby Encino, in a rustic house overlooking the San Fernando Valley, with a pool that was of natural stone, seemingly carved by Mother Nature herself. They were very house proud, so the first time we took Clyde with us on a visit, we had to leave him in the car. The next time we brought him in with us, and Clint and Maggie immediately flipped for him. Before long they decided they had to have a basset hound of their own, so they adopted a female they called Sylvia. We adored each other's company and loved taking the sun around their pool on weekends, sipping margaritas, watching our dogs run around and laughing at their ridiculous antics.

It occurred to us that if we mated Clyde and Sylvia, we could take the pick of the litter and give away the rest. We waited for a day when Sylvia was in heat and then took Clyde over to their house to let them go at it.

When we arrived, Clyde picked up her scent and started getting it on with the furniture. We placed him in position with Sylvia but poor Clyde had absolutely no idea what to do. He aimed for her ear, her nose, everywhere but the right place. It was a disaster. We never *did* get them connected right—we were laughing too hard.

Burt and I had been living together for several months, both working regularly on our TV shows, when he came home one night and made an announcement.

"This living together just isn't good enough. I think we ought to get married." I felt so close to Burt already, it never occurred to me that marriage could make me love him any *more*.

"That's okay, Burt," I said to him, "you don't *have* to marry me. Everything's fine as it is, don't you think?"

"Except that I don't know how to refer to you anymore. I would like to be able to say 'This is my wife.'"

"How about just saying 'This is my old lady'? Or even 'This is my old cow'?"

He didn't laugh. "So you don't want to marry me, is that it?"

"Of course I do, Burt. What I mean is I don't want you to feel pressured into marrying me."

"I don't feel pressured. I just want to share my life with you. Do you want to share your life with me?"

"Yes . . ."

"Then I want you to be my wife. It's that simple."

Burt was *very* serious about the whole thing. Once I saw how important it was to him, it became important to me too. I was suddenly excited by the thought and couldn't wait to become Mrs. Burt Reynolds. I went over to him and took his face in my hands.

"Okay . . . when?" I whispered.

"We'll figure that out tomorrow," Burt said, picking me up and carrying me into the bedroom.

Our lovemaking that night reached a new level of physical and emotional joy. My fulfillment was complete—I now had his total commitment, and he had mine. I felt a release inside myself and a feeling of safety that I had never known. Marriage *was* going to make me love him more, after all.

The following day we started planning how to go about the procedure. We ruled out eloping without telling anyone, so we took turns calling our parents with the news. They were delighted and probably a bit relieved, since living together out of wedlock was not quite as acceptable in 1962 as it is today.

"Do it up right, Joyce," my dad said over the phone from England. "I'll pay for it, just don't go *mad!*"

Burt wanted a quiet, simple wedding, as did I. "Nothing too far out. I'll be the groom, you'll be the bride, dressed in white, that kinda stuff. . . ."

"Me? In *white*? Try pale gray!"

"Very funny . . . now what about a church?"

This was a good question. First, we had to figure out what religion we were. Oddly enough, that issue had never come up in the six months we had known each other.

"What are you?" I asked Burt.

"I'm not sure, what are you?" he said.

"I'm ordinary," I replied.

"What the heck is ordinary?"

"I dunno, Church of England . . . I guess that makes me Protestant."

"Well, that's what I am."

"Great—then it's settled!"

Our next task was selecting a church, and that didn't take very long either. We walked into the one closest to our house, the First Methodist Church on Tujunga Avenue, and asked to see the minister.

"Do we have to be Methodist to be married here?" we asked him.

My Buddy

"No, my children, you don't," he said with a gentle smile.

"And *you* can marry us, even if we're not Methodist?"

"That is correct. You see, the Methodist ceremony is a simple one. We don't go in for a lot of what you would call frills."

"That's perfect, Reverend, that's just what we want."

These Methodists were all right—not only was the church close to our house, but they'd let us get married without a lot of pomp and ceremony. We were ready to convert.

Once the date, time, and place were all set, we sent out the invitations. I soon found out how naive I was about traditional American wedding procedures. There was the matter of the pre-wedding parties, for instance. The only showers in England involved water, so when Arlene Needham told me I had to have one, I was worried.

"Am I going to get wet at this thing, Arlene?"

"No, silly, we shower you with *gifts!*"

That sounded good. The women would have a shower for me, the men would have a bachelor's night for Burt, and then there would be a big couples shower for the both of us. I wanted to know what would take place during these curious pre-wedding rituals.

"What do guys do on their bachelor night?" I asked Burt.

"We go out and get rip-roaring drunk and do crazy things like go to strip joints."

"And what do the girls do at the bridal shower?"

"You stay home, wear nice dresses, and drink punch."

"That's not fair. I think I'll go out for drinks with Arlene. We'll have the first *women's* stag night!"

"No, you won't. It doesn't work that way. How's it gonna look, you and Arlene sitting at a bar drinking together?"

"Very *attractive!*"

Maggie Eastwood hosted my bridal shower, and as Burt had said, we *did* sit around wearing nice dresses and drinking punch. It began to get a little boring, but then gifts started to appear—a toaster here, a blender there, all the things we needed. This was much better than going to strip joints.

The following night was Burt's bachelor dinner, but I don't think he enjoyed it very much. He was so crazed thinking about what *I* was doing, because I told him I would go out with Arlene instead of needlepoint class, as *he* had suggested. I never panicked about what

Burt was doing without me because I trusted him completely, but he was prone to unfounded attacks of jealousy—something that would cause problems later in our marriage. When he got back from his stag night, I wanted to know if he had fun.

"So what did you do, Burt?"

"Guys don't have to tell girls what they did."

"Well, then, just think of me as one of the guys."

"We just had a few beers, a few laughs, sat around, watched some films . . . no big deal."

"Films? What kind of films?"

"Oh, this guy Bill from the studio had some blue movies. It was nothing, really."

"But I'm fascinated. Can *we* watch those films sometime too?"

"Of course not!"

"Oh, come on, *please*?"

"No, that's *sick,* forget it."

I let the issue slide for the moment, but I hated that double standard of things that guys could do and girls couldn't.

On the Saturday night before our wedding, Hal and Arlene hosted our couples shower at their ranch, and their generosity was overwhelming. It was a major bash: They decorated their pool area with banners and streamers—it looked like Mardi Gras in the San Fernando Valley. There was a lavish spread of food, an unending flow of liquor, and much laughter, dancing, and carrying on until the early hours of the morning. It took us a full hour to load our presents into the car.

"Burt, I think the Americans are on to something with all this shower business," I said, stuffing the last few gifts into the trunk.

When our parents arrived that Monday, our living room was so strewn with gifts that it looked as though we'd looted a department store. There were kitchen appliances that my mother had never even conceived of, and my dad had a difficult time trying to figure out what he could give us that we hadn't already received. They'd brought with them some wonderful English china and silverware, but they wanted to get us something else, something really special.

My dad had always been a TV freak, ever since buying the first one available in Northampton, when I was a child. Burt and I had a small black-and-white set with a lousy picture, so the choice seemed clear: a brand-new *color* TV. Dad insisted on spending extra money to get a custom-made Early American maplewood cabinet that he knew Burt loved.

Burt's parents and my mum and dad all stayed in a nearby Hollywood hotel, and I think Burt, Sr., and Fern were at first taken aback by my parents' down-to-earth, almost abrasive way of speaking, but after the initial shock they got along famously. I think they probably helped Burt's parents loosen up—but then Mum and Dad were always great at breaking the ice.

They got along so well, in fact, that years later, after our divorce, my parents decided to visit Burt's parents on a trip to Florida. I told them I thought that it might not be such a hot idea.

"Why the 'ell *not*?" my dad said indignantly. "I told Burt 'n' Fern if I was in Florida, I'd call 'em, and that's exactly what I'm gonna do! It's got nuthin' to do with *you* two—I'm a man o' my word!"

My mum was a little more apprehensive.

"But 'arold, won't it be a bit awkward?"

"Don't be stupid—we got nothin' against them, they got nothin' against us. What those kids did wasn't *our* fault!"

They spent two weeks traveling in Florida and did actually go to see them. Later, when they'd returned to England, I called to see what had happened.

"Well, let's hear it—did you talk about Burt and me?"

"Yeah, we said, 'Ain't it a shame?' and then went out and had ourselves a good time!"

How civilized, I thought.

On Thursday night the rehearsal was held for the wedding ceremony. Both sets of parents were there, along with my maid of honor, Sharon DuBord, a friend that I'd made at Desilu, and Burt's best man, Dudley Remus, an old pal who had flown in from Florida. Burt had to come straight from the "Gunsmoke" set, so there was no time for him to change. He made a great comic entrance as he arrived, huffing and puffing, dressed like Quint the Blacksmith in his half-breed Indian makeup.

"This is the first Methodist cowboy wedding on record," he joked.

Burt and I found it amusing that like a show, you had to rehearse weddings, and we tried to resist our temptation to crack a lot of dumb jokes about the whole thing. The organist didn't show up at rehearsals, so as we started walking down the aisle, a short bald man with a mustache came out and started to hum in a nasal tenor voice.

"Dum dum, de-dum! Dum *dum* de-dum! Dum dum de-dum dum, de-dum dum de-dum!" At this I went over the edge and burst out laughing.

"Cut!" Burt yelled.

"Makeup!" I shouted.

"Which camera do I look into?"

"Where are the cue cards?"

"Hit your mark!"

"Speak when the reverend says 'Action!' "

After we settled down a little, the minister explained to Burt at what point the ring was to be put on my finger. "Propman," Burt whispered as we tried to suppress our laughter, to no avail.

We took our parents to dinner after the rehearsal and then drove them back to their hotel before returning home to Hermit's Glen. It was late, and we were exhausted.

"I'm going to make up the bed in the den," Burt announced.

"The den? Are you expecting company?"

"No, I just don't think it's right for us to sleep in the same bed tonight. We're getting *married* tomorrow."

"Oh, really? Thanks for reminding me!"

I told him that he was being silly and old-fashioned by insisting that we sleep apart the night before the ceremony. We had already been living together for six months, for God's sake. But after thinking about it, I understood what he meant. It was a sweet gesture—he wanted the night before our wedding to be different, to make the next day special.

"You're right, Burt, it's very beautiful and symbolic that we don't sleep together tonight."

"Plus we'll want to make up for it *tomorrow* night!" he said.

There was a wonderful sense of anticipation in the air as we kissed good night and went to our separate rooms. As I lay in my bed, I could think only of how much I loved him, how much I wanted to be falling asleep right next to him, and what a wonderful life we would have together. It *was* going to be a special day.

* * *

My Buddy

Shortly after eight o'clock on Friday, June 28, 1963, in the First Methodist Church on Tujunga Avenue, in North Hollywood, California, the Reverend William Merwin pronounced us man and wife.

The wedding went smoothly and as planned. Burt looked terrific in a simple dark suit and straight tie, and I wore white silk, with an elaborate net veil arrangement. It was a small, intimate gathering—not counting the press. There seemed to be more of them than our family and friends put together.

The photographers had a field day as the guests arrived at the church. Amanda Blake, Milburn Stone, and Ken Curtis, from "Gunsmoke," were there, as was Burt's friend Jimmie Rodgers, a popular country and western singer who sang at our ceremony.

My parents were a bundle of nerves through most of the last-minute preparations. Years later they revealed to me the drama that had gone on behind the scenes. At one point Burt, Burt, Sr., my mum and dad and I were all preparing for the ceremony, but Fern—Burt's mother—was nowhere to be found. My mum went searching for her and finally found her alone in a room, sobbing. My mother tried to comfort her and asked what was wrong.

"I'm frightened," Fern sobbed. This seemed natural enough on her son's wedding day.

"You're frightened about your Burt?" my mother asked.

"No," Fern said, "about your Judy. I just hope Burt can control his temper with her."

I knew nothing of that exchange at the time.

Our reception was held at our favorite French restaurant, Coolibar's, which catered a twelve-course dinner for us and the thirty-two guests in our reception party. After a wonderfully festive night of toasts and congratulations, Burt and I made our getaway.

We left just after midnight. It was warm enough to keep the T-Bird top down as we drove north along the winding Pacific Coast Highway, stopping now and then to get out of the car and admire the breathtaking beauty of the ocean below. Standing at the edge of the cliff, we held each other, our love as boundless as the Pacific, wanting the moment to last forever.

As dawn broke we arrived at our hideaway, the Highland Inn in Carmel-by-the-Sea, wearily checking into the bridal suite. As soon as the door was closed, we dropped our luggage, tore off our clothes, and got into bed.

I was mesmerized by his eyes as they stared directly into mine during our lovemaking. I saw in them the purest love I had ever known as we celebrated the supreme commitment we had just made to each other—marriage.

The next day Burt discovered to his dismay that since the hotel was nestled in the hills, it could not receive the television broadcast of Sunday's big all-star football game from Monterey. He insisted that we cut the honeymoon short and return home to Los Angeles and our fabulous new color television. It wasn't a very romantic notion, but I didn't mind, since it meant seeing more of my parents, who were staying at our house for a few days before returning to England. After all the hoopla, they were surprised when we casually strolled in on Saturday evening.

"Hi, we're back!" we announced humbly.

"See, 'arold?" my mum joked. "I *told* you it wouldn't last!"

Once we were married, Burt wanted to change me even more.

"Now you are my *wife*. You must behave like a lady—no more boyish clothes, pixie hairdo, or bad language. I don't want my wife being thought of as one of the boys."

I obliged, because I wanted to make him happy and proud of me. I even wore an uncomfortable push-up bra on occasions—something I would never have done otherwise and have never done since. My hair grew past my shoulders, and I curbed my language admirably. But after a while it made me feel uneasy—I wasn't being myself. I wanted to say "shit!" now and then.

I began to realize that my sense of freedom was something that Burt didn't really understand at all. It frightened him. If I wanted him—which I truly did—I'd have to conform to his way of thinking, which wouldn't come easy after so many years of living my life *my* way.

As Hollywood's latest newlyweds, Burt and I were an irresistible gossip item. We found ourselves on fan magazine covers and the subject of numerous articles, many of which took the liberty of assuming I would be turning in my tap shoes to become a housewife.

My Buddy

For the time being, at least, we were *both* the breadwinners, so we decided to get a house of our own, with plenty of room to settle down.

Buying a house was such a *married* thing to do. After much perseverance we found an enchanting house in Studio City, set into the hillside with a glorious view of the San Fernando Valley. It was on Laurelcrest Drive, at the top of a series of hairpin turns, built on an acre of steeply inclined land. The garage was at street level, and stone steps led down from the gate to the front door.

The ivy-covered house was greatly in need of repair, but we saw the potential for a comfortable home. When Burt saw the living room wall, he visualized his gun rack; when he saw the spacious veranda, he envisioned a game room; when he saw the patio, he imagined outdoor barbecues. When I saw the disheveled-looking tree house, I envisioned a disheveled-looking tree house—but one that would make the coziest of love nests.

Without much hesitation, we bought the house for $38,000. We split everything down the middle, including a $12,000 home improvement loan which we used to knock down a wall and make the living room larger, install a bar, and replace the tiny bedroom windows with sliding glass doors leading out to a balcony.

From Hermit's Glen we brought only Burt's king-size bed and a few antiques I had accumulated, so we shopped for odd bits of furniture that we needed. Everything had to be the same Early American style that Burt loved, and in my eagerness to embrace Americana, I tried to develop a taste for these pieces of roughly hewn maple.

As our decorating shaped up, my only worry was that there was no place in the house that was mine alone, except the kitchen—it was Burt's den, Burt's living room, Burt's bedroom, and *my* kitchen. Thanks to the wedding gifts, that kitchen was at least fully equipped.

We naturally brought the beautiful color TV that my father had given us. In knocking down the living room wall, we had exposed a closet that was perfect for rows of shelves, and Burt set his heart on moving the TV into one of those compartments. He discovered to his dismay, however, that the TV was far too big. I was stunned when he walked through the front door the next day with a gigantic chain saw that he had rented, and I was even more flabbergasted when I saw him pick it up and start sawing off the legs of the beautiful cabinet. It was like a knife going through butter. I stood aside and didn't argue; I wasn't *about* to differ with him as long as that chain saw was on the premises.

Burt lifted the set to the shelf, but it was still too wide, so he buzzed his way through one side of the cabinet, then the other. He proudly slid the set into the wall compartment, only to realize that the set was too *deep*—it protruded a foot out from the shelf.

Burt scrutinized this dilemma as I swept up the mound of sawdust left over from the carnage of our set. He came up with a brilliant solution: he'd simply knock through the wall into the closet behind it. I stood back and cringed as he went at the wall with a sledgehammer, filling the room with a cloud of dust. When all was said and done, the television *did* fit nicely and it was a convenient way of saving space; I just didn't know how I was going to explain it to my dad when he next visited us and saw his expensive wedding gift cut down to its bare picture tube.

In addition to his taste for Early American decor, Burt was a monogram fiend, putting our names or initials on almost anything with room to bear them: coasters, place mats, silverware, and wastebaskets.

We had "Burt and Judy" towels, and all his shirts bore some variation of his name, be it Burt, Buddy, or BR. He gave me turtlenecks with "Judy" sewn in script, and he even spent an afternoon labeling each of my thirty-odd cookbooks with tiny stickers that read "From the kitchen of *Judy Reynolds*."

Burt outdid himself with a splendid leather director's chair for me to use on the set, with "Mrs. Burt Reynolds" engraved on the back. Everyone loved to kid me about it, and I finally had to stop taking it to work when they threatened to change my name in the credits!

One of my contributions to our new home was a set of satin sheets. They were very sexy and sensual at first, but we soon found out the hard way that *staying* in them was a problem. The pillows were the first to slide off while we made love, and we would gradually slither onto the floor in the throes of passion, landing with a thump.

Clyde would waddle in and lick our faces as we lay there, and I'd burst into hysterics watching Burt, with his obsession for stunts, ham it up by taking naked pratfalls off the slippery bed.

Burt's sense of humor knew no bounds. Jonathan Winters was one of his idols; he owned all of Winters's records and knew his material by heart, often doing perfect imitations of his characters and routines, complete with the uncanny sound effects.

Burt finally got the chance to meet his hero when he found out that his agent also represented Winters. A meeting was arranged, and Burt excitedly drove up to Winters's house. He got out of his car and was greeted by the sight of Jonathan lurking behind a tree in his robe and pajamas, holding a shotgun.

"Hold it right there, buddy," Winters commanded in a hillbilly accent. Burt chuckled.

"This here's pur-i-vate property, boy! I could *pop* you for this!"

"Hey, that's a great bit," Burt said, creased with laughter. But Winters kept threatening, and never broke from that character, until finally his wife came out and retrieved her husband. Burt returned home convinced more than ever that Winters was a comedy genius.

When Burt and I went out socially, we often worked like a comedy team, feeding each other straight lines and doing takes. It wasn't contrived, it was just the natural way we responded in public.

Burt would introduce me in his deadpan style: "Do you know Judy? Sure you do. *Everybody* knows Judy. Do you like Judy? Sure you do. *Everybody* likes Judy. English accent, great legs, sure, sure . . ."

I would needle him in front of other people in a good-natured way because I knew his reactions would get big laughs. If someone asked me, "Is this your husband?" I would drive Burt crazy by saying, "No, he's my *Buddy!*"

He would retort by dredging up my given name in front of everyone. "I believe your name was *Joyce,* right? Aha. Joyce . . . no *wonder* she changed it. . . ."

When Burt and I were "on" together, there was nothing quite like it. We were a magnet to everyone around us, but it was clear by our chemistry that no man or woman could come between us.

Burt enjoyed socializing with older, more established figures in show business. He'd done a telethon with Patti Andrews, of the Andrews Sisters, and they got along so well that she invited us over for dinner at her sister Laverne's house.

After Burt and I admired their spacious home, they told us the sad story of their previous house, which was destroyed in a famous

Beverly Hills fire. They were neighbors of Fred MacMurray at the time, and as the fire spread, it was headed for his house; the way the winds were blowing, the Andrews Sisters' house was not in danger.

In a panic to save his home, MacMurray refused to be evacuated and instead called Walt Disney Studios, where he was under contract. He demanded that four large ritters—wind machines used to simulate hurricanes in films—be sent to his house, along with a team of technicians to operate them.

They arrived just in time to erect two of them in the fire's path and two more on the roof of the house, as MacMurray raced around turning on his sprinklers. The ritters changed the path of the blaze, sending it directly toward the Andrews Sisters' property with no warning whatsoever. They could salvage only their jewelry and gold records by throwing them into their pool. The rest of their home burned to the ground as Fred MacMurray stood proudly on his roof, safe behind the howling wind machines.

We continued to spend a lot of our time with Clint and Maggie Eastwood. Not long after we'd settled into Laurelcrest, Clint came over with the script for a movie he had been asked to do in Italy. It was a western, and Clint was intrigued by the script. He asked Burt and me if we'd read it and give him our opinion before he decided.

It was an unusual part. Clint's character was almost always on camera but he only spoke about one word for every cowpoke he shot to death. The script had a certain appeal, though, and Burt and I told Clint he should do it—the fewer words he spoke, the more countries it would play in. Besides, it would mean a free trip to Italy for him and for Maggie, and if the movie bombed, it would fade into obscurity without damaging Clint's career.

Clint took the part and a whole new western genre was born: The movie was *A Fistful of Dollars,* directed by Sergio Leone, and it set the trend for a string of dusty, low-budget spaghetti westerns. It was the film that introduced the raspy-voiced, tight-lipped persona that captured the world's imagination. We kidded Clint that he had two expressions on the screen: intense and *more* intense. He was the first one to laugh at this kind of ribbing, because he was secure and self-confident about his talent as an actor.

72

My Buddy

Clint and Maggie were fond of parlor games, as were Burt and I and another couple we were close to—Channing and Jozy Pollock (she was from England, he had a stunning magic act featuring disappearing doves). When we gathered socially, we grew tired of Charades, so one evening over dinner we devised a similar game but with more intricacies, which we dubbed "Allusions." We made up all kinds of rules and perfected it to the point where we actually approached the Goodson/Todman company with the idea. We were convinced it was better than the popular game shows on television at the time.

They agreed to let us come in for a demonstration, so we showed up at Goodson/Todman armed with clock timers, buzzers, and elaborate cards indicating topics and points. We explained the concept, divided ourselves into two teams, and started playing. After twenty minutes of fervent play, we finished and looked over at the stonefaced executives. "Thank you for coming in," they said, "we'll let you know. Next, please!"

We walked out of there feeling pretty stupid. It was definitely a "don't call us, we'll call you" situation.

Ryan O'Neal and his wife, actress Joanna Moore, were another couple with whom we were good friends. Ryan was then working on his TV series, "Peyton Place," and like Clint, he would soon make his transition into movies, while Joanna had already appeared in a number of films of her own.

Burt and I were at the hospital with Ryan when their daughter Tatum was born. The birth was effortless, because Joanna was in such fantastic physical shape—she swam laps in her pool right up until the day she entered the hospital.

Ryan was a fitness buff, and Burt often worked out with him at his house, as he did with Clint. Burt and Ryan loved to be watched as they worked out, hamming it up with grunts and groans. Clint, however, *hated* being observed; he considered it an *invasion*. To him, working out was a solitary, meditative experience.

Most of Burt's closest friends were actors from the other TV westerns. They formed a kind of brotherhood: Doug ("The Virginian") McClure, Bob ("Wagon Train") Fuller, Lee ("Big Valley") Majors, and, of course, Hal Needham, who was on *all* of the shows. When they hung out together at Hal's ranch, the talk was six-guns, saddles, and stunts.

"You shoulda seen that guy do a triple back flip. . . ."

"How high were those flames . . . ?"

"He needed *six* mattresses. . . ."

"How many flights of stairs . . . ?"

"I didn't time the punch right, and goddamn if he didn't go flyin' across the room!"

Stunts were their *lives.*

We always hung out with Burt's crowd, so I had little opportunity to pursue friends of my own. I also learned that Burt preferred not to hear about my past social life, especially when it came to the men I knew in London. Whenever I volunteered a story I thought would amuse him, Burt winced and said he'd rather not know. I could understand that to a certain extent, but it hurt me to see his reaction to my dear old friend Stirling Moss, whom I invited to dinner when I heard he was visiting Los Angeles. It was one of my only attempts to incorporate anyone from my past into my life with Burt.

It was wonderful to see Stirling looking so well, completely recovered from his near-fatal crash at Goodwood. His face had been flawlessly reconstructed, and his memory was intact. Over dinner Stirling mentioned how much my visit to his bedside in the hospital had meant to him.

Instead of appreciating my joy at being reunited with such a close friend, Burt made the evening miserable. He hated the notion that I had been with other men before him, let alone having to sit across the dinner table from one of them. Burt pouted throughout the meal and rudely retreated to the bedroom when we finished eating. It was terribly embarrassing. Feeling that he had caused a rift, Stirling excused himself and left right after dinner. I walked him out to his car and tried to apologize.

"Stirling, I'm so embarrassed. I don't know what's gotten into Burt. I'm sorry you had to sit through that. . . ."

"Hey, don't worry about *me,* kid," he said. "I'm worried about *you.* I hope you can handle him."

* * *

My Buddy

There were other aspects of my past that I had to edit out for Burt. Having first tried marijuana in London when I was eighteen, I enjoyed it at parties if it was offered. Burt had also tried it during his early days in New York, but it made him uneasy. He wouldn't even *talk* about it, so I didn't push it.

On one occasion the subject came up unexpectedly. We spent a weekend at a ranch belonging to one of the wranglers in charge of the horses on "Gunsmoke." There was a lot of talk about "turning on" when we arrived, and upon hearing this, Burt drew me aside for a lecture.

"If you're going to smoke that stuff, it's going to be with me, and *only* with me," he said earnestly. "And what's more, if I find out you *have* been smoking it with anyone else, I'll *kill* you!"

I didn't argue. I realized that he was trying to share something with me that was very foreign to him. In doing so, however, he had to lay down some ground rules.

We spent a fabulous weekend at that ranch, wandering off into the woods and getting high. It was fun, but Burt seemed too nervous and uncomfortable to really enjoy it—perhaps because his father was a police chief.

Despite these differences in our personalities, our love for each other prevailed and our married life began to settle down nicely. Then we lost our jobs.

Even though unemployment is inevitable for actors and actresses, it unfortunately happened to both of us at the same time. "Fair Exchange" actually had been canceled after our first season, but a large amount of mail in support of the show convinced the network to put us back on in the hopes that our ratings would improve.

The fundamental problem with the show was that it was an hour long; only westerns and police dramas were an hour—not sitcoms. Desilu tried to salvage the show by shortening it to a half hour, but the condensed format just couldn't accommodate the complicated trans-Atlantic plot. After airing thirteen more episodes in the fall of 1963—including one in which I received my first screen kiss from a young actor named Jack Nicholson—CBS took "Fair Exchange" off its schedule for good.

Burt originally had joined the cast of "Gunsmoke" to help fill the void that Dennis Weaver created after leaving the show the year before. Burt's character of Quint the Blacksmith was somewhat limited, however, and he started to appear in fewer and fewer episodes. It came as no surprise when CBS didn't renew his contract.

Burt wasn't exactly heartbroken, though, since he was now free to consider other parts. What he missed most was leaving his group of pals from the show and the camaraderie he had built up. Hollywood being as cruel as it is, the news got around that he was "dropped," as if he had failed in some way, instead of the truth, which was that his part had simply reached a dead end. For the first time, Burt felt he was a step behind the rest of the brotherhood.

Christmas had always been a dismal affair for me, because my parents' shop was so busy during the holiday season that they were utterly exhausted by the time Christmas Eve rolled around. This year promised to be different, however, as Burt and I looked forward to sharing the celebration in Florida with the Reynolds clan.

On the plane to Florida, Burt warned me to be on my best behavior. His family was very conservative, since football and police work were their main interests and occupations at the time. When we arrived, I was afraid to open my mouth at first, but they were so warm and friendly, I soon felt very much at home.

Burt had lapsed into his best good ol' boy accent, with a big "Howdy, y'all!" for everyone. I'm the same way when I return to England, but hearing Burt suddenly speaking this way took some getting used to.

"Why aren't you in the kitchen with the womenfolk?" he asked me before our Christmas dinner.

"The *womenfolk*? What is this, 'Wagon Train'?"

All the womenfolk around Burt's home had two names, like Nancy Lee, Betty Sue, Cindy Lou, and Billie Jo.

Whenever one of them handed me a baby, I was mortified. "I'm not very good with babies," I said, as even the calmest of infants howled once it was placed in my arms. I was asked when *we* would be having a child. "Ask Buddy," I said.

Burt and I had talked about having children ever since we first decided to get married, but it had not been a realistic possibility as long as we both were working. Burt's freckle-faced niece and nephew were perfectly behaved, all-American kids. Their example, combined with the beautiful way in which Ryan and Joanna had handled the birth of Tatum, inspired me more than ever to have a child.

Burt was obsessed about the idea. It was a foregone conclusion to him that our child would be a boy, and that he would grow up to play football just like Daddy. Heaven help the poor boy if he expressed a preference for ballet.

I was actually terrorized by the act of giving birth. My mum used to say, "I'd rather *die* than have another child," an attitude that didn't have me running to the obstetrician. I wanted to be a good mother, though, and I thought we should wait until we had enough money set aside to give our child a good education. If we were going to do it, I wanted to do it right, and I felt we had plenty of time.

In the meantime we added to our family by buying a dachshund puppy after our return to L.A. He was a good companion for Clyde, and we named him Festus, after the character on "Gunsmoke."

For a while, being unemployed at the same time gave us something in common—not to mention loads of time together. We would go for job interviews and come home to commiserate about what a rotten business we were in. As long as we were *both* out of work, we tried to make the best of things and remain cheerful.

Just as despair began to set in, I was heartened by two jobs that came along in succession. I played an Irish nun on "Bonanza," which was my first appearance on a western and an excellent opportunity to do a straight, dramatic role. Then came a small part in a movie written by Paddy Chayefsky, *The Americanization of Emily,* starring James Garner and James Coburn. When Burt found out that one scene with Garner and Coburn required me to be partially nude, he flew into a rage.

"Don't worry, Burt," I said, trying to calm him down. "I'll have my back to the camera at all times."

"I don't care about the camera. What about the crew? And *Coburn?* And *Garner?*"

He was so incensed, he called the wardrobe department at MGM studios to insist that I be covered adequately. I couldn't blame him for being concerned, but he created such a stink that I felt embarrassed, because my part in the movie wasn't that big—and neither were my boobs. I ended up wearing paste-ons, which weren't very comfortable, and all the fuss only added to my anxiety about doing the scene to begin with.

Later that spring, I was considered for a part on a comedy series called "The Baileys of Balboa," playing the daughter of a wealthy California yachtsman. Burt worked with me on polishing my American accent. Thanks to his coaching I won the role and had the producers convinced I was born and raised in the U.S. of A. When I showed up for my first day of work speaking in my natural accent, the director was flabbergasted.

Burt was thrilled I'd found a job, but I could tell deep down he was impatient and frustrated. I always believed in him and knew he would be a huge star someday. In addition to his brilliant comedic talents, he has always had that special ability to make his acting look so effortless, to make even the weakest dialogue sound genuine.

Luckily, he soon found some work in a low-budget movie filmed in the Orient, *Operation C.I.A.* When he returned home from a month of shooting there, he was bubbling over with a fantastic story about "a friend of his" who had experienced something truly remarkable on a visit to a geisha house.

Burt went into great detail about how this "friend" had been massaged and tantalized with exotic oils and the tender hands of a half-dozen geishas all expertly trained in fulfilling a man's every fantasy. His "friend" was brought to the edge of orgasm by these girls, but just as he thought he would explode with ecstasy, they suddenly left the room. But he was not alone.

A beautiful young Eurasian girl was suspended from the ceiling, sitting in a basket, with a hole in the bottom that revealed her genitalia. The girl was lowered by the cables that held her basket aloft, until she hovered over him. At that point two geishas appeared to help the young one onto him. Once he was inside her, they began to rotate her at great speed, until his resulting orgasm—aided by her specially trained inner muscles—lifted Burt's "friend" about a foot off the bed.

I *loved* that story and lived it along with him as he told it, but Burt described it all with such enthusiasm and attention to detail that it was obvious no such "friend" existed.

My Buddy

"You don't have to pretend it wasn't you, Burt," I told him. "It sounds like an incredible experience. I'm envious!"

Saying that was a *big* mistake. Burt was shocked at me for approving of such a thing.

"If I *had* done it," he said, "and I *had* admitted it to you, I'd be disgusted with your reaction. This is probably your way of setting me up so *you* can screw around!"

What I said had completely backfired. It was ironic that Burt was now furious at *me* and *my* response to *his* fooling around with the geishas. I couldn't win. The capper was when he said, "I find it amazing how free you are with my body. It doesn't bother you at all hearing about my sexual encounters with another woman. Oh, no, you find it exciting! That's *sick!*"

I couldn't be as possessive of Burt as he was of me. If a man so much as *looked* at me in the wrong way, Burt had him up against a wall by the throat, threatening to kill him if he did it again. It was no joke. He mentioned it in an interview for the Chicago *Tribune*:

> . . . There was a time when I really did play tough guy. . . . It was a way to get girls and be somebody. But fortunately I married a girl who was Peter Pan. She was English, and I remember one night when a guy got intellectually smart with me and I didn't know how to handle it, I picked him up and hung him on a coat hanger. I thought she'd think that was wonderful.
>
> Well, she didn't speak to me for about ten days. And when she did, she told me she thought it was the most disgusting thing she'd ever seen. And it was then that I realized that if I had attacked this guy with humor—instead of my fists—she would have thought I was terrific. . . .

There was one bizarre instance, however, when his grounds for jealousy were *very* understandable.

Burt had gone home to visit his parents in Florida and I planned to join him when my "Baileys of Balboa" filming was completed. During the two weeks we were apart, I was up every morning at 5 A.M. for the drive out to Balboa to film on location. Our dressing rooms were seedy trailers, and there were outhouses instead of bathrooms—not the glamorous side of television work.

When I arrived in Florida, Burt and I made love that night with the special zest that comes from being deprived of one another for any length of time.

Late the following afternoon as we got ready for dinner, Burt emerged from the bathroom with a stern look on his face. He went over to the bedroom door, bolted it, and wedged a chair up against the doorknob so that no one could enter. He strode over to me, seething.

"Okay, strip down. I wanna know who you've been with. . . ."

"What?"

"C'mon, I mean it!"

"Burt, what is this?"

"I've got something that only *you* can give me. Ever had crabs?" I was totally mystified. "What do you mean, seafood?"

"*You* know what I'm talking about. I've got 'em, and the only way I coulda gotten 'em is from *you.* Now *who* have you slept with?"

Burt was livid, but tight-faced, because he had to control his temper while in his parents' home. I was frightened because I honestly had never heard of such a thing. He explained that crabs only came from sexual contact with unclean people, and that he hadn't been with anyone else. I hadn't, either, but I didn't know how to convince him of that.

"All right now, strip down," he insisted. "I'm going to have to examine you." I did so, and he led me into the bathroom where the fluorescent lights and a magnifying glass would aid in his search.

"Burt, this is ridic—"

"Just do as I say!"

"Burt, there's nothing there."

"Well, they're tough to spot. . . ."

"No kidding!"

"They're just eggs on you, but they're moving on me. Take a look at *this.*" In the palm of his hand were some tiny white specks. Burt claimed these specks had "hatched" on him overnight.

I couldn't believe I had transmitted such a terrible thing, especially since I'd had no sexual contact with another man. I asked Burt if it was possible I could have picked them up from rented costumes on the "Baileys" set, or perhaps even the grimy outhouses on location in Balboa.

"Don't give me the old toilet seat routine," he said harshly. "I'm not a chump. There's only one way to get 'em, and that's how you *got* 'em!"

I was saved by the fact that we were in his parents' home. He couldn't yell. Instead, he screamed at the bottom of his lungs, through clenched teeth. I was in tears.

"Put your clothes on, we're going to the drugstore. We'll tell my mom that we're going for a little drive."

We drove into town and I waited in the car as he bought the necessary lotion in the drugstore. When he got back in the car, I tried again to get through to him.

"Burt, you've got to believe me, I don't know how—"

"Don't open your mouth. I'd rather you didn't even talk at all if you're just going to give me the same old bullshit. We're going home to put this stuff on and kill those things. *Then* we'll see if there's anything left to talk about."

We returned to the house where his mother was busy preparing dinner. Once safely inside the bathroom with the door locked, he continued to give me orders.

"Now strip down again and put your clothes in a pile over there."

It was as if I were being deloused. It was vile, but I did as he said as he removed his own clothes and put them in the same pile.

"I'll do you, then you do me," he instructed. "This stuff stings, so make sure you don't get it on any of the sensitive areas."

He worked gently and gingerly, like a painter at his easel, finally stepping back with a satisfied look and handing me the ointment.

"You've got to cover every single hair with this stuff, otherwise the eggs will hatch and start to crawl around."

I started to work on him cautiously, but when I reached his crown jewels, I didn't realize some of the lotion was on my hand. I touched him and he exploded with pain.

"*AARRGGHHH!!!*" he cried, stuffing his fist into his mouth to muffle the noise.

"Burt, I'm sorry, I forgot about the ointment—"

"*You're* sorry!"

He put his ear up to the door to see if his yell had been heard, clutching his groin in agony. "This is all your fault," he muttered.

We had to wait about fifteen minutes for the ointment to do its work before we could wash it off.

"Burt, let's go see a doctor about this. It's all so disgusting."

"No way."

"But we can go to someone who won't *tell*."

"I'm telling you this stuff will work, just relax."

After washing up in the bathtub, it was time for the final inspection, so out came the magnifying glass again. Suddenly, there was a knock at the door. It was his mother.

"Buddy! Judy! Dinner's almost ready!"

By now I couldn't contain myself any longer. "If your mother's cooked seafood, I'll *die*," I said.

"We'll be right out!" Burt shouted, letting out a giggle.

"You've got to admit, Burt," I said, "this *is* a ridiculous scene."

By now he was laughing so hard he had to agree, and I knew the worst was over. That night our lovemaking was splendid. As we lay in bed, shaking and shivering after a particularly emotional climax, I whispered, "After *that*, Burt, how could I even *think* of being with any other man?"

He smiled, and I thought at last he understood.

In the summer of 1964 Burt traveled to Montgomery, Alabama, to participate in a fund-raising drive for underprivileged children. The charity event had been organized by local dignitaries, such as the mayor of Montgomery, and Alabama governor George Wallace.

The civil rights movement was peaking in America, and there had been ongoing race riots in Alabama. Wallace was hated by the blacks for his segregationist views and his stand on voting rights. Police brutality and racist murders by the Ku Klux Klan had all combined to raise the racial tension to a boiling point.

I had seen news reports of demonstrators being beaten and fire-hosed, but this was far from my mind when I got the call from Governor Wallace's office telling me that Burt had been taken ill. Because the doctors hadn't been able to diagnose what appeared to be a serious illness, they suggested that, as his wife, I should be by his side. It would all be arranged for me: An official government car would be waiting to take me straight to the hospital.

When I arrived at the airport, a chauffeur met me in a stretch limousine with darkly tinted windows. I stared blankly out at the streets as we drove, wondering what news would greet me about

Burt's condition. As we neared the hospital, I noticed an increasing number of angry blacks lining the sweltering streets, shouting, raising their fists, and crowding closer and closer to the car. The limousine was forced to a stop by the teeming crowd, and the faces pressed against the window, looking distorted through the glass. I heard the crash of their fists on the hood of the car.

The driver—who was black—told me to lie down on the floor and cover myself with his jacket. He comforted me by saying that we were close to the hospital and that help was on its way. In my panic it dawned on me that they must have thought I was the mayor, or perhaps even Wallace himself.

I saw people mount the trunk of the car and heard the thump of footsteps on the roof. The limousine then began to rock from side to side, and I pulled the driver's jacket over my head just in time to protect myself from a shower of shattered glass from the back window.

Suddenly I heard the wail of sirens. I peered out to see riot police descend upon the retreating crowd, catching stragglers by the collar and bludgeoning them with clubs. I had been grateful at first to see the policemen, but when I saw the awful brutality they used on the handful of demonstrators who were left behind, I felt nauseous.

Suddenly the door of the limousine flew open and a helmeted officer poked his head in.

"You all right, Miz Reynolds? We're sorry 'bout all this trouble. We're goin' take you straight to the hospital now."

I was swept into a waiting police car, and a motorcycle escort was quickly rounded up. With flashing lights and screaming sirens, we drove the two remaining blocks to the hospital.

I was still in shock when they showed me into Burt's room, but the doctors advised me not to mention the incident to him. Burt was feverish and delirious, but he smiled when I kissed him on the forehead and held his hand.

Fortunately, the doctors had been able to diagnose his mysterious illness: While filming a fight scene in the Orient, he had accidentally swallowed contaminated river water and contracted a vicious bug that had infected his blood.

It would take a few days to filter Burt's blood and bring his fever down, and since my hotel was in the middle of the riot zone, the doctors offered to have a cot brought into his room. I spent the next three nights there, until we were finally able to return to the safety of Laurelcrest, quite shaken by the experience.

In the fall, my parents arrived to visit, this time accompanied by my uncle John and aunt Alice. Although I was thrilled to see them, I dreaded my dad's reaction when he saw the chain-saw massacre Burt had performed on the cabinet of our television set while trying to fit it into the shelf. Luckily Burt would not be home until later, giving me time to break the news gently.

I gave them a tour of the house and they were impressed with the improvements we had made since their last visit. But it wasn't long before my dad started looking around the living room curiously.

"Where's the telly, Joyce?" he asked me.

"Um . . . we're a bit short of space, so it's in there. . . ."

"Where?"

I pointed at the closet, the doors of which I'd purposely closed.

"Well, let's see it, then."

I revealed the set, snugly placed in the shelf. "It's in here to conserve space."

"Well, where's the bleedin' cabinet?"

"It's . . . *gone,* Dad."

"Gone?"

"You see, in order to get it in there, we had to trim it a bit."

"You had to do *what*?"

"We had to take the cabinet off. . . ."

"Well, you saved it, didn't you?"

"Not really . . . it got sawed off. . . ."

"You sawed that bloody expensive wood right *off*?"

"Not really, Burt had to saw—"

"Now let me get this straight," my dad said, "that silly sod asked for a telly in this special bleedin' wood that I go to the trouble of buyin', and he saws it to bits, and now it's in *there*? You believe this, Kath?"

Just then Burt returned home, and the subject was dropped while they greeted their son-in-law. Uncle John and Aunt Alice were especially thrilled, not having met him before. Nothing was mentioned about the TV until dinnertime.

At age nine *(Sunbeam Photo Limited, Margate)*

My first professional picture, taken at age sixteen *(Houston Foger, London)*

Stirling Moss visits me in Edinburgh after
On the Brighter Side, with paparazzi on
his tail. *(Beaverbrook Newspapers,
Edinburgh)*

Burt's and my wedding day
(Judy Carne Collection)

Burt and I entertain after the wedding *(from left)*: Dad, Uncle John, Aunt Alice, and Mum, in 1964. I'm wearing a beehive between Maggie and Clint Eastwood. *(Judy Carne Collection)*

Mr. and Mrs. Harold Botterill

request the honour of your presence

at the marriage of their daughter

Judy

to

Mr. Burton Leon Reynolds

on Friday, the twenty-eighth of June

at eight o'clock in the evening

First Methodist Church of North Hollywood

Forty-eight thirty-two Tujunga Avenue

North Hollywood, California

The invitation

Burt and I outside Laurelcrest, after the honeymoon (*Judy Carne Collection*)

The Reynolds family:
Burt, Judy, and Clyde *(Gene Trindl)*

(Gene Trindl)

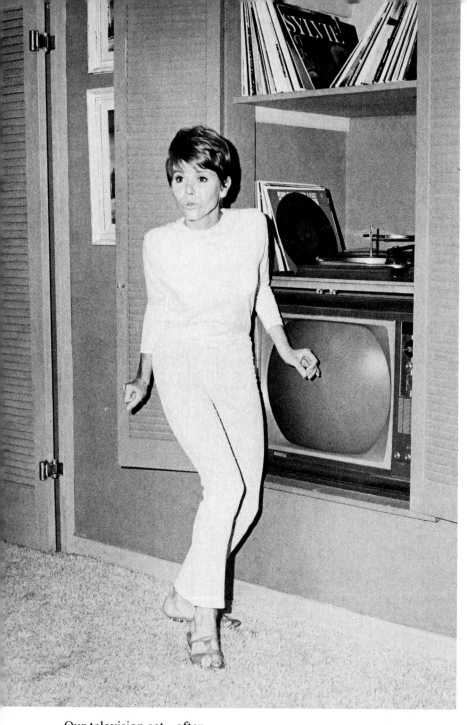

Our television set—after
Burt's chainsaw remodeling (*Roy Cummings*)

My Buddy

I was in the kitchen preparing an English roast when I heard the click of the television knob and a commercial start to blare. Uh-oh, here it comes, I thought.

"Burt, I've been meanin' to ask you," I heard my dad start. "Remember the cabinet that telly used to be in? You still got it, have you?"

"No, we threw it out. . . ."

"Threw it . . . *out*?"

"Well, Pop, you see, it was a question of space."

"Oh, I see . . . pity you didn't save the wood. Kath and I could have used it for somethin', seein' as it was that nice *maple wood*. . . ."

My mum tried to keep the peace. "My, but it's tucked out of the way, ain't it, 'arold?"

Before long we were all laughing about it. It became a running gag for the rest of their stay.

"If you haven't got anything to do, Burt, find something with legs on it and saw them off. If you need work, maybe you can find a job as a lumberjack."

Burt was able to laugh about it, too, but after a while it got to him. He took me into the bedroom for a lecture. He sat in his swivel chair with his feet up on his rolltop desk.

"First of all, tell your dad to lay off about the damn TV set!"

He listed his grievances, one of which was having to drive us all to a "Baileys of Balboa" press party. It was in honor of the series debut, to be held aboard the yacht where we filmed the show. My parents had been looking forward to the party since their arrival.

I understood why he didn't want to drive to Balboa to attend a tedious press function for a show he wasn't appearing on. He just didn't realize that as one of the show's stars, my presence was imperative. "I know you don't fancy it, Burt, but how about if I take my folks and we'll see you when we get back?"

He certainly wasn't going to let me go unescorted, so he grudgingly agreed to drive us. At the party I tried to include him while being introduced to members of the press, but every time a TV executive dragged me away to meet someone else, I could sense Burt's thunder growing heavier and heavier. When the introductions were over, I felt his grip on my arm. "Let's go," he said.

"But Burt, the party's just starting. There's dinner and dancing yet to come."

"We leave *now,*" he growled.

Not wanting to cause a scene, I excused myself, rounded up my folks, Uncle John and Aunt Alice, and we left.

Burt's bedroom lectures continued throughout my parents' visit. Sometimes they lasted for hours, and my mum and dad would see me emerging from the bedroom in tears. I tried to cover up for my parents' sake, pretending nothing serious was going on. But it was.

Burt's frustration about being out of work was eating him up inside. I could hardly blame him; when I'm out of work, I tend to dramatize my *own* life, which can be destructive. Some days Burt's mood sank so low that I had to put his dinner on a tray and bring it to the bedroom. The next day, however, he'd be back to his old self.

On his good days Burt knocked himself out to please my parents. Knowing how much my dad loved sports, Burt volunteered to take him and my uncle John to their first American football game. It was an outing that my dad talked about for years to come.

They set off for a Rams game, my dad and Uncle John dressed in their Sunday suits and ties. Burt, clad in his Florida State sweatshirt, began explaining the rules on the way. When they arrived at the Coliseum, Burt pulled up to the ticket booth.

"Stand in line and get three tickets, I'll park the car and meet you in front," he said.

"Cute, Burt . . . that's the oldest trick in the book! *You* park the car, and *we* pay for the tickets!" my dad joked.

Burt wanted them to experience the true spectator side of his favorite game, so he bought them large tubs of popcorn and beer from the vendor. In those days popcorn didn't exist in England, so my dad and Uncle John didn't know whether to eat it or throw it in the air like confetti.

"Say, Burt, I don't wanna seem stupid, but what do we do with this?" pointing at the popcorn.

"It's popcorn, something we all eat at games."

"Tell you what, John," my dad kidded, "we'll watch 'im eat some, and if 'e don't keel over, we'll 'ave a bite."

My Buddy

"I know the English like beer at room temperature," Burt said, "but you just taste these frosties."

They each took a sip.

"That's nice, Burt, but would a Scotch be out of the question?"

As the game went on, Burt explained every play to them as only an expert could. My dad and Uncle John loved every minute of it, and the following Sunday before their departure, they spent the entire day watching the televised games on our conveniently shelved set.

Burt's good moods seemed to come fewer and farther between. We weren't communicating with each other as we used to. A case in point came when I made a guest appearance on "Twelve O'Clock High" with a handsome young actor named Andrew Prine. The script called for numerous romantic scenes between us, so we had to spend many hours wrapped around each other, hugging and kissing. As can easily happen in this situation, a noticeable attraction developed between us.

When the shooting finally ended, I was afraid he would approach me in some way. When I saw him walking toward me before leaving work that last day, I got into my car and drove away as fast as I could. I didn't even dare say good-bye.

I was happy to see Burt's smiling face when I got home. I told him about how the circumstances had induced an attraction to my co-star, and that I was proud of my ability to analyze the situation and come to the conclusion that what I loved most was my marriage to a man in whom I could confide my deepest emotions.

Burt was furious. He totally missed the point of what I was saying. All he heard was that I'd been attracted to another man, not understanding that I'd totally rejected it upon reflection. Burt just wanted to tear him apart.

A similar reaction occurred when I decided to take up tennis. My doctor had recommended that to ease tension, I develop an interest in something other than acting, perhaps a sport; I've always suffered from not being able to divert my attention away from my work, from not having enough so-called hobbies.

Our neighbors on Laurelcrest, Ed and Dorothy Parham, were tennis fanatics. They had always encouraged me to take it up. In light of my doctor's advice, I thought, Right—tennis! I mentioned the idea to Burt, but he wanted no part of such a "sissy sport."

Undaunted, I went out, bought all the cute outfits and equipment, and started going to the Lake Encino Tennis Club, where the Parhams played. I took lessons from the pro, "Gorgeous" Gussie Moran, and after a while I was good enough to play with the people I met at the club. But when they started calling me to arrange times to play, Burt went absolutely nuts.

"I know what goes on at these tennis clubs," he said to me with grotesque paranoia. "There's more drinking at the bar and screwing around with each other's wives than tennis."

It became difficult getting out of the house to play, especially if Burt was in a bad mood. It was even worse when I returned.

"Who did you play with? For how long? What did you drink? Who did you leave with?" he demanded.

I finally invited him to come along to the club to check it out for himself, but when he did, he spent the entire time wondering which of the men I had flirted with.

As time went by the issue of my supposed liaisons at the club became so blown out of proportion that I finally hung up my racket.

One reason for Burt's insecurity was a problem that had been plaguing him for years: a rapidly receding hairline. When I met him, Burt was already wearing a half-inch hairpiece on "Gunsmoke," but off the set he just had what I called the "Comb-Over Blues"—the fine art of subtly combing the hair forward. The makeup people at "Gunsmoke" started giving him wider and wider toupees as he lost more hair, and in private, he went through a hat-wearing phase.

He was able to joke about it with his friends, making cracks about the billiard-ball look, but with me, he was panic-stricken. The first hair-counting session happened one day when I heard him scream from the shower, "Judy, come in here! Look at my *hair*! *Look at it*! It's not on my head anymore, it's going down the *drain*!"

He spent many days angrily cursing his predicament. Adding insult to injury were his good friends, Clint and Ryan, whose full heads of hair showed no signs of loss. Burt thought perhaps it was because they took vitamins and drank carrot juice, so he followed their example. In his desperation Burt was ready to try almost any home remedy that was suggested. For a while he washed his hair every

My Buddy

day; when that failed, he went days *without* washing it. As a fellow actor I sympathized with his predicament. It wasn't just vanity; he was concerned because it posed a major threat to his career.

"Burt, with looks like yours, who needs hair?" I said, trying to make him feel better. Unfortunately it didn't help.

Burt's hair wasn't the only thing going down the drain: Our savings were dwindling and we suddenly found ourselves struggling to make ends meet. The money I earned on "Baileys of Balboa" went straight into our joint checking account. Since most of our money was tied up in the house, it was the only steady income we had.

Each month Burt sent two checks home out of our joint account: one to pay the mortgage on his parents' ranch, and another to contribute to the Lake Worth Playhouse Scholarship Fund, which he had founded. When unemployment set in, these payments became increasingly difficult. On top of our mortgage and home improvement loan, we had to make the payments on our cars. Our financial status was in peril.

Burt would have been devastated if he couldn't make one of those payments home, not only because he cared so much about the people in his community, but because it would have made him look like a failure in their eyes. I was only too happy to help, but Burt didn't grasp the reality of the situation—we were flat broke. I didn't dare bring up the subject because I knew it would only create more problems.

Many of these problems stemmed from Burt's belief that the husband should *always* support the wife. Now that just the opposite was happening, if only temporarily, Burt's depression grew more serious. He started to have what I used to call his "Black Days."

Both Clint and Ryan tried to console him by revealing that their wives had supported *them* through their early years. Joanna Moore was a prolific actress before Ryan came into his own, and Maggie Eastwood brought home the paycheck before Clint found steady work. Clint was so concerned, he took Burt out for dinner to give him a pep talk.

"What did you do with your time, Clint?" Burt asked him.

"I got *ready*, that's what I did. I worked out, got my body in shape. I had *plenty* to do!" When Burt came home from that dinner, he was praising Clint's pragmatic outlook, and his spirits were raised for weeks. If only he could have known then that he was on his way to being a *superstar.*

Doing a series is a time-consuming job. Each day I rose at 5:30 in the morning to drive to Balboa for a 6:30 makeup call followed by a full day of filming. I stopped for groceries on my way home, returned in time to cook dinner, ate with Burt, learned my lines for the next day, and went to bed early.

Meanwhile Burt's insecurities grew. He became morose. Even his sense of humor was bitter, and double edged.

"How was your day, Burt?" I asked, arriving home from work.

"Oh, it was okay. I woke up. I combed my hair—that is, what's *left* of it. I got in the car and drove down Ventura Boulevard, took a right . . ." In his deadpan style of delivery, it was *very* funny. But when I laughed, he turned on me.

"So it's *funny,* is it, that I'm driving around, doing nothing, while you're working? God, I *hate* my days. . . ."

A familiar dread for me was coming home at night to find Burt in the dark, the curtains drawn, his head buried in his hands—having a Black Day. I began to recognize these days in advance and tried to adjust accordingly. My first approach was to make light conversation—anything to avoid asking how his day had been.

"Gosh, Burt, they didn't even use me today. I sat around in the trailer and played cards with the makeup guys."

"*Really?*" he said. "D'ja *screw* any of them?"

I'd fumble around for something to say, trying to be patient, knowing Burt's hair-trigger temper could be particularly explosive on those Black Days. Unfortunately, I invariably said the wrong thing—like "Shut up!" for example. "Drop dead!" also came to mind when he started accusing me that way.

Wham! I got a powerful, backhanded slap across my face. It was easy enough to knock *me* down. His lashing out seemed to release some of his pent-up anger and frustration, but something was very wrong; he began striking me harder and harder, with alarming regularity.

A row could occur over something as simple as watching a football game on television. Our weekends were usually geared around the televised games. He spent all day Saturday and Sunday glued to the

My Buddy

TV, and it was my job to keep a steady stream of beer and snacks coming from the kitchen. This was fine with me, but he made the mistake of trying to force me to understand the game, which was hopeless. When you have a passion for something, it's only natural to want to share it with someone you love, but in this case, I just didn't take to it. This frustrated him no end.

"Take a look at this—they're about to score a touchdown."

"But Burt, I don't understand it."

"That's why I'm *explaining* it to you!"

"But Burt, I just don't like the game."

"You're not even trying—you don't *care*."

He took it as an affront, a personal insult, and started to get angry. It got to the point where I dreaded hearing the constant roar of the crowd blaring over the TV. All it took was an ill-timed complaint, or back talk, and I'd get hit.

Either way, without fail, Burt broke down and wept after hitting me, promising never to do it again. He also made it up to me when we made love that night. The intensity of his passion during sex seemed directly related to the intensity of his violence earlier that day. This is why I put up with the abuse for so long. I loved Burt so much, and wanted our marriage to work—I just wouldn't admit to myself that his promises to change could be broken.

After being knocked down enough times, I learned to hit the floor fast—and *stay* there. I'd even play dead. I turned it into an acting exercise, holding my breath as long as I could, careful not to flutter my eyelids. I knew I was safe when he fell to his knees in tears, panic-stricken about whether he might have seriously injured me.

If I was lucky, he'd take his aggressions out on other things. Sometimes his dinner plate would go flying. "Keep it up, and next time it'll be *you!*" I was only too happy to clean up the mess; thank God it *hadn't* been me.

The walls also took a beating. I would put pictures over the telltale fist marks, making for rather curious hanging arrangements. Friends would come by to visit and notice a picture in an unusually low position. I'd make excuses and jokes like, "Oh, I *like* it down there—it's easier to see with my bad eyesight!"

Hanging our wedding pictures three feet off the ground certainly looked odd. Even Burt would make excuses, claiming the holes were caused by Clyde crashing into the wall at full speed after someone had called his name and diverted his attention.

My former roommate, Suzan Kroul, was the only one who knew the actual cause of the holes, but even with her I would try to cover up, always hoping it was just a passing phase. As long as I had enough pictures, I figured I could keep my secret.

I gave Burt some gym equipment with a punching bag for his birthday, hoping it would help him work out his aggressions. He spent hours flailing away at that bag, but it didn't seem to help. I lived in fear of Burt's hostility from one day to the next, afraid to put the key in the door when those curtains were drawn. . . .

I remember that last day so well. It was summer, and very hot. We had no air-conditioning and I was wearing a light cotton dress to keep cool. Inside the house it was hot but not sunny, since Burt had drawn all the curtains and sat, slowly burning his fuse, which was particularly short that day. I don't even know what finally set him off that time; he grabbed the front of my dress, which ripped easily in his hands, and gave me a sudden backhander. It was bad luck for both of us, because I fell back against the fireplace and hit my head on the brick mantel. I curled up on the floor and lay there, dazed, until suddenly I felt the wetness of Clyde's tongue licking my face. I looked up and Burt was gone.

I ran. I ran right up Laurelcrest Drive to the Parhams, who drove me to the hospital, where I was treated for a mild concussion. I stayed with them and called Burt the next day. I didn't know what to say, so I just said the first thing that came to mind.

"Burt, what are we going to do?" I rambled. "Is *divorce* the only solution to our problems?"

I said it in desperation, to shock him into realizing we needed help. I was staggered when all he said was, "Okay, if that's what you want, go ahead, see the lawyers. I'm sitting right here in this chair waiting for you to come home. . . ."

I suggested we try to get some form of counseling, a third party to listen to our problems. This just infuriated him more.

"Me? *You* go! *I* don't need that! I'm sitting here waiting for you to come home!"

Mentioning divorce was a blind threat that I was forced to carry out, otherwise it would have meant walking into that house and not knowing what to expect from day to day. I went to see a lawyer, although it was the last thing I wanted.

I faced the painful task of calling my parents to tell them the news. I dreaded this, because I felt as though I'd let them down. After a few days of procrastination, I finally plucked up enough courage to place the call. My mother answered.

"I have some bad news, Mum," I said nervously. I could hear her breathing stop on the other end of the line. "The marriage hasn't worked. Burt and I are getting a divorce."

My mum was wonderful. She confessed that she'd always been intimidated by him since the day of our wedding, when Burt's mother had told her about his temper.

My dad simply said, "Do whatever you think is right, Joyce. Your mum and I are behind you all the way." I knew deep down he was sad to hear the news. He respected Burt's strength of character and thought of him as a "man's man," someone who would see to it that his daughter would always be safe. They had a great rapport; Burt always gave my dad a big hug when he saw him.

Burt described breaking the news to his parents in an interview with A. E. Hotchner (later printed in Hotchner's book *Choice People* and quoted here by permission):

> . . . When my marriage to Judy collapsed, I called my mother and I told her that I had failed—the first person in our family to get divorced. "Tell Dad he's right about me—I'm never going to make it." My father is a big, gruff man, who has been a police officer all his life, and we always had a military school relationship. . . . He was a tough disciplinarian, and not much emotion had ever been exchanged between us.
>
> But this time he got on the phone and said, "Burt, come on home, I've got something to tell you." Dad picked me up at the airport, and I anticipated a long lecture, but he didn't say a word driving to our house. Then, when we got there, he poured a couple of glasses of brandy, and that was the first time in all my years he had ever offered me a drink.
>
> He told me that everyone failed at one time or another, and that all that counted was the love and understanding of the people who cared about you as he cared about me.
>
> There were tears in his eyes, and all of a sudden we were in

each other's arms, holding tight, shedding tears of love. That moment gave me a strength that I'm sure I can always draw on. . . .

"Have you . . . thought this *through,* Miss Carne?" the judge asked me during the divorce proceeding.

"Yes, your honor, I have. I truly have."

"And you understand the divorce laws in California, and the meaning of *community property?*"

"I do."

The judge was surprised that I wasn't asking for support from Burt, but the truth is I just don't believe in alimony. I've never thought it right for a woman who could support herself to be entitled to any of the earnings—present or future—of her ex-husband. I simply did what I thought was right: I paid Burt for his half of our house and assumed responsibility for our home improvement loan.

During our wedding ceremony the minister had said the usual line, "If anyone can show just cause why this couple should not be joined, let him speak now or forever hold his peace." I fantasized that this would happen during the dreadful divorce proceedings, that Burt's voice would pipe up from the back of the courtroom, saying "Hold it! Stop this, I don't want it! It's all going to be all right. . . ."

We thought our marriage would last forever, but somehow, as we struggled for survival in Hollywood, that marriage disintegrated.

Perhaps Burt felt threatened by a wife whose concept of a "woman's place" was not what he was brought up to expect; although I was a devoted nest maker, I was also a fellow actor, and our careers at that time seemed more important than having children.

I was still in love with Burt when I filed for divorce, and part of me will love him forever. "There's only one true love in anyone's life," he was recently quoted as saying.

Perhaps he was right.

6. On the Rooftop

As I readjusted to single life, I started to revert back to my old, preferred habits. I cut my hair short and took childish pleasure in screaming my favorite obscenities at the top of my lungs, hearing them echo off the bare walls where Burt's guns and knives had been. I redecorated the house, filling it with antiques and the most feminine decor I could find. I played my Beatles records at full volume, sending their music blasting into the hills.

Unfortunately I also resumed my habit of sleepwalking during times of stress. This time, however, I began to charge around in my sleep to a dangerous degree.

Late one night the police found me strolling down Laurelcrest Drive, fast asleep. With my short haircut and oversized T-shirt, they mistook me for a little boy.

"Does your mommy know where you are?" one of the officers asked.

"My *mommy*?" I said, waking from my daze. "She's in England, for God's sake. . . . I'm almost *thirty years old!*"

That first night they saw me safely home, but my sleepwalking became such a frequent occurrence that the police grew accustomed to it. They drove me home without waking me, put me to bed, and called me in the morning to tell me what had happened.

I also began having traumatic nightmares, dreams in which someone was trying to murder me—I could actually see the hands stretching out to strangle me.

I was lonely and isolated after the divorce because I'd met most of my friends through Burt. They had to make a choice, and their loyalties were with him. I felt like a foreigner all over again.

To make matters worse, I was a new addition to Hollywood's Just Divorced and Totally Vulnerable list, and many of Burt's cronies were eager to jump into his barely cold bed with me. Every time the telephone rang I thought: Oh, great, someone to talk to in my time of need. But no. It was usually someone wanting a little romp with "Burt Reynolds's old lady."

Ryan O'Neal was one of the first to call. He was going through a divorce of his own at the time, so this gave us a lot to commiserate about. We had a quiet dinner together, laughed about old times, and then he proudly produced a pair of tickets.

"Guess what these are for," he said, waving them in front of me.

"Let's see . . . the Bolshoi's in town?"

"Nope. These are tickets to one of the best fights of the year!"

"A *fight*?"

"Yeah, boxing . . . a *boxing* match!"

"Oh . . . a *boxing* match!" All I knew about boxing was that my dad treasured an autographed picture of Rocky Marciano that Burt had managed to get for him.

"You'll love it, Judy, I've got ringside seats."

"Far out, Ryan. . . ."

The arena was jammed to capacity, and a fog of cigar smoke engulfed us as we squeezed into our seats. When the fighting began, burly men and buxom women screamed at the top of their lungs, "*Kill* him! *Murder* him! He's a *bum*!"

I looked over at Ryan, who was caught up in it all, his fists in front of him, mimicking the action. I watched in shock as the two fighters battered each other, sending a shower of blood and sweat onto the canvas in front of us. As the rounds progressed, I began to sweat. I grew queasy and had to find the ladies' room in a hurry. After depositing most of my dinner in the loo, I returned to my seat, grateful to see that the fighting had stopped.

"You're just in time for the last round, Judy," Ryan yelled.

"Oh . . . *great,*" I said. By now the faces of the combatants were pulplike, swollen, and bloody. Ryan and the rest of the crowd loved every minute of it, but I was horrified. It took me weeks to get the awful memory of that violence out of my mind.

I started to pursue interests and activities I had been repressing with Burt. I got a Yorkshire terrier named Whitney. Coming out from under Burt's influence, I felt liberated, a free spirit once again.

I started to practice tennis with a vengeance. I was greatly encouraged by Nancy Zimbalist—Efrem, Jr.'s, daughter—who played at the club. She was warm, bright, and amusing, and her friendship meant a lot to me as I adapted to being single once again.

I started going to clubs and discotheques more often. One night a friend called to ask if I'd like to check out a new club that people were talking about—a club whose clientele was exclusively female.

My curiosity was aroused, so off we drove to the club on Pico Boulevard. There were lots of masculine-looking women playing pool in one corner, and a few feminine women watching them. This was no lady's bridge club. This was a world without men.

My friend steered us to a table and then went to the bar to order us drinks, as I sat nervously trying not to look at the female couples dancing and necking. I reached for a cigarette and before I could even get it into my mouth, four women offered me a light. Wow, I thought, all this attention—I must stay cool and act casual. I don't want them to think I'm Mary Poppins.

When my friend returned with the drinks, I knocked mine back in one gulp. Suddenly I noticed a woman at the bar with a drink in her hand and a long, slow-burning cigarette in her mouth. Being nearsighted, I squinted to see more clearly. Her image was captivating.

"What are you squinting at, Judy?" asked my friend.

"Do you see that woman over there at the bar? Who is she?"

"Oh, that's Ashley . . . she comes in here a lot."

I was told that Ashley's father, now deceased, had been one of the most powerful forces in Hollywood, notorious for his womanizing.

I was fascinated, and put my glasses on for a better look. She was slim, with short auburn hair and finely chiseled cheekbones. She wore a buttoned-down shirt and cream-colored jeans tucked into leather boots and belted with a huge brass buckle.

"Do you want to meet her?" my friend asked.

"Well . . . maybe if the right moment arrives," I said. I found myself constantly gazing over at Ashley in wonderment, and soon enough we were introduced. It was a curious sensation—I had what felt like a schoolgirl's crush on her.

For the next few days I couldn't stop thinking about her, so I decided to go back to the club, hoping to see her again. This time I went with a different friend, who, unbeknownst to me, was emotionally unable to cope with it. As we entered the club, my friend saw the women dancing close and kissing, and went into shock. When we reached our table, she fainted. Everyone turned and stared as I helped her up, my face beet red with embarrassment. When I got her to her feet, I felt a tap on my shoulder. It was Ashley.

"Having a bit of trouble, dearie?"

"Oh, hello . . . uh, my friend isn't well," I stammered, trying to come up with an explanation. "She's, uh . . . having a bad period!"

Ashley smiled. "Having a bad period, eh?" she said skeptically. She offered to assist in getting my friend home. I quickly said yes, and we dropped her off.

"It's okay, I know the club freaked her out," Ashley said. "Some women find a visit to a gay club too much to deal with, it's not unusual. How come *you* didn't faint?"

"I've seen it all before and it doesn't faze me," I lied.

She flashed a knowing smile that attracted me to her in a most powerful way. When she drove me home, we sat for a while in the car, talking. I was certain she'd at least try to kiss me. But she didn't.

I was oddly devastated. Was there something wrong with me? Did she think I wasn't attractive? How was I going to *handle* this?

To my relief she offered me her phone number and told me to call if I wanted to see a movie or go out to dinner.

"Great. How about tomorrow night?" I said, almost too quickly. I thought to myself, Judes, you fool, don't sound too eager—Ashley might be turned off. She told me she was busy but to stay in touch.

For some reason I couldn't bring myself to call her over the next few days, but I waited by the phone each evening in anticipation of a call from her, which never came. Finally I got up enough nerve to dial her number.

When I heard her voice I panicked, and hung up the phone. Then I *really* felt silly, so I dialed her again and greeted her warmly.

"Did you dial my number a few minutes ago?" she said almost immediately. It took my breath away, and I explained that indeed I had, but I didn't get through.

"Really?" she said suspiciously. I was obviously dealing with a no-bullshit person, so after dithering a bit I finally asked if I could see her.

She was having a small party at her house the following evening, and told me to stop by. I was nervous, yet excited at the thought, and brought her a bottle of champagne, which I'd been told she adored. As I drove to her house I thought, Judes, what are you doing? Where do you expect this to lead?

These were questions I couldn't answer. I only knew that for the first time since separating from Burt, I had met someone who kindled an emotional response inside me. The fact that it was a woman was something I'd have to deal with later.

When I arrived at her house, I heard lots of music and laughter coming from inside.

"It's open, come on in!" someone shouted. It was a warm and comfortable cottage, and I smelled incense burning. There was a group of women—some of them strikingly beautiful—sitting around talking, smoking weed, and listening to music. They were playing my favorite records at the time: the Four Tops, Martha and the Vandellas, and Smokey Robinson and the Miracles.

I felt awkward, but tried not to seem out of place. Everyone seemed bright and witty. It was as though Ashley were the Queen Bee, with her drones gathered around to amuse her. I didn't mind becoming her new drone, because I felt an unmistakable physical attraction toward her.

I started to see Ashley regularly, but just as a friend. I always brought her gifts in my effort to please her, but she never showed any affection other than an occasional kiss hello or good-bye. Eventually I was bold enough to invite her over for dinner.

I spent all afternoon preparing so that everything would be just right: fresh flowers for the table, some fine champagne, and the best

Cordon Bleu meal I knew how to cook. Ashley could hardly boil an egg, so she was truly flattered when she saw the feast I'd prepared.

We had similar tastes, especially when it came to music. She loved my modern "hi-fi"—the new thing in 1965—so after dinner I played an Ike and Tina Turner record at full volume. Before long we found ourselves clinging to each other, immersed in the music.

Ashley had a lovely figure, with long legs and delicate breasts. When she first kissed me, her mouth seemed so small—but then, I'd never before been kissed so passionately by a woman. She gently touched and caressed my body, knowing intuitively how to satisfy me. It was a revelation to feel so safe, to be in the hands of a sensitive woman. There was no threat, no invasion. After that night together, we were inseparable.

Ashley was very young and still trying to figure out what she wanted to do with her life. Within a month she came to live with me on Laurelcrest Drive, arriving with her Doberman, three cats, and some personal belongings, which included a treasured family album.

She rarely mentioned her father, but in those moments when she discussed her upbringing, she revealed that she worshipped him despite his faults. As a child growing up in his house, she'd been exposed to many of his infamous sexual escapades. Witnessing these multiple affairs made it impossible for her to relate to a man in any way. She wasn't bitter, though; it wasn't that she disliked men so much as she just found it easier to communicate with women. She was secure in her sexual identity, and that was that.

I didn't really miss being with a man during this time because I was given lots of love and attention, and was sexually satisfied. I didn't feel incomplete as a woman, and I was surprised at how easy it was relating to Ashley in this way. I felt nothing but closeness, warmth, and understanding.

Ashley had a passion for riding motorcycles, and she convinced me to give it a go. I loved the sense of freedom, so I purchased my own two-cylinder Honda a few weeks later. I was in pig heaven when it came to all the slick accessories and bike fashions.

We joined some biking friends for excursions all over Orange County, usually ending up at the shore, in places like Laguna Beach. We numbered eight or ten and gathered early Saturday mornings at someone's house before leaving as a group.

On the Rooftop

One weekend Ashley arranged for everyone to meet at my house. One by one the other women started to arrive, until finally we were assembled and ready to roll. The sound of ten motorcycles starting up together was deafening. The vibrations were so strong that my house, nestled in the hills, began to shake. People all over the neighborhood came out of their homes to see what was causing this minor earthquake; it must have registered at least a 3.5 on the Richter scale.

"That's the last time we meet *here!*" I shouted to Ashley over the din, as we sped off for parts unknown.

The year 1966 started with an audition for the lead in a new sitcom called "Love on a Rooftop," being produced by Screen Gems, the highly successful TV division of Columbia Pictures. The part called for an American girl, but my agent knew I could handle the accent after my charade on "The Baileys of Balboa."

For the audition they paired me with a handsome young actor who looked vaguely familiar. His name was Peter Deuel, and he was very outgoing, with a magnetic smile. As we waited our turn, we realized that we had indeed worked together before, on an episode of "Gidget," with Sally Field. Peter was under contract to Screen Gems, one of their stable of actors who attended in-house acting classes and appeared on their various shows.

Peter had a great sense of humor, so we hit it off immediately. The producers sensed our chemistry, and we were cast as David and Julie Willis, struggling newlyweds living in a tiny San Francisco apartment that boasted a roof with a spectacular view. Julie was an art student, and Dave an apprentice architect, and they survived on his weekly paycheck of $85.37, refusing to accept any money from Julie's rich parents, who could never understand how their daughter could be content to live on love alone.

Rich Little, the gifted impressionist, played our next door neighbor Stan, a struggling young writer who supported himself and his wife (Barbara Bostock) by writing restaurant menus.

Our executive producer, Harry Ackerman, was responsible for hit shows such as "Bewitched" and "The Flying Nun," and he had high hopes for us. To begin with, the show was to be shot in color, which was a big deal in 1966. The pilot had a charming script by Bernard Slade, and we were directed by a talented and energetic man named

E. W. Swackhammer, whom we called "Swack" for obvious reasons.

"Love on a Rooftop" was picked up by ABC and slated for a desirable slot on Tuesdays at 9:30 P.M. I was thrilled: Not only would I be working with a talented group of people, but everyone thought the show was destined to be a hit.

In my private life I had a little domestic comedy of my own going on. My home now housed seven animals: Whitney, Clyde, and Festus, as well as three cats and Sabre, Ashley's Doberman. Whitney, my four-pound Yorkshire terrier, thought he was also a Doberman. One afternoon as the dogs were playing on the stairs, things got a bit out of hand. Clyde bumped into Whitney and knocked him down a flight of steps, breaking his pelvis and his rear left leg. The vet had to put him into a body cast for two months, and poor Whitney never knew which leg to raise when he had to wet. He'd try leaning on the injured leg, fall down, try the other leg with no success, and just end up squatting.

The veterinarian warned me that, with the crowd of animals at my house, there were likely to be more problems in the future. I gave it some thought and decided to see if perhaps Burt wanted to take Clyde and Festus. I called his publicist, Nancy Streebeck, who got back to me immediately, saying Burt would love to take them. I arranged for them to be sent to Florida. Although it was sad to see them go, I knew Burt would take good care of them.

With them went the last visible trace of my marriage, and it was even more symbolic than the actual divorce decree. I had now embarked on a new marriage—a television marriage.

Peter Deuel and I spent more time together than people who were actually married. We had a 6:30 makeup call every morning, and filmed all day on the Screen Gems set that simulated our tiny apartment. The scripts called for an endless number of scenes in our minuscule bathroom, where we retreated to have a word with each other in private whenever guests were in the living room. There was endless hugging and kissing, and after doing this five days a week, we developed a love/hate relationship.

The hate part was nothing serious, just the result of working long hours in close quarters. We made sure we never left for the day bearing a grudge.

On the Rooftop

"I love Peter dearly," I told *TV Guide*. "It's just that I can't *stand* him most of the time!"

"Judy, baby," Peter interjected, "if you call this loving me dearly, I dread to think how you'd *hate* me dearly!"

I spoke in my normal British accent around the set, which never failed to startle Peter. I'd whisper something dirty to him in my Cockney best right before a take, and then go right into all-American Julie Willis as soon as Swack yelled "Action!"

Peter would cover for me when my Americanese faltered. If he heard me mispronounce a vowel, he'd make a mistake on purpose. "Sorry, Swack," he'd shout, shouldering the blame. "Careful, Judy," he'd whisper, "you're sounding a little mid-Atlantic."

Peter and I confided in each other about our personal lives. He was the first man with whom I felt comfortable enough to discuss my relationship with Ashley. He was fascinated when I told him about it.

Some men were drawn to me when they learned I was having an affair with another woman. They were aroused by the challenge of being the one to "save me" from my evil ways. Peter was not in that category. He cared on an emotional level. It was a revelation to him to be able to talk to a woman about this, and he felt it somehow enriched his understanding of the feminine mind.

Peter was fiercely protective of me if he thought I was being mistreated by anyone. One day during a break I was going over my lines and Peter was chatting to someone in another part of the studio, when suddenly a commotion broke out. I saw some members of the crew trying to restrain Peter, who was pummeling the fellow he'd just been talking to. I was shocked, because it was so unlike him to exhibit any kind of violence.

He stormed off to his dressing room without an explanation, so I followed him. I was determined to find out what had set him off, but he was evasive.

"Peter, you don't have to bullshit me. What did that guy *say* to you to get you so crazy?"

"He was talking about you—he called you a dyke."

Tears welled up in my eyes. The incident had left him shattered. I was so moved by this display of compassion that words failed me, and I hugged him tight. There are friends, and then there are *friends*.

* * *

I got into the habit of riding my motorcycle to work, traveling through Laurel Canyon to the Screen Gems studios with Whitney perched in a basket. Before long Peter showed up at work on his motorcycle, which he'd dug out of his garage. We would often go for a spin during our breaks, to clear our heads.

Every six weeks we traveled to San Francisco to film the exterior shots for each episode done in the previous weeks. Peter and I were housed in luxurious hotels, and since we didn't know anyone in San Francisco, we usually just headed back to the hotel after work for a sumptuous meal and drinks.

On one of those trips we ended up in my room after dinner, pleasantly drunk, and started to roll around on the plush carpet. Peter made me laugh with his imitation of a whale, which involved lying on his back, filling his cheeks with water, and spouting a thin stream high in the air which splashed back down into his face.

It had been a long time since I'd felt a desire to be held and kissed by a man. But here was dear Peter, my TV husband, so close to me, making me laugh and teasing me when I withdrew, gently drawing me close enough to kiss, then releasing me to clown again. With Peter I felt my instinctive responses not only replenish themselves, but well up to the point of overflowing.

"Do you realize we are lying to the American public? We owe it to our fans, darling!" he said as we climbed up onto the luxurious bed. We undressed and he held me. His body was firm and muscular, and he soothed me by whispering, "You're not afraid, now, are you?"

I wasn't any more.

The next day we filmed a scene involving a brass bed that Peter was to wheel from an antique shop to our apartment as I rode on it, giving him directions. One by one we went up and down the steep hills of San Francisco.

We'd just reached the top of a hill and were about to start down when I heard a loud snap. The cable securing the bed to the camera truck had broken. I sat on the bed helplessly as it began rolling down the hill, gathering speed rapidly.

I screamed, and before anyone else could react, Peter ran ahead of the bed and planted his feet firmly, letting it crash into his back. His arms and shoulders buckled but the crew caught up with us and pulled the bed to safety, as Peter crumpled to the pavement in agony. He was the hero of the day—a few seconds more and the bed and I would have raced downhill out of control. He had acted quickly and bravely, straining his back and shoulder muscles in the process. But within minutes he was back on his feet, shrugging it off and making jokes.

"Without me, gang, there would be no *Julie Willis!*"

There would have been no Judy Carne, either. Within twenty-four hours, Peter had "saved" me twice—and both times it happened on a bed.

Although I couldn't tell Ashley what had happened between Peter and me, it didn't matter; the experience in San Francisco made me realize that I was with Ashley out of choice, and not out of fear of commitment to a man.

Ashley wasn't interested in my "Love on a Rooftop" stories, anyway. She rarely watched television and was totally bored by show business.

Gradually, however, I began to feel isolated by the gay life-style and its exclusive social circles, far removed from my work. When the invitation to a Hollywood premiere read "Judy Carne and guest," I naturally took Ashley, which turned out to be a mistake. One of the columnists the next day wrote, "At the premiere was JUDY CARNE, with a handsome young female companion. . . ."

The article mentioned Ashley by name, played up our relationship, and talked about my recent divorce from Burt. The innuendo had the "Love on a Rooftop" publicity department in a spin. I was called in for a meeting with the studio executives, headed by Jackie Cooper, then vice-president of Screen Gems.

"Judy, we're not telling you how to live your life," they told me, "but the fact is, you're on television and in the public eye. We don't need this kind of publicity and neither do you."

They were nice about it, in a protective, family way. They said they'd be happy to help me meet new people and reorganize my social life. I accepted their advice, and from then on, my escorts to public functions were carefully chosen by the studio.

The only place Ashley and I could go in public was the club on Pico Boulevard where we first met, certain that the paparazzi would not be hanging around *there*. But even that became a problem.

One night as we were saying good-bye to some friends outside the club, a police car swept up beside us and two officers jumped out. They read us our rights and told us we were being arrested on charges of "lewd conduct," whatever *that* meant. We may have been acting affectionate, but it hardly warranted police harassment.

It was my first time inside a police car, and I was terrified. Fortunately, after talking to us for a few minutes, the cops changed their minds and let us go. Although we were now two miles away from our cars, we weren't about to complain—we were just thankful that we weren't going to make the next day's headlines. The gossip columnists would have had a field day.

Not long after that incident Ashley accepted the inevitable—I was once again attracted to men. There were no rows or ugly scenes; we simply agreed to live apart for the sake of our friendship. This motivated her to pursue her own career, and she went on to become a special effects artist for one of the major film studios.

In September my mum and dad came over for their annual visit. Having already been to Disneyland, Malibu Beach, and other such tourist attractions, they were quite content to take a flask of tea, a couple of folding chairs, and spend their days watching me work on the "Love on a Rooftop" set.

They also came along with us on location to San Francisco. It was Columbus Day, and I had been chosen to be the Queen of the Columbus Day parade. The mayor, a chubby, balding man with a ruddy complexion, escorted us around town in a limousine with a full bar, something my father had never seen. We visited historic monuments and street carnivals, where the mayor took great pleasure in using the siren and watching pedestrians jump out of the way.

It was the most fun my parents had in all of their travels in America. Later that night the mayor asked my dad if he wanted to visit a strip show to see some "tits and ass."

"Thanks, but I don't think so," my dad replied. "My wife's got all that I can handle!"

Determined to show my folks a good time, the mayor ordered his driver to take us to Finocchio's, the famous nightclub featuring drag queens. When we arrived, the club was overflowing with the holiday crowds.

"Are you sure we'll be able to get in on a night like tonight?" I asked the mayor.

"Let me put it this way—if we don't, I'll *close down* the joint!"

My parents were overwhelmed. Who would believe it: Here they were in San Francisco, with the mayor and a police escort, watching a drag show. At the end of the night, my dad thanked him.

"It was a lovely Columbus Day, but I don't know what all the fuss is about. You say he 'discovered' America. If Columbus set off in this direction from Spain, he'd have to have been an idiot to bleedin' *miss* it!"

Peter and I were the sweethearts of San Francisco. We always got the red-carpet treatment and could do no wrong as far as anyone was concerned. But we tried.

The hotel's public relations man was always bending over backward to make us feel comfortable, saying, "Anything you want, call me."

One night we were longing to smoke a joint, so I dared Peter to call the guy and ask him for some pot. Peter flashed a grin and dialed the phone.

"Hi, this is Pete Deuel. Remember when you said that if I wanted anything, I should call? Well, I've got sort of an unusual request. . . ."

"You want to meet some girls?" the man said.

"Well, I wouldn't say no to that, but it's not exactly what I had in mind. I wanted to get hold of some smoke. . . ."

"Some 'smoke'?"

"Yeah, you know, the kind that gets you . . . how shall we say, 'potted'? It's not that I *need* it or anything, it's just that I'd be a lot happier if I had some."

I watched Peter's face. Suddenly he hung up and burst out laughing.

"Whad he say, whad he say?"

"He said—get this—'I'll forget you said that, Mr. Deuel!'"

Peter and I often slept together on our trips away from home. After waking in the morning, I'd turn to him and plant a gentle kiss on his cheek.

"Good morning, TV husband," I'd whisper.

"Good morning, TV wife," he'd say, opening his eyes.

Our television marriage was a divinely unusual relationship that we consummated on those trips to San Francisco, removed from our regular lives in Los Angeles.

By the time we finished shooting the last episode of the season in the spring of 1967, ABC had not yet told us whether the show would be renewed. This was unusual, since our reviews had been excellent and the ratings as strong as another new show on ABC, "That Girl." After weeks in limbo the network announced it was canceling "Love on a Rooftop." It had obviously been a tough decision—at the time, ABC was the poorest of the networks financially, and we had simply been unable to outrate our principal opposition, NBC's "Petticoat Junction."

Peter and I were devastated. It wasn't just that we were out of work, it was the frustration of losing out to such dubious competition. ABC received a flood of mail in protest of our cancellation, but it was to no avail.

I've often wondered just how the course of my life would have changed had "Love on a Rooftop" been more successful. I only know that I wouldn't have been looking for work that June day when I got a call from my old friend Digby Wolfe, whom I'd known for years in England. He was a comedian with a very flamboyant, fast-paced sense of humor, and during the early sixties he'd had his own successful television show in Australia. Now he was working as a comedy writer in Hollywood.

"Judy, I've been writing this special for a producer named George Schlatter," Digby said. "It's a very wild concept. We're trying something totally different. I've been telling Schlatter about you, because you're perfect for it, with all your intimate revue experience. That's the style we're going for: sketches, songs, dancing, you know . . . but *different.*"

Digby explained that Schlatter knew my work from "Rooftop" and was interested in seeing more.

"Just come in for a chat," he said casually.

"I'd love to, Digby, but will it be like an audition? Will I be expected to *do* anything?"

"No, no, it'll be very relaxed. George is really a far-out guy, you'll see. Trust me."

In Hollywood when people say "trust me," that's usually a cue to be on your guard, but I'd known Digby a long time and knew that he meant it.

"Should I come looking any special way?" I asked.

"Just come as *you*, love."

The following day I went to see George Schlatter and his co-producer, Ed Friendly, at their offices in a modest one-story red-brick building in downtown Burbank. It was an unusually loose meeting, with lots of joking around, as Digby had said it would be.

Ed Friendly was a former vice-president at NBC and true to his name: an affable, impeccably dressed, white-haired gentleman. Schlatter preferred a sloppier, rolled-up-sleeve look, and always had a pencil behind his ear. He was attentive and picked up on everything I said. His piercing eyes, combined with thick eyebrows, mustache, and goatee, gave his smile a sinister quality. I was mesmerized when he spoke to me.

"I know Digby's filled you in about this show we're all involved in. At the moment it's only a special, but with any luck it could be a series. Have you heard of the comedy team of Rowan and Martin?"

I told him I had. They had already made a name for themselves on the nightclub circuit, and I had recently seen their summer replacement series for "The Dean Martin Show."

"It's loosely based around them, Judy, but nuttier, so we're looking for a cast of nuts. It's a bit like the revues you've done in England, which Digby has been telling me about. I understand you like doing accents and playing all sorts of different characters. . . ."

"I *love* it."

"And you're not . . . how shall I put it . . . *uptight?*"

"Hardly!"

"I ask this, you see, because Dick Martin is . . . well, he's a little weird. He insists on making *whoopee* with all the women in the cast."

"Well then, I'll just have to give him a boff to shut him up and get on with the job!" I said, without missing a beat.

George laughed so hard he fell out of his chair. Whether or not Dick Martin was a womanizer, I knew Schlatter was just trying to test me. He wanted to see how I'd react; if I had gasped, he would have thought I was inhibited. He was simply looking for a certain kind of response, and I gave it to him.

"Great, Judy. We start in three weeks. You'll get a call."

"Oh . . . great!" I said thankfully, getting up to leave.

"By the way," George said, walking me to the door, "did you ever see 'That Was the Week That Was'?"

"Of course. I loved it. That's my kind of thing."

"How about any of the old Ernie Kovacs shows?"

"No, but I've heard a lot about them. . . ."

"Good. I've got this idea, you see," George said. "My wife Jolene was a regular on the Kovacs show, and every week she got a pie thrown in her face. As a result she received a tremendous amount of sympathy mail. I want to stretch out that idea of a pretty lady getting a pie in the face. Judy, this means I'm going to be doing some really terrible things to you. You'll probably say, 'What are you doing this to *me* for?' All I can say is you're just going to have to trust me." By now George had the crazed look of a mad scientist.

"America will love you, Judy—you will have the sympathy of the entire *nation*!"

His words were ominous. I wasn't quite sure what it all meant, but I left the meeting on a cloud.

When I got home, I wondered what had just hit me. I hadn't performed for them—not a song, nor a dance, nor even a reading. Insecurity set in: Did I really have the job or was it just a case of some producer talking big? I had been to plenty of meetings that sounded great but led to nothing.

There was, however, something different and exciting about what George Schlatter had said, and I couldn't get his words ("sympathy of the entire nation!") out of my mind. Whatever this show was, I wanted to be part of it.

The following week I got a call from my agent, Sandy Gallin. He'd negotiated an excellent contract with Schlatter/Friendly. I would appear as a guest on a one-hour variety show entitled "The Rowan & Martin Special," airing September ninth. If it led to a series, I would be a regular performer.

This was cause for celebration, so that weekend I joined a group of friends on a three-day excursion to the Monterey Pop Festival, an outdoor event organized by record producer Lou Adler, and John Phillips of the Mamas and the Papas. From all indications it was going to be a "happening".

We booked rooms in the motel where the musicians would be

staying, and drove up to Monterey, caravan-style. Someone brought a quintessential hippie van, covered with painted flowers and loaded with food and drink—and mescaline. Numerous tabs were ingested by all of us on the way to the concert. The hallucinogen, I was told, would take effect in a few hours. We would be "peaking" as the music got into full gear.

Fifty thousand people were assembled for an extraordinary succession of musical talent from all over the world. We were able to secure a V.I.P. parking section close to the stage, and for the next three days, confusion reigned. No one knew what acts would be appearing, or when; the fun was watching it all happen, as the mescaline took effect.

Our van became a popular place to congregate, a psychedelic chuck wagon for the musicians and their friends. On the stage, Simon and Garfunkel are delivering their quasi-baroque folk songs, as John Phillips and Mama Cass Elliot stop by our van. Cass is far out, we get into a good rap . . . she tells us to watch out for a fantastic new guitarist named Jimi Hendrix, as well as "the chick who sings with Big Brother and the Holding Company."

Saturday we take more mescaline and watch African drummers pounding a beat as Hugh Masekela trumpets forth. I wander through the sea of people . . . everyone on some kind of trip; mushrooms and peyote are popular. People are touching each other, getting off on the texture of flesh and hair . . . people are selling arts and crafts everywhere . . . twice my portrait has been drawn by artists who don't even want money for their work.

Big Brother and the Holding Company is introduced. Their singer, an earthy woman in gold-knit bell-bottoms and tunic top, is named Janis Joplin. She leads the band into a blues number, "Ball and Chain." Her voice is raw, then majestic, then rasping, shrieking, then suddenly gospel-like as she spreads her soul out over the crowd.

Around midnight Tommy Smothers appears onstage and introduces Otis Redding, who takes charge with a fervent rhythm and blues beat.

"This little song is one o' mine, a song that a girl took away from me—a good friend of mine. This girl, she jus' took this song, but I'm still gonna do it anyway," he says, referring to Aretha Franklin's hit,

"Respect." He works the song up to a fever pitch, and by the end he is shouting:

> *Respect, baby . . . respect!*
> *Everything I want, give it to me!*
> *What I need, baby, give it to me!*
> *Give it to me, sock it to me!*
> *Sock it to me, sock it to me!*

His set is a sensation. Everyone is drunk with rhythm and blues. He is a hero. . . .

Come Sunday, supplies are scarce . . . matches and tissues are valuable commodities. Even water . . . a girl is crying because her dog's tongue is hanging out from dehydration. Water, quick, in the van. He starts lapping it up and the girl cries out of joy.

Enter the Who. The mescaline enlarges all sensations and perceptions . . . the image of Daltrey and Townshend multiplies, forming visual echoes floating up to the sky as the music rages and roars. . . .

Women everywhere are breast-feeding their babies. I stare in astonishment—so that's what it's like!

A young girl wanders aimlessly, holding a sick baby with a gray pallor. The mother is only a child herself . . . she says she is lost, on acid, and unable to feed her baby. Her breasts no longer give milk. The baby's mouth is chapped and dry . . . something must be done.

I climb behind the wheel of the van . . . we begin to move, lurching back and forth. I have never driven a stick shift—much less a bloody van—but I hear my dad's voice: "Let the clutch out nice and slow, Joyce. . . ."

It works. We make it back to the motel, an ambulance is called, and mother and child are taken away to the hospital.

When I return to the festival, my friends are freaking out, thinking the van was stolen, that I was kidnapped. All of this while the Who is going berserk, smashing their guitars onstage and flinging them into the crowd. It is a wild, destructive climax.

By nightfall, musicians from the other bands file down to the front of the stage to look and listen, as Jimi Hendrix starts his set. He weaves his music into our consciousness. For his finale he kisses the microphone, and the band begins a heavy rock dirge. The rows of amplifiers pump out thick sheets of electronic sound as he sings "Wild Thing."

On the Rooftop

Hendrix lays down his guitar and kneels by it. He squirts lighter fluid onto it and sets it ablaze, beckoning the flames upward like a pyromaniacal snake charmer . . . then he slams the guitar into the bank of amplifiers as he leaves the stage. Hendrix is now a legend.

The mood changes again as three Indian gentlemen quietly seat themselves onstage among an intimate setting of pillows and sitars. Ravi Shankar begins his hypnotic maze of drones and quarter tones, catching everyone in its trance. . . .

It was a fitting end to a now-historic festival that promoted consciousness on all levels, as the "flower power" movement was peaking. I returned to L.A. spiritually enriched. I'd also made a new friend—Cass Elliot lived nearby in the hills, so we stayed in touch.

On a scorching, smoggy Monday morning in early July, I got into my new '67 Mustang and took the Ventura Freeway to Burbank, where the first rehearsal for "The Rowan and Martin Special" was held at the Schlatter/Friendly building.

When I arrived, I noticed several familiar faces from TV sitcoms: Barbara Feldon ("Get Smart"), Ken Berry ("F Troop"), and Larry Hovis ("Hogan's Heroes"). I also recognized Dan Rowan and Dick Martin: Dan smoked a pipe and had an air of calm about him, while Dick walked about with a naughty grin, looking as if he'd just come over from the Playboy mansion.

The show had a name: "Laugh-In." How clever, I thought—it was like a "sit-in" or a "love-in," but with comedy.

George and Ed milled about, introducing the cast to one another. I met an elfin man named Arte Johnson and a fiery Italian woman named Ruth Buzzi. There was an attractive blonde, Pam Austin, a soft-spoken Henry Gibson, and a large and raucous Jo Anne Worley.

We all took seats around a couple of converted Ping-Pong tables and George hushed everyone before addressing the group.

"Hello, gang, and welcome to the 'Laugh-In.' Now we've got this script here," he said, dropping it on the table with a loud thud. It was a foot thick. "As you can see, there's a lot of stuff to shoot. It's gonna seem crazy, but you're just going to have to hang loose, and swing with it. It's a one-shot special, so let's *make* it special."

He stressed that we should give it our all, that we had nothing to lose.

"If you've got any suggestions, I want them *all*. Characters, jokes, pratfalls, facial expressions, sounds you can make, accents you can do, I want them. Do not edit *anything* for me. I'll judge what I can use and what I can't. Be outrageous!"

Arte Johnson piped up. "You mean we can *swear*, George?"

"If that's what you want to do, be my guest."

Arte let loose a flurry of profanities, and I added a few that he'd left out. We sounded like obnoxious twelve-year-olds.

"Yeah!" said George. "That's it, go crazy. We'll protect you. We'll *edit* you."

With this inspiring chat, George had us buzzing. He couldn't have assembled a more eager and responsive group.

"As you can see from the script," he went on, flipping through the pages, "the theme of the show is 'Up, Up, and Away.'" The song with that title was then a hit by the Fifth Dimension, who were the musical guests on the show. "Most of the jokes and sketches are built around this theme. Let's go through it page by page and see what we've got."

The script was slowly dissected, with George guiding the process. "He'll do this, she'll do that . . . you guys try this . . . who thinks they can do that? We'll never get away with *this* . . ." and on and on.

By the end of the meeting, parts had been assigned and we were given a detailed schedule of the days to come.

The week was a hectic one, full of costume fittings, music rehearsals, and sketch blocking. We spent a few days filming on location around Burbank, making costume changes in the rest rooms of grimy gas stations. I rode my motorcycle dressed in black leather, as the cameramen filmed crazy shots, with wild pans and quick zooms. Other cast members frolicked along the sidewalks in tights and tutus. We certainly had fun filming it, but no one knew how George planned to use this bizarre footage.

During the taping Rowan and Martin did their stand-up routines, and some of the cast used characters from their own acts. Arte Johnson was Mr. Rosmenko, a pop singer from behind the Iron Curtain who sang Broadway show tunes with Russian lyrics, believing them to be ancient folk melodies from his homeland. Henry Gibson recited short and silly poems that were profoundly hilarious. Jo Anne Worley spoofed an inept ventriloquist, drinking a glass of water and throwing her voice with hysterical results.

One of my segments was referred to in the script simply as the "body painting sequence." I was supposed to dance to rock music wearing a bikini, with graffiti painted on my body. A shy man named Art Trugman arrived in the dressing room, carrying paint bottles and brushes. As I stood there in my bikini, watching and waiting with fascination, I could tell he was ill at ease trying to decide where to begin his work.

"Look, I've never done this before," he said bashfully. "You'll have to bear with me." The brush tickled as he began to paint. As one of the letters of a word reached below my navel, I noticed that his hand was shaking. I decided to break the tension.

"While you're down there, would you do a friend a favor?"

He looked up, stunned, then smiled and blushed.

"I just hope your wife doesn't walk in right now!"

"I must say, it's a far cry from painting scenery," he admitted.

The entire process took almost three hours, during which time George and a group of men came in and out, arguing in hushed tones as they reviewed Art's progress. They were members of the NBC Broadcast Standards Committee—the censors.

I overheard snippets of conversation referring to my navel. Apparently, a bikini was not allowed to be worn on television, even though they were the rage at the time. NBC had already been over this ground with Barbara Eden's costume on "I Dream of Jeannie," and she was required to wear a flesh-colored navel plug. Network policy was that the American public wasn't ready to view the bare female navel on their TV screens.

George was not about to give up that easily. He promised the censors that if they let me wear the bikini, my navel would be disguised. "We'll paint an eyeball on it or something. C'mon, fellas, have a heart," he begged them.

They reluctantly agreed, and a doorbell was painted on my navel below the words *Postman Ring Here*. America was about to see its first televised navel.

The end of the show involved a psychedelically painted "joke wall." Our job was to pop out of little doors like cuckoos, delivering everything from knock-knock jokes to limericks and more—the stranger the better. George shouted instructions from behind the cameras to generate energy and spontaneity.

When we'd finished, Schlatter's comedic master plan was still somewhat mysterious. Although we wouldn't get to see the show until it aired, we all felt a special rapport and looked forward to the prospect of working together again. NBC would not decide until air date, September ninth, which meant a sweat out of nearly seven weeks.

One thing kept me busy during the wait: I couldn't get that bloody doorbell off my navel. I didn't know what kind of paint they used, but it took a week of daily scrubbing in the bathtub before the graffiti completely disappeared.

I found myself with a welcome flurry of acting assignments over the next few months: an appearance on "Run for Your Life" with Ben Gazzara; a guest shot on "Man from U.N.C.L.E."; I even filmed an episode of "The Big Valley," with Linda Evans, Richard Long, and Lee Majors, whom I hadn't seen since my marriage to Burt. It was a special thrill working with Barbara Stanwyck, whom I had admired as the femme fatale in so many great films, like *Stella Dallas* and *Double Indemnity*. My mum and I used to cry our eyes out over her at the Ritz Cinema in Northampton.

In my scenes with Miss Stanwyck I was struck by her slight stature, since her screen presence had always been larger than life. When I heard her deep, sexy voice, I was entranced. She was very kind to me and insisted on staying late to repeat her lines to me off-camera while they filmed my close-ups. It was a classic example of "the greater they are, the nicer they are."

On the night of September ninth some friends gathered at my house to watch the "Laugh-In" debut. All those bizarre things we'd filmed came together magically for a hilarious hour of insanity, and when it was over, my phone didn't stop ringing for hours. People I hadn't seen in *years* called to give their congratulations.

I later realized something: George had made no mention of those terrible things he was going to do to me that would give me the "sympathy of the nation." I wasn't sure if he had dropped the idea, but I knew I would have a chance to find out. There was no question in my mind that "Laugh-In" would be picked up by NBC, and trade papers like *The Hollywood Reporter* confirmed my feeling:

> Not since Ernie Kovacs has there been such electronic insanity . . . a lightning paced marathon of running gags, blackouts and colliding non-sequiturs on film, on tape, and painted across the female anatomy. . . .

The following day Sandy Gallin happily informed me that I would be a regular performer on the "Laugh-In" series. I was ecstatic. Before rehearsals would begin, however, he'd lined up a guest appearance on "The Smothers Brothers Comedy Hour."

On the show with me were Kenny Rogers and the First Edition. I sang a number Kenny and Mason Williams had written, as well as the Beatles' "When I'm Sixty-Four" with Dick Smothers. Tommy and I talked about the excitement of Monterey Pop. He and Dick were trying to extend their variety show format to include a younger audience by featuring rock groups like the Who and the Doors.

It was a productive time for me. I was about to start a series with an unusually talented group of people, and I was filled with confidence. At this exciting juncture of my life, I started to venture out into the Hollywood social scene more often.

The Factory was one of the most fashionable clubs at the time. It was a swank, recently converted warehouse on Santa Monica Boulevard, the first members-only club to combine a discotheque and restaurant. It was a joint venture of a number of show biz folk, including my old pals Tony Newley and Sammy Davis, Jr. At one of its many star-studded bashes, I found myself standing next to Frank Sinatra at the bar. He was nursing a drink and had his back to me.

He didn't notice me as I ordered from the bartender. Just as I summoned up the courage to introduce myself and mention that I knew his wife, Mia Farrow, Sinatra was approached by a rather loud and tipsy partygoer.

"Hiya, Frank," he said, patting him on the back. "Groovy party, don'cha think?" Sinatra just stared at him, nodded, and sipped his drink. Then the guy leaned closer.

"Say, Frankie . . . you got any *grass* on ya?"

Sinatra tensed. "Yeah, pal, I got plenty of grass," he said. "It's at home—on my *lawn*."

Within seconds Sinatra's bodyguards surrounded the crass fellow, smoothly lifted him by the elbows, and escorted him out. Having watched this little drama, I decided it didn't seem like an auspicious time to meet Ol' Blue Eyes, so I discreetly mingled back into the crowd.

Suddenly I heard a soft, familiar voice calling me. I turned around and saw Mia Farrow, trying to make her way toward me through a sea of people.

"Mia!" I said, greeting her with a warm hug. "I've just seen your other half at the bar. I wondered where you were."

She seemed unusually nervous, and quickly led me into the ladies' room to tell me what was going on. "It's Frank," she said. "I can't seem to get away from his bodyguards. They're watching every move I make. I'd love to smoke a joint—do you have one?"

"Sure, love . . . but we can't do it here."

We found our way out onto the fire escape undetected and lit up. We recalled the fun we used to have when Burt and I visited the set of "Peyton Place," where she was working with Ryan O'Neal.

We talked about our current activities, and Mia described the movie she was finishing, *Rosemary's Baby,* directed by Roman Polanski. She was enthusiastic about it, but admitted that it had taken its toll on her personal life. I didn't have to ask what she meant by that.

She mentioned an exciting trip she was planning to take to the Himalayas where she would join the Beatles on their pilgrimage to meet the Maharishi Mahesh Yogi, the founder of Transcendental Meditation, who lived on an ashram in the remote wilderness of northern India.

"It's really going to be splendid, Judy," she explained. "My brother and sister are coming along, as well as Mike Love, of the Beach Boys. You should join us—you'd love it."

I relished the thought of taking part in what was certain to be an unforgettable adventure, but in the meantime, we had to get back to the party. We tried the door, but it had locked behind us. We were both quite stoned, and I saw terror wash over Mia's face, afraid of the reaction she was likely to get from Sinatra.

I took her hand and we slowly groped our way down the fire escape and around to the front of the club, where we made a giddy re-entrance amid a blaze of flashbulbs.

When I later contacted Mia about the trip to India, she said it was planned for late February. This made it impossible for me to go along. I was firmly committed to an adventure of my own: "Laugh-In."

7. A Stunt Runt
Is Born

NBC gave us a "kamikaze" time slot, as our fearless leader, George Schlatter, liked to call it: Monday night at 8 P.M., opposite "Gunsmoke" and "The Lucy Show." Even the popular "Man from U.N.C.L.E." failed in this slot, causing NBC to cancel it at mid-season.

And so it came to pass that George Schlatter was given the chance to produce the show of his dreams. With Rowan and Martin a stabilizing force as the hosts of the show, George was free to expand the variety show format by assembling a company of players that could explore the outer limits—for 1968—of television comedy.

"Laugh-In" formed its identity in its first half-season—fourteen shows, from January to May—climbing swiftly to the top of the ratings and earning the distinction of being the first show in history to topple Lucille Ball in the ratings. Taking part in those first shows was as mind-boggling for me as it must have been for the viewers to absorb. Thanks to four little words, my life would never be the same again.

"Remember those 'terrible things' I said I would do to you, Judy?" George asked me during the first script meeting.

"I wondered when you were going to bring that up, George."

A Stunt Runt Is Born

"Well, the writers have suggested we use an old musician's phrase, 'Sock it to me' . . . have you heard of it?"

"Sure," I said, the memory of Monterey still vivid in my mind. "It's on that Aretha Franklin record, 'Respect.' She sings it in the middle section . . . *sock-it-to-me, sock-it-to-me, sock-it-to-me, sock-it-to-me!*"

"Yeah, that's it," said George. "We'll make a gag out of it and 'sock it to you,' *literally.*" The sexual implication of the phrase titillated George's imagination. He wanted to develop it into a catchy phrase that would be unique to my personality and identifiable with "Laugh-In."

"Now, Judy," he said to me, "how would you present this in a typically English way?"

I thought for a moment, and replied in a Cockney accent, "And now, folks, it's 'Sawk it to me time!' "

"Perfect! That's when we let you have it."

"With what, George?" I asked.

"I dunno, anything . . . how about a boxing glove?"

As long as it was funny, I wasn't about to argue. For the first "Sock It To Me" the glove punched through a backdrop behind me, and I ducked. Countless variations were soon to follow—including falling through the ever-popular trapdoor.

This stunt required precision and timing. It was essential to keep my knees bent when the doors flew open and dropped me onto a stack of mattresses below. Rigid knees could have resulted in a broken leg. I also had to keep my arms by my sides to prevent them from hitting the sides of the trap as I fell. A few guest stars learned these lessons the hard way when George sent them down through those dreaded doors.

I was sawed in half by a magician, became the target of a knife-throwing act, and as a lion tamer, had my chair bitten apart. I even put my head in a guillotine—which nearly led to tragedy.

This particularly gruesome "Sock It To Me" called for my decapitation. Before the director could shoot it, however, the guillotine had to be tested, so a cabbage was placed where my neck was to go. We all gathered and watched as the blade was released, slicing the cabbage neatly in half. There was momentary panic as we all realized it could have been *me*! George chewed out the propmen, and tried to convince me that the mishap had all been a joke. But I knew better.

"No way, George . . ."

"Aw, c'mon, Judes, a joke's a joke!"

"Why don't *you* put your head in it, then?"

"Okay, I *will*!" He looked at the guillotine for a moment, then knelt down and put his neck in the blocks. "Whatever happens, tell my wife I love her!" When the blade fell, his eyes bulged in their sockets, but his head stayed attached to his body.

"Okay, George, you win . . . I guess I'm just a *stunt runt* to you!"

George loved practical jokes, and I was his favorite target. During one "Sock It To Me" in which I remarked to Dan and Dick, "It may be a space capsule to you, but it's a *rocket to me,*" I was flown up to the ceiling by wires attached to a body harness, with a smoking rocket strapped to my back.

"Awright, gang, that's a wrap!" George said. "Lunch break!" The lights dimmed and everybody quickly disappeared. I was left swaying helplessly, high above the studio floor.

"Hello . . . ? I want to come *down* now! It's lunch for me too!!"

Dead silence. "Can anyone hear me?!" I yelled, verging on panic.

Suddenly the studio doors flew open and the entire company tumbled back in, letting loose the laughter they'd been stifling in the hallway.

"Gotcha!" George yelled.

"You bastard, get me down!"

"I'd love to, Judy, but our rigger just went to lunch, and he's the only one who knows how to work the damn thing!"

"I'll get you for this, George!" I shouted, although I found it hard to stay mad after they lowered me to the ground—it *was* a bloody good laugh.

It didn't take long for water to become the most popular form of socking it to me.

I quickly learned the dos and don'ts of taking a bucket of water. From the corner of your eye you can see the propmen poised with their buckets, and the natural reaction is to flinch as they throw them. The trick is to ignore all of this, and look surprised when the water hits.

Sometimes I was doused with two or more buckets at the same

time, to increase the impact—and presumably the laughs—as waves of water hit me from all sides. The propmen became quite proficient at it. They *had* to be, because if they accidentally got their hands into the shot, it all had to be redone, causing expensive delays: Stage hands had to mop the set, and my makeup and hair had to be redone while my dresser fetched a duplicate dress.

I frequently caught a chill after getting doused with the cold water in those buckets. I had to dash from under the hot lights through the air-conditioned studio to my dressing room with wardrobe ladies toweling me off as I ran.

Finally, when a bad case of the sniffles affected my singing voice, George was concerned. "Hey, Judes, what's with the cold?"

"It's the freezing water in those bleedin' buckets, George!"

From then on the water was heated—he didn't want his "Sock it to me" girl coming down with pneumonia.

I did my best to contribute ideas that were outside the "Sock it to me" realm. One day during a break I perched on George's lap and pretended to be a ventriloquist's dummy, much to his amusement.

"I love doing dolls and dummies, George . . . mechanical humor. I think it's an untapped area."

"Yeah . . . I like that. Let's kick it around and see what we can come up with."

On the next show I introduced the "Judy Doll," a running gag that I usually did with Arte Johnson. Standing immobile in a doll's dress, with white knee socks and bows in my hair, I spoke only when Arte pulled the string attached to my back: "Ha-low, I'm your Judy Doll . . . touch my little body and I *hit!*" I would then knock Arte down to the floor. We did a multitude of variations, such as "Ha-low, I'm your Judy Doll . . . you can play catch with me, you can play house with me, but try to play doctor with me and I'll break your face!" and "I don't mind being on the shelf with Chatty Cathy, but please don't put me in the washing machine with G.I. Joe!"

The doll idea evolved into a more extended feature, "Robot Theater." Arte and I portrayed poorly programmed robot Thespians whose ill-timed movements usually resulted in the destruction of the set.

We were encouraged to contribute our own ideas, and many of them became fixtures of the show. Arte Johnson was extremely prolific at this. In addition to Mr. Rosmenko, he was Rabbi Shankar, the proverb-spouting Indian mystic, and the German soldier—a character he invented spontaneously, emerging one day from the NBC wardrobe room squinting through a monocle, dressed in the helmet and uniform. He found a potted palm, peered through its leaves, and in a thick German accent purred "Verrry interesting!" It was an instant classic.

Arte also invented Tyrone F. Hornigh, the dirty old man. Tyrone was a perfect foil for Ruth Buzzi's character, Gladys Ormphby, the frumpy spinster. Each time Tyrone mumbled his desire for her on the park bench, Gladys attacked him with her handbag.

Ruth played one of the best drunks I've ever seen. In a running gag with Dick Martin, they played a pair of barroom lushes, a portrayal so frighteningly realistic that NBC only allowed them to do it once every few weeks, and *then* only in the second half of the program, when fewer minors were presumed to be watching.

Jo Anne Worley didn't need to play characters, she *was* a character. "Boring!" was her reaction when the pace slowed down. At an early script conference, she saw a joke and commented, "That's another chicken joke!" Only Jo Anne could make such a ridiculous phrase funny enough to use on virtually every show from that day on.

Jo Anne's raucous personality met its match when Alan Sues was added to the cast. Alan was so naturally hysterical, he got laughs by just rolling his eyeballs. His campy, crybaby style of delivery gave life to Uncle Al, "the kiddies' pal," the riotous children's show host, and Big Al, the wigged-out sportscaster who never did a "featurette" without ringing his little bell ("My tinkle, my tinkle, I *loooove* my tinkle!").

My closest friend in the cast was Henry Gibson. I'd known his wife, Lois, when she was a story editor at Desilu Studios. Henry and Lois lived on the beach in Malibu with their three children, Jonny, Charlie, and Jimmy. Whenever I felt depressed or insecure, I'd spend a weekend with the Gibsons and find out who I was. Then I'd race back to L.A. to tell everyone else.

Henry's special contribution to the show was his poetry: "My Potato Is Falling Off," "I Think I Don't Have a Giraffe," and "Is the Frog the Farmer's Friend?" were a few of his more memorable works. He was the philosopher-king of "Laugh-In."

There was a constant flow of talent in and out of the lineup. After the first few shows we were joined by a lady who quickly became a member of the family—Goldie Hawn. She was an excellent dancer and extremely lovable, but her "Laugh-In" persona didn't come into its own until one magic day when we were lined up to read jokes from cue cards. When Goldie stepped up and read, she inadvertently reversed a couple of words. After a few seconds she realized her mistake, and let out a divinely silly giggle.

"Hey . . . did that make sense?" she asked innocently.

Everyone in the studio was enchanted. We had all witnessed Goldie's uncanny ability to be adorable, and it was spellbinding.

George jumped up out of his chair. "Goldie, if you *ever* lose that quality I'll *kill* you," he shouted.

After that Goldie's cue cards were deliberately sabotaged to induce that same captivating reaction. One day she blurted out an instant classic: "I forgot the *question!*" It was written in for her, and quickly became one of her trademarks.

Goldie gained her reputation as a featherbrained blonde, but we knew the other side of her. "Yeah, Goldie's dumb," we used to say, "dumb as a *fox.*"

We were all in our dressing room one afternoon when Art Simon, Goldie's manager, arrived with some important news. Art was softspoken, but his well-chosen words carried a great deal of weight, and Goldie trusted him implicitly. He told her that the Coca-Cola company was offering her $100,000 to star in their new commercial. Goldie was understandably overwhelmed by the magnitude of the offer.

"Fantastic, Art . . . that's great!"

"Goldie," Art said, looking her straight in the eye, "I want you to think about something. What do you want to *be*? Do you want to be known as 'The Coca-Cola Girl,' or do you want a long-range career in films?"

"Art, you don't understand, I have no clothes, I have no car . . ."

"You'll be all right, Goldie, you'll get them soon enough," Art said calmly. "I don't think we should accept the offer."

Goldie saw how serious he was, and she began to cry. "But *why?*"

"Look, I know it seems like a lucrative offer right now, but if you want to save yourself for movies, you've *got* to turn it down!"

It was the most brilliant managerial advice I'd ever heard, and it took a lot of faith on both their parts. If I had been advised by people with *half* Art's foresight, I would have been spared a lot of blunders in the years to come.

The "Laugh-In" work week began each Thursday at 2 P.M. with a script meeting at the Schlatter/Friendly offices. It was a late call, since the night before, we'd been taping the previous week's show well past midnight.

George presided at the head of a long table, perched on a stool above us. Dan and Dick sat on either side of him, along with that week's guest star. Each week a different entertainer joined us in our songs and sketches—such as Sonny and Cher, Diana Ross, Tony Curtis, Connie Stevens, Don Rickles, Peter Lawford, Dick Gregory, Kaye Ballard, Flip Wilson, Davy Jones, Robert Culp, Sally Field, Bobby Darin, and Marcel Marceau, to name a few.

Our head writer, Paul Keyes, was positioned near George, and at the far end of the table sat our musical director, Billy Barnes, our choreographer, Hugh Lambert, and our indispensable propman, the aptly named Gary Necessary.

There was a lot of joking around at these script readings, but beneath the laughter was a layer of tension. If you didn't read a line convincingly the first time, it would be assigned to someone else. It wasn't a competition, though, because the foremost thought in our minds was what would be best for the show. We traded parts that didn't feel right, because it was better to give them up than to have them fall flat.

George was rarely without his attaché case, which contained bulging binders, crammed full of material. He worked around the clock, driving everyone as hard as he could—especially the writers, whom George kept locked away in a motel across the street.

Allan Manings, who became our head writer during the second season, used the metaphor of a luxury liner to describe the relationship between the writers and the cast. "We're down in the hold, shoveling coal, and we know that somewhere above the decks, there's a huge party going on," Allan once told me. "All we hear is the constant voice of the chief engineer—George Schlatter—screaming, 'More coal, Scotty, more coal!' "

The writer's motto was "Let us be naughty, but never vulgar!"

Meaningless words were created that were *wide* open to interpretation (*bippy, nurn, nurdle,* etc.), as were the catchphrases, such as "You bet your sweet bippy," "Ring my chimes," and "Blow in my ear and I'll follow you anywhere."

Some of the phrases came up quite accidentally. When a writer was asked to define one of these nonsense words in an early script meeting, he blurted out, "Look it up in your Funk and Wagnalls!" The phrase became so popular, it gave new life to the Funk & Wagnalls dictionary company.

On Monday rehearsals began at 10 A.M. in Studio 4 at NBC, with most of the sets still under construction. When we broke for lunch, I usually dashed across the street with Jo Anne Worley, Henry Gibson, Billy Barnes, and Alan Sues to the Carriage House. There, the lights were low, and the Bloody Marys were made to order by the generous bartender.

After lunch came the first run-through. This was not only for our benefit, but also for that of the censors. They sat in the shadows with their faces buried in the script as we ran through each joke. George paced nervously, trying to assess their reactions and doing his best to distract them whenever a controversial line came up.

On Tuesday, taping began promptly at 10 A.M., starting with the segments featuring Gary Owens as our "off-stage announcer," cupping his ear and delivering introductions, jokes, and assorted non-sequiturs. Gary taped all of his bits that morning, and we regretted seeing so little of him. A chat with Gary was an oasis of calm during the course of a hectic day.

We taped blackouts, sketches, and running gags all day long until the dinner break, after which came the prerecording of the musical numbers we would be lipsynching the following day.

My answering service woke me gently at 8:30 on Wednesday mornings. After a bath, some toast, and a protein drink from my blender, I was off for the taping, which began at noon. Wednesday was the *killer* day—over twelve hours of videotaping.

The "cocktail party" always came first. It was a tension-filled taping because so many people were involved, and a flubbed line would momentarily halt the momentum. After one run-through, the cameras were rolling. A script could be constructed that would read as follows:

COCKTAIL PARTY

CAST, CHER

HENRY (As Parson)
The fact that the Lord giveth and the Lord taketh away does not make Him an Indian giver.
MUSIC: UP TWO BARS AND OUT

JO ANNE
Boris says that capitalism isn't working; but then again, neither is Boris.
MUSIC: UP TWO BARS AND OUT

ARTE (As Shankar)
It is written that he who maketh the Viper crouch low whilst the flute of life plays, shall have his asp in a slink.
MUSIC: UP TWO BARS AND OUT

CHER
You know, Dick, Blacks have a really tough time in the Union of South Africa.

DICK
I know, Cher, it's tough being a minority.

CHER
Yeah, especially when there's more of *you* than *them*.
MUSIC: UP TWO BARS AND OUT

JUDY
My classmates and I can't decide what to take this semester, but we've narrowed it down to either the administration building or the library.
MUSIC: UP TWO BARS AND OUT

DAN
Perhaps the reason more women don't run for the Senate is because every six years their seat is up for grabs.
MUSIC: UP TWO BARS AND OUT

128

A Stunt Runt Is Born

RUTH (As Gladys)
Marriage is a union. But then so are the teamsters.

SUPERIMPOSE:
1. LLOYD BRIDGES . . .
2. DON'T CROSS JOAN RIVERS

After lunch we returned for the "Mod Mod World" musical number, the weekly tribute to a social institution, written by Billy Barnes and staged into a lavish production number by Hugh Lambert. Billy and Hugh were two of the program's unsung heroes, as each week they churned out, in effect, a mini-musical.

It then became time for George to step in and direct the sketches. Although he was our producer, George acted as a director in the cinematic sense: He was always by the cameras with his script, creating an atmosphere in which we could "play."

"Tape is cheap," was George's battle cry. He rarely stopped rolling the videotape, because he knew that with this group, a mistake was likely to produce more laughs than what had been written.

In the late afternoon a well-stocked bar was wheeled onto the set—a signal that the cameo guests would soon be arriving. These were the celebrity walk-ons, which became a "Laugh-In" trademark. Working with the cameos was always a thrill, because George effectively tapped the constant stream of stars that flowed through the NBC studios for appearances on "The Dean Martin Show," "The Jerry Lewis Show," and "The Andy Williams Show."

Douglas Fairbanks, Jr., was the first guest to be recruited in this way. George bumped into him in the corridor and convinced him to drop by the set to tape a few one-liners. The success with Fairbanks set a precedent, and George used his innate wheeler-dealer technique to reel in the biggest stars in the business.

John Wayne was the most celebrated cameo guest to appear on "Laugh-In" during our first season. A clever plan had been devised to lure him on.

"Ladies and gentlemen," Dick said each week in the monologue, "we're very happy to have John Wayne with us tonight."

"Dick, that's not true," said Dan. "John Wayne is *not* here tonight. . . ."

"Aha! He didn't show up *again*. . . ."

After weeks of this needling, word reached the Duke, who tuned in to "Laugh-In" and loved it. He broke his own rule of never doing TV by agreeing to appear, and the results revealed his superb sense of humor. After John Wayne's appearance, the flood-gates were opened and "Laugh-In" became the "in" thing for stars to do.

The cameo guests had no idea what they would be asked to do on the show. If they asked in advance, George only said, "We'll give you two hundred and ten dollars and a lot of love!" The element of surprise was essential.

We never knew exactly who would be showing up. When a guest arrived, we dropped what we were doing and did our best to put them at ease by being friendly and making them laugh.

Lena Horne recited variations of "Sock it to me" in her divinely sexy voice, and I remember Dinah Shore rapidly repeating, "Sock it to me sock it to me sock it to me sock it to me . . . oh go sock it to *yourself!*" She was involved with Burt Reynolds at the time.

I felt privileged to work with legendary comedians Jimmy Durante, Jack Benny, George Burns, and Bob Hope, as well as younger geniuses Peter Sellers, Sid Caesar, Mel Brooks, and Jonathan Winters.

George loved to get established movie stars to utter nonsense words and phrases, which he edited later for maximum effect.

"Lake Titicaca?" asked Greer Garson.

"I bet *my* sweet bippy and *lost* it!" giggled Liberace.

Zsa Zsa Gabor insisted on knowing the meaning of everything she was asked to say. "Bippy? But vat does dis *mean?*"

"Don't worry, we probably won't even use it," George told her.

"I von't say things ven I don't know vat zey mean!" Zsa Zsa insisted. George aired the clip of her saying just *that!*

Personalities outside show biz were also recruited, such as William F. Buckley, who, when asked to appear, was said to have remarked, "I not only won't appear, I resent being *asked!*"

When Billy Graham appeared, we all behaved as though we were in Sunday school. You could hear a pin drop.

Jack Lemmon was absolutely brilliant when he made his appearance. We gathered excitedly behind the camera, but noticed that he was having trouble getting into it at first. George threw a few jokes at him, but Lemmon looked off camera when he repeated them.

"Jack, we need you to look right *into* the camera," George said.

"Oh? I see . . . well, George, I'm used to looking into somebody's face when I say a line," Jack responded. In movies, actors rarely look directly into the lens of the camera.

I went over to George and whispered, "Tell you what . . . if I put my face really close to the side of the camera, he could look at *me* when he says his lines."

George approved, so I pressed my cheek against the lens. With someone to look at, Jack felt more natural, and soon he started improvising lines that were much funnier than the original ones. It was a fascinating look at a great actor surmounting unaccustomed circumstances, and his last line was quite fitting: "This isn't a television show, it's group therapy!"

If a joke on "Laugh-In" didn't make sense, it was usually because the meaning was simply too "inside".

> ROBERT CULP: I'm a secret agent.
> JUDY: Oh, you must be with William Morris!

"George, they'll never get that joke," someone commented when it came up in the script.

"If they don't get it, they'll *ask!*" said George. It got even more inside than that. Every now and then a sign in the background of a sketch would read "C.F.G. Airlines" or "C.F.G. Automat." Only people who worked on the show knew that C.F.G. stood for "Crazy Fucking George," the nickname he'd earned as a result of his maniacal hunger for new material and the way he drove everyone crazy trying to produce it. He was so proud of this title, he had the initials put on his combination-lock attaché case.

C.F.G. loved to get away with risqué jokes. The viewers were teased by having lines like "Put some fun into your wife," "Down Pluto! Up Uranus!" and "The KKK is full of sheet" flashed on the screen barely long enough to read what was written. Carolyn Raskin, our editor and associate producer, was responsible for much of the show's brisk pace.

The body painting was another of George's great teases. Graffiti, caricatures, and free-form designs were displayed on our undulating flesh in provocative ways. Goldie was included in the body painting soon after her arrival but she never seemed to enjoy it. She was a good sport, though—until she tried to get the paint off after her first session. She called me right away.

"Judy, I've been scrubbing and scrubbing. This stuff won't come *off*," she said.

"Don't worry, Goldie," I reassured her, "it'll come off. It usually takes a few days." I explained to her that the artists used paint that was resistant to our perspiration.

"But Judy, I can't walk around with *bippy* and an eyeball painted on my body!"

"You know, Goldie, you're right . . . we've got to talk to them about this," I said. There *had* to be an alternative. We decided to take a firm stand with George on the matter, and it worked—before long, the artists were using washable paint.

In the early days I stood as they painted me, but by the time Goldie arrived, we lay on boards as two artists worked on each of us. This gave Goldie and me time to get to know each other.

We had a lot in common. She had been through years of ballet training, was a homebody, and loved to cook, so we often swapped recipes. The girl talk inevitably got around to our love lives.

At the time, Goldie was involved with an aspiring writer/director, Gus Trikonis. He was dark-haired and gorgeous, but very shy when it came to appearing at "Laugh-In" functions.

Goldie was a voracious reader, always carrying a book, usually something Freudian. She told me that she had been in analysis for some time. Judging by the sense of security and self-confidence she displayed on the show, it was obviously working for her.

One day George told us of an unusual development: Salvador Dali, the surrealist painter, enjoyed "Laugh-In" so much that he was interested in painting our bodies personally! Goldie was apprehensive about the idea, but I thought it was wonderfully outrageous that one of the world's most renowned artists wished to express himself on human canvases and televise the result. It would be an artistic *event*. Alas, it became a question of logistics: The process would have been too time-consuming for our schedule, so the idea was dropped.

Soon the censors became preoccupied with the entire body painting issue. Having lost the "navel" battle, the censors sent down a memo stating that the artists were not allowed to paint the insides of our thighs. The calves, knees, and outsides of the thighs were fair game, but the insides were a kind of no-man's land. To establish this demilitarized zone, we were actually *measured*. Goldie and I just wanted to get the bloody thing over with; what we *didn't* want was lengthy discussions on whether a paintbrush was allowed two or three inches from our groins!

These taboos seemed ridiculous for television in 1968, as Americans were bombarded each evening with graphic newsreel footage of the war in Vietnam. This was one of the arguments George made to the censors. "We're just trying to do a job here, George," they responded. "Never mind the war and the riots, you do your job, we'll do ours."

"But you don't understand—we're breaking new ground," George told them.

"We're all for innovation, George," the exasperated censors argued, "but on the other hand, it's a *family* show."

George presented outrageous material for their approval that he knew didn't stand a chance of getting accepted. His scheme was to desensitize the censors so that the less-risqué sketches would seem tame by comparison.

"I agree with you guys, some of these things *are* pretty wild," he'd tell them, "but the problem is, you've snipped out nearly twelve minutes that I've got to make up here. I don't have to tell you what twelve minutes of air time *costs*."

George usually ended up bartering with them. "All right, if you won't give me the gay joke, you *gotta* let me keep the nun joke." And they would.

"Life is one giant double meaning!" was George's philosophy, Swhich was exemplified by the notorious "bald" joke. The script called for me to appear bald, and George wanted it to look so authentic that he called in a makeup expert from 20th Century-Fox. It took three hours, and he did a perfect job. Over this bald pate I wore a wig that looked exactly like my own hair.

An invisible wire was attached to the wig, and when I said "And now, folks, it's 'Sawk it to me time!'" the wig was yanked clean off my head. "Oh!" my line was. "I've never been *bald* before!"

The censors didn't get the double entendre during the run-through. George had done a good job of distracting them by saying, "Can you believe how funny she'll look with that bald head? Ha ha! It'll be *hilarious*!"

The day after the bald joke aired, the censors stormed onto the set.

"Everyone in the country knows what 'to ball' means, George! You must think we're idiots!"

C.F.G. just looked at them with an expression of shock.

"You know, guys," he said, "you're not going to believe this, but honest to God, I never thought of it that way. I'm up to my neck in material and I can't catch *everything* that goes by. I'm *grateful* that you pointed it out to me. From now on I promise I'll always look for those double meanings."

The censors shook their heads and exited in frustration. George deserved an Oscar.

I was also at the center of the controversy surrounding the first dope joke on "Laugh-In." I knew that some of our writers got high, and they knew the same about me. George must have known this, because one day he took me aside to ask my opinion about a sketch on the subject.

"Judy, I want to pick your brain. Feel free to answer honestly, because I'm not here to judge."

"Sure, George, what is it?"

"We've got this bit, y'see, where two hippies greet each other in a park. One says 'Hi.' The other one says 'You too?'"

"That's cute, George . . . but will they get it?"

"That's where you come in. I want you to tell me how to present it so they *will* get it. Tell me what they should wear, how they should speak."

We went to the NBC wardrobe and I assembled what I thought to be the authentic garb. Long-haired wigs, of course, peace symbols, some beads (but not *too* many), bell-bottomed jeans, open-toed sandals, and a hanging roach clip. Henry Gibson was my fellow hippie in the sketch, and we looked as though we'd just come from Haight-Ashbury.

The joke went right past the censors, but the day after it aired, they stormed onto the set again, seething, and pulled George aside.

"You must really think we're a bunch of schmucks, George!" I heard one of them shout. "How do you think I felt when my kid turned to me this morning over breakfast and said, 'That dope joke last night was really *cool,* Dad!'"

"Well, if that's what your kid said," George said without flinching, "you'd better keep an eye on him!"

A Stunt Runt Is Born

When letters poured in from the nation's youth, NBC realized that maybe dope jokes were funny after all. They sent down a memo saying that "only Judy Carne" was allowed to do dope jokes. They figured that since I was British, it would be less offensive. Later on, of course, jokes about pot were *de rigueur.*

I was the only member of the cast who actually smoked pot—even though a majority of the American public believed *everyone* on the show was "turning on."

I only smoked grass socially, usually in the privacy of my own home. I preferred the serenity of its high to the sloppy, aggressive high of booze, but I always had a very firm rule: I *never* mixed it with my work. That was courting disaster. I'd learned that lesson the *hard* way.

Flip Wilson was our guest one week and the two of us got together in my dressing room for a celebratory joint when the taping was over. We took all the precautions: towels under the door, spray deodorants; we even exhaled into the ventilation system. Suddenly there was a knock at the door. "Judy? Are you in there?"

Flip and I exchanged paranoid glances, fearing the worst. I exhaled a lungful of smoke and said, "Just a minute, I'm not dressed!"

I opened the door a crack and saw one of George's production assistants, with an apologetic look on his face.

"I'm sorry to disturb you, Judy, but there's just one bit with you and Flip that needs to be redone. We promise it won't take very long. By the way, you don't happen to know where Flip is, do you?"

"Flip? Flip *who . . .* ? Oh! You mean *Flip!* No, I haven't seen him . . . I'm sure he's around somewhere, though . . . uh, tell you what, if I see him, I'll tell him you're looking for him."

"Great, Judy . . . we're really sorry about all this."

"Oh, that's okay . . . now . . . I'll be out in a minute." I went back to Flip, who was hiding behind my costume rack.

"Shit, mama, we're on!" he said.

"Okay . . . now . . . let's pull ourselves together."

"Right. I'd better get outta here." He opened the door and poked his head out, looking both ways before stealthily creeping down the corridor to his dressing room.

I arrived on the set first and then Flip showed up. "Hey, Judy," he said, acting surprised. "I thought you'd gone home already!"

"Sorry about this, guys," George said, "but we just forgot to do one of the quickies, it'll just take a second."

By now it was 2 A.M., and we were punchy, exhausted, and stoned. We could hardly look at each other for fear of laughing, so we did it in one take.

"That's a wrap. Thanks, you two can go home now," George said.

When we got outside to the parking lot, we slapped each other five, clicked our heels, and danced all the way to our cars.

"Well, all right, Flip!"

"That was a close one, but we did it, mama!"

We really thought we'd pulled it off. That is, until the show aired three weeks later.

I had forgotten about the incident by then, and all of a sudden, during a flurry of quickies, there we were, seemingly in slow motion. We looked disoriented and our timing was pathetic. The phone rang, and I wasn't surprised to hear Flip's voice on the line.

"Did you see it, mama?"

"Sadly, yes . . ."

"Never again, right?"

"*Never* again!"

Flip's guest appearances on "Laugh-In" allowed him to perfect some of the characters he later brought to his own hit show—such as Reverend Leroy and Geraldine. George loved him because he could deliver racial jokes in an inoffensive way. Only Flip could lend benevolence to lines like "We'll stop marrying your sisters if you stop stealing our music!" and "When we take over, we're gonna have to kill some of *us* too!"

Another person who could get away with racial humor brilliantly was Sammy Davis, Jr. In his first guest appearance on our eighth show, he immortalized another "Laugh-In" catchphrase: "Here come de Judge!"

On an earlier show the writers had come up with a wealth of courtroom sketches featuring British comic Roddy Maude-Roxby as a powder-wigged English judge. "You've been brought here for excessive drinking," he'd say to the defendant, usually Henry Gibson.

"Okay, your honor," says Henry. "Let's get started!"

Wham! Henry would get hit with a giant inflatable gavel.

These jokes were ancient. Many of them were supplied by Henry's wife, Lois, who'd discovered them in an old vaudevillian's filing cabinet. When Sammy came across "Here come de Judge" during the script meeting, he looked as though he'd seen a long-lost friend.

"'Here come de Judge'? Far out, man, that's Pigmeat Markham's line!" he cried, referring to the black comedian he'd worked with as a child. Sammy launched into dozens of Pigmeat's courtroom jokes, and "Laugh-In" had a new judge.

When we taped the show, they scheduled twenty minutes to shoot his first routine, but once Sammy was in front of the cameras in that robe and wig there was no stopping him:

> Lock de door, hide the key,
> De judge is comin' an' he's comin' for thee!
> Tap your toe, jump and shout,
> Here come de judge, let it *all* hang out!
> Here come de Judge! Here come de Judge!
> Order in the courtroom, I *am* the Judge!

"Laugh-In" was a perfect showcase for Sammy, and the jokes poured out of him. He reveled in the workshop atmosphere: He sang "When the Saints Come Marching In" as Mr. Rosmenko's brother; he joined Henry for a poem, demonstrating how to recite it with *soul*; and he and I sang "Singin' in the Rain" (what *else*?) before getting soaked.

George wasn't sure how he would react to taking a bucket of water, but not only did Sammy agree to it—he showed up for the taping in one of his finest silk suits.

"Hey, Sam, are you sure you want to get wet in *that*?" I asked him, knowing how the water had ruined so many of my costumes.

"Dig it, Judes, when the audience sees me in this silk suit, man, they ain't never gonna believe I'm getting it socked to *me*!"

Sammy and I reminisced about his visits to London. "Vidal, Newley, and you, man, we got you *all* over here now," he said. "London must be *dead* without you cats. You and that groovy roommate of yours had that town on *fire*!"

Sammy asked me if I'd thought about making a record. I told him it was one of my dreams.

"You've got to *use* this 'Sock it to me' thing, babe. It's big, man, really big. You could get a hit record out of it. In fact, tell you what, I've got a recording session in a few days—we could lay down a quick track for you at the end of the session and play around with it. How about it, Judes?"

"That's smashing, Sam, I'd love it!"

I spent the next few days on a cloud. Sammy Davis, Jr., had just asked me to *record* with him, and what's more, he thought it would be big—*really* big.

I went along to the session full of anxieties—what would the song be like? Would I be able to learn it in one afternoon? I arrived and was taken to the control booth, where I watched Sammy soar through the last few takes of a number.

"When Sammy is finished, we'll do your tune," I was told.

"How will I learn it that fast?"

"There's nothing to learn. You'll just keep saying 'Sock it to me' over the track."

I sat nervously in the sound booth, listening to Sammy doing his thing, and then my time came. The rhythm section laid down a simple rock beat, then the horns came in with some background riffs. Every four bars I came in with those same four words. I improvised a few variations, but before I knew it, the tune was over.

"Is that it?" I asked. "Are you sure we have enough?"

The arranger said it was fine, that they would add some special effects later. I thanked Sammy and kissed him good-bye as he left with his entourage. Within minutes the studio was almost deserted. My recording debut had been a disillusioning anticlimax.

As I gathered myself together, I noticed a young man packing up his camera equipment. He'd been taking pictures of me throughout the session. He approached me with a big smile, and with his ruffled shirt and sensitive face, he resembled a poet.

"Hello, I'm Dean Goodhill. I was sent to photograph you making this record."

"So I noticed. What did you think?"

"Well, I was busy taking pictures, but it sounded fine to me. How do *you* feel about it?"

"I'm not too sure, actually. It all happened so fast. . . ."

"Well, just know that I got some great shots of you—really candid stuff with you and Sammy."

He asked me if I wanted to go for coffee, and I happily agreed, not feeling up to the post-session party.

A Stunt Runt Is Born

Through no fault of Sammy's, the record turned out to be a gimmick and a disaster. It was done in a hurry and without much forethought, so it didn't *deserve* to do well. But I did get something out of the session: I met Dean Goodhill.

At that time in my life I was eager for a relationship with a man, yet still slightly intimidated by the thought. I responded well to Dean because of the soft and gentle quality of his appearance and personality. He was fine-boned and slender, with delicately formed artist's hands. He was strong but not threatening.

We went through a rather accelerated courtship; we nuzzled in the car that night after the recording session, and we started seeing a lot of each other. When I saw how well his pictures of Sammy and me came out, I was able to arrange work for him on "Laugh-In."

Dean showed up on the set with a motor drive attachment for his camera—a rare accessory in those days—and captured, frame by frame, the process of me getting soaked by a bucket of water. George was so impressed, he hired Dean as one of the "Laugh-In" photographers, an arrangement that allowed us to be together most of the time.

When "Laugh-In" broke for the summer, our popularity was reinforced by the reruns. The press began to increase its coverage on us, some of which was disturbing. A Sunday newspaper magazine supplement carried this profile of me: "An unrepentant extrovert off screen as well as on, Judy's invitation to 'sock it to me' was taken seriously recently by California police when they arrested her for appearing in a 'too-brief' bikini on Malibu Shores."

I *had* once been told to "cover it up" by a Malibu lifeguard as I sunbathed topless, but that was a far cry from being booked and fingerprinted. I usually limited my sunbathing to my home, and enjoyed inviting friends over on weekends. Sometimes Nancy Zimbalist came over with her stepmother, Stephanie, a slender and strikingly beautiful lady with a superb wit, who was only a few years older than Nancy. She occasionally brought along her ten-year-old daughter, Stephanie, Jr., who was the very image of her mother.

On one of these occasions Nancy left for a tennis date, leaving Stephanie and me to bask in the sun. Stephanie told me about the status of her marriage to Efrem, Jr. He was heavily involved with meditation at this time, and although they lived separately, there was a great deal of love between them. How civilized, I thought. After a while Stephanie checked in with her answering service and then came back out onto the sundeck.

"Judy, would it be okay if a friend of mine came over to visit?"

"Sure, Steph. Anyone I know?"

"I'm not sure. Do you know Kirk Douglas?"

I laughed. "Oh, yeah, I know Kirk! Tell him to come on over. And have him bring Burt Lancaster along too!"

My doorbell rang about twenty minutes later. "That must be Kirk," said Stephanie.

"*Sure* it is," I said sarcastically.

"Then go ahead and answer the door just as you are, I *dare* you!"

"Okay, I *will*!" I was only wearing the briefest of bikini bottoms, with a boy's baseball cap on my head. But Stephanie had dared me, and under these circumstances I've been known to do almost anything. I walked up to my front gate and opened it, expecting to see Nancy returning from tennis. There stood Kirk Douglas, in all his dimpled splendor.

"Oh! Hello," I said, covering myself up. "Come on in. Sorry about the way I look . . . just think of me as a little boy!"

"I'll try," he said, "but if you're a boy, I'm the Queen of England!"

I put on a T-shirt and fixed him a drink. "I'm sorry, but I honestly didn't expect you to be standing there," I said.

"Listen, that was the highlight of my day," he said with a wide grin. We'd had a lot of cameo guests on "Laugh-In," but Kirk Douglas was the first one to appear in my own *home*.

It was good to see everyone when we returned to work. Over the summer Dan and Dick had taken the show on the road with the help of Ruth, Jo Anne, Goldie, and Henry Gibson.

"Judy, it was amazing," said Henry. "In Vancouver I read my poems at a candlelight demonstration against the war. Then, at the hotel, there were masses of people clawing and grabbing at us, as though we were the Beatles!"

I'd had a similar experience when Goldie and I were honorary guests at the annual Soap Box Derby in Akron, Ohio, along with Herb Alpert and Jean-Claude Killy. Chevrolet organized a grand ticker-tape parade and we were told that over 100,000 people had turned out for the event. I was amazed. I'd only seen such response in newsreel footage of troops returning from the war, but here we were, a trumpet player, a skier, and two "Laugh-In" girls.

By the time we reached the presenting stage, the multitudes were frenzied, cheering and screaming, "Say it, Judy! Say it!"

"And now, folks," I bellowed through the mike, hearing my words echo out over the sea of faces, "it's 'Sawk it to me' time!"

As the deafening cheers resounded back at me, I was awestruck by the impact of that phrase and its ability to ignite the crowd. I looked at Goldie, who was trembling as much as I was. I took her hand and said, "Let's keep a grip on ourselves. It's only a TV show . . . we've *got* to keep it in perspective."

"Right, it's only a TV show," she repeated. "It's only a TV show . . . it's only a TV show. . . ."

8. Cuckoo, Laugh-In World

This is a groovy life, this is a lot of fun
I may be black and blue before the season's done
In spite of chicken jokes, we're telling everyone
That it's a Sock-It-To-Me, Verrry Interesting
Cuckoo, Laugh-In *world*

Billy Barnes

Our first show of the 1968–69 season began with a "Sock it to me" extravaganza. One by one the cast had it socked to them in a variety of ways, until the camera settled on me, happily remarking, "Well, what do you know? For once they didn't sock it to *me!*"

I had spoken too soon. In rapid succession I was pelted with Ping-Pong balls, struck by a clock, zapped by lightning, stunk by a skunk, clubbed by a caveman, and then sent down through the trapdoor. But it didn't end there. I climbed back out and my dress was torn off, a backdrop fell on my head, and a torrent of water knocked me to the floor. The water shrank my silk crepe slip, and I tried to cover my body, but to no avail. This footage became the highlight of our Christmas parties, as George gleefully pointed out the three frames in which my nipple popped out on national television.

Cuckoo, Laugh-In World

This subliminal titillation on that first show was followed by the historic cameo appearance of presidential candidate Richard Nixon.

Our head writer, Paul Keyes, had written jokes for Nixon's speeches over the years, and he had suggested to the campaign staff that an appearance on "Laugh-In" might show the lighter side of Richard Nixon, which couldn't hurt in the upcoming election against Hubert Humphrey. NBC was agreeable as long as Humphrey was offered equal time, but the Vice President declined, thinking it undignified. C.F.G. was thrilled to set the stage for such a media event.

The studio was turned upside down by Nixon's visit. He arrived with an entourage of aides and Secret Service agents who looked like a fleet of Ken dolls in their matching blue suits and crew cuts. Paul Keyes conferred with Nixon and his aides, filling him in on the procedure for the cameos as the Ken dolls fanned out through the studio to secure the premises.

Nixon looked out of place in front of the camera. His eyes darted around the studio as he tried to make sense of his new surroundings.

"Mr. Nixon," George said politely, "we'd like to have you repeat some of the phrases from the show that the people love. For instance, would you say, 'You bet your sweet bippy'?"

"You bet your *what*?" Nixon asked, blinking in the harsh lights and looking around for his aides.

"The line is, 'You bet your sweet *bippy*.' "

Va-*roomph*. Nixon's aides surrounded him, as if to protect him from this alien word. After a quick conference, a spokesman emerged.

"Mr. Nixon would like to know—what's a 'bippy'?"

"Never mind," George said diplomatically. "We'll try another one. How about saying 'Good night, Dick'?"

Va-*roomph*. Once more the aides rushed to the rescue. Further deliberation ensued, and then the spokesman announced the verdict.

"No, no, I'm afraid Mr. Nixon couldn't possibly say 'Good night, Dick.' It carries the wrong connotation altogether."

George suggested a few other phrases to Nixon, all of which were rejected. Finally, to our amazement, Nixon simply looked quizzically into the camera and said, "Sock it to *me*?"

It was the only thing he agreed to say. When he was elected President six weeks later, political observers pointed out that his appearance on "Laugh-In" might well have helped him defeat Humphrey, by proving to America that he had a sense of humor. One thing is sure: Nixon won the election by under a million votes, while nearly *fifty* million viewers watched that unforgettable "Sock it to *me?*"

According to the Nielsen ratings, one out of every four Americans was watching "Laugh-In" during the '68–69 season. Gary Owens often gave us reports on how the show was doing; one of his statistics pointed out that "Laugh-In" was watched by more people each week than had ever seen *Gone with the Wind*. We learned that bars all across the country were empty at 8 P.M. on Monday nights, and that Tuesday morning commuter trains were abuzz with references to the show.

With this kind of popularity the "Laugh-In" merchandising empire was born. It started with a "Laugh-In" magazine, complete with order forms for any number of "Laugh-In" accessories: lunch boxes, "Sock-it-to-me" T-shirts and raincoats, coasters, inflatable gavels, jigsaw puzzles, neckties, chewing gum, school supplies, beachware, sleeping bags. There was even a comic strip, and a chain of "Laugh-In" fast food restaurants that proclaimed "Here come the Fudge" and served "Bippy Burgers," among other dishes. I was even measured for a "Judy Doll" that Mattel toys planned to market.

Alas, none of our original contracts contained clauses covering such merchandising—our reward was that we were the stars of the number-one show on television.

My mum and dad arrived in October and they were delighted by all the fun and excitement behind the scenes. Whitney, my Yorkshire terrier, knew the layout of the NBC studios so well that he could lead them from the parking lot, through the corridors, to my dressing room.

Their visit coincided with a week in which we presented a "Salute to Old Age." George hired special makeup men from 20th Century-Fox to make everyone in the cast look 100 years old, the same artists who aged Dustin Hoffman for *Little Big Man*. Our makeup was so authentic that my parents were jolted by the uncanny sight of their daughter looking at least forty years their senior.

We hobbled through some sketches and a musical number in which we all ended up passing away. It was around 2:30 in the morning, and my parents had already gone home. I pulled off my wig, stepped into my jeans, and hopped into my car without bothering to take off the geriatric makeup.

I was doing 70 mph on Ventura Boulevard when I saw flashing lights behind me. I pulled over, and a policeman approached my window.

"Good evening, ma'am, driver's license and registra—" he said, stopping short when he got a good look at me. "Lady, what are you doing driving that fast this late at night?"

"Officer, I know this is going to sound silly, but my name is Judy Carne and I've just finished work on 'Laugh-In' . . . this isn't *me,* you see . . . by that I mean, I'm made up to look *old*—a hundred years old, for the *show.* . . ."

"Let me get this straight, lady. You want me to believe that you are Judy Carne of the 'Laugh-In'? That's pretty weird, if you ask me."

"You've got to believe me," I pleaded. I got out of the car and started jumping up and down, pulling some of the latex wrinkles off my face. "You see? I'm young! I really am! It's *me!*"

The officer just stared at me, dumbfounded, as I began to tear my face off, until the shock of recognition hit him and he realized I was telling the truth.

"Now I've seen everything," he said. He gave me a warning and told me to slow down. I thanked him and got back in my car.

"By the way, Miss Carne, could I trouble you for an autograph for my kids? They're not going to *believe* this!"

C.F.G. took great pleasure in watching the "Sock it to me" phenomenon sweep the country. Watching me get hit was something the viewers could count on each week, without fail.

Whenever it seemed we had exhausted every possible way of socking it to me, the writers would come up with yet another variation. Looking up from a copy of Homer's *Odyssey,* I remarked, "It may be an epic poem to you, but it's a *saga to me!*"; as a Japanese waitress, I said, "It may be rice wine to you, but it's *saki to me!*"; wearing a helmet and shoulder pads, my line was, "It may be football to you, but it's *soccer to me!*"; and I even told a grocery boy that "It may be 'bag it' to you, but it's *'sack it' to me!*"

When C.F.G. saw how willing I was to comply with the stunts, he tried to see just how far I'd go.

"Whatcha got this week, George," I asked, "the same old stuff?"

"This time, Judes, I've got something *really* different. How would you feel about . . . parachuting out of an airplane?"

"Now that *is* different! Of *course* I'll do it!" As always, I was eager to please. Besides, I'd always wanted to free fall. George couldn't believe it, and kept asking me if I was *sure* I wanted to go through with it. "This means giving up your Saturdays, to take lessons, you know." My answer was still yes.

George fessed up that he was bluffing. He'd made a bet with the writers that I *wouldn't* agree to do it. He lost.

While C.F.G. was betting on my gullibility, friends like Henry Gibson were becoming increasingly concerned that the stunts I was doing hadn't been properly tested. He'd seen me get hurt a few times.

The most frightening injury I sustained occurred during a "Sock it to me" in which I played a soldier peering out from a trench, dressed in full camouflage with a helmet and rifle. The script called for me to be shot at by machine guns and the bullet holes were to be simulated by tiny explosives lined up in the sand bags at eye level in front of me.

The cameras rolled, the explosives triggered, and after a quick burst of smoke, my face was stung by a spray of sparks, snapping my head back and knocking off my helmet. When I felt blood on my cheek, I screamed and went into shock. The sparks had missed my eye by fractions of an inch.

George went pale and ran to my aid, and the NBC nurse was quickly summoned.

After she helped me to my dressing room, the nurse cleaned my wounds and calmed me down by telling me that it wasn't serious. My face would not be scarred.

On another occasion the script called for me to be shot out of a cannon. I climbed into the barrel in the human cannonball outfit and said my line. Then I curled up in a ball, and was catapulted out onto a pile of mattresses, amid a cloud of smoke.

Unfortunately the smoke chemicals had been mixed incorrectly. As I was ejected from the cannon, I got a deep whiff of the fumes. I lay on the mattresses, choking and coughing. I was blinded.

Cuckoo, Laugh-In World

"Help! I can't *breathe!*" I cried. "I can't even *see!*" Once again the nurse was summoned. My eyelashes had been fused shut by the fumes; she flushed out my eyes with water and my sight returned.

A few weeks later another "Sock it to me" was shot with smoke and explosives, giving me a grand opportunity for revenge.

After the explosion I fell into a dead faint, so when the fog cleared, all George could see was my body lying in a heap.

"Oh, my God!" he screamed, running over to me in a panic, ashen faced and on the verge of a coronary.

"Gotcha!" I yelled, sitting up and laughing in his face.

"Dammit, Judy! I know I'll laugh in a few minutes, but *shit,* you really zinged me . . . !"

Seeing the terrified look on George's face for just a few seconds gave me great satisfaction. For once I had turned the tables on him.

Being the stunt runt meant having to stay late on Wednesday nights to tape a "Sock it to me" that had gone wrong earlier in the day. Everyone had gone home and it was just me, the crew, and those buckets of water. I rarely got to leave before two in the morning.

After one particularly late night I returned home and noticed my front gate ajar. When I entered the house, I was shocked to find it empty, except for a few pieces of furniture. I walked back outside in a daze, to make sure I had the right house.

It was a violent scene: My stockings hung from the chandelier, what little furniture remained had been slashed, and my publicity photos had been ripped up and scattered around the room like confetti. Everything of value was gone. All that remained was the television set that Burt had wedged into the shelves. None of it had been insured.

I called the police, who were on the scene in minutes. They searched the premises and dusted for fingerprints, but there wasn't much they could do until morning, when they would talk to my neighbors. In the meantime they stationed a patrol car nearby.

Goldie and Ruth arrived the next morning to give me moral support and take me to work, since I didn't feel up to driving. They were disturbed, as I was, about the depraved way in which the burglars had violated the home of the "Sock it to me" girl.

My neighbors told the police that a moving van had been parked outside my house for hours, and that three men wearing overalls and carrying clipboards had spent the afternoon loading up my belongings. It was such a convincing act, the neighbors thought I was actually moving. The burglars obviously knew my schedule well enough to strike when they were sure I would not return home until late in the evening.

Henry Gibson was so distraught by the robbery that he appealed to the NBC brass to help me out. He figured that since RCA was their parent company, they might be able to spare at least a record player until I could replace my belongings.

Henry got no response. Even though they sympathized, the reaction was, "If we do that for her, we'll have to do it for everybody."

"But I'm not talking about *everybody*," Henry said, "I'm talking about *Judy*!"

At the end of the week Henry came to me, choked up, with his paycheck in hand. "Here, Judes. Lois and I have talked it over. We want you to have it."

I was so moved by this, tears welled up in my eyes. Here was Henry, with a family to support, handing me his week's pay. He was insistent, but I couldn't accept it. I told him that the offer itself was more than enough—a profound gesture of love and friendship.

There was a special camaraderie between Jo Anne, Ruth, Goldie, and me. Our styles and identities were so varied that there was no sense of competition, and we got along famously.

The dressing room we shared was quite a scene. It was normally used by a dozen chorus girls, so when we took it over there was plenty of space to stretch out, with lots of room for our costume racks, each holding the two dozen costumes we wore every week.

"We need the girls for a special fitting tomorrow night," the costume designer told us one day, as we reviewed our schedules. We groaned in unison, as it meant going home after work and then having to return after dinner.

"Why can't we do it along with our other fittings?" someone asked.

"This is the only time the den mother can make it," he said.

"The *what*?"

"The den mother from the Bunny Hutch at the Playboy Club. She's going to fit you for your bunny outfits."

George had arranged with Hugh Hefner to have the head den mother of his entire organization come over and make us look like authentic Playboy bunnies. Suddenly we were filled with curiosity. Would the den mother be an older bunny with a little gray tail?

When we arrived for the fitting, the den mother turned out to be a friendly woman in her mid-forties, with a figure that was still quite impressive. She had a rack of outfits in all colors and sizes.

"This isn't going to work very well with *my* body," said Goldie.

"Nor mine," I added, looking down at my chest. "These fried eggs are going to get *lost* in those things!"

"Just you wait and see what I'm going to do for you," she told us. "You will be transformed."

The inside of the Playboy outfit looked as though an architect had designed it. Built-in foam rubber shelves lifted our breasts, pushing the nipples upward, and excruciatingly tight corsets hugged our waists. With the cuffs, ears, and tail in place, the transformation was complete.

When Jo Anne tried on a costume with the shelves, she looked like the Hindenburg disaster, and we howled with laughter.

"I'd love to go home to Dean in this getup," I said, looking at Ruth and Goldie, whose eyes gleamed as they realized what fun we could have with these outfits in the privacy of our homes.

Jo Anne wanted no part of it. "I don't want to gross Roger out!" she cackled, referring to her husband, actor Roger Perry.

We asked the den mother if we could borrow them overnight, but she was hesitant.

"All right, I'll tell you what: After we use them tomorrow, we'll let you take them home for the night."

We never got to take her up on it—those costumes were on their way back to the Playboy Hutch the minute we stepped out of them.

The press naturally loved to write about the behind-the-scenes lives of the " 'Laugh-In' Girls." We all received a good deal of coverage, but after a while the words began to hurt. A few stories began to insinuate that Goldie and I were involved in heated competition with one another, battling it out for female dominance on "Laugh-In." One story proclaimed: "The 'feud' rumors are only whispers now, but they're getting louder, and it looks like a certain blonde and an English lass are heading for a showdown."

Nothing could have been farther from the truth. Goldie and I were good friends and we loved working together. I'd been able to ignore this kind of journalism in the past, but after a while insecurity set in and the stories started to eat me up. I began to wonder if perhaps something *was* going on that I knew nothing about.

When I approached Goldie with my worries, she admitted having gone through the same trauma over the stories. It was a tremendous relief to talk it out with her, to realize that this conflict had been the fabrication of gossip columnists. We made a pact, agreeing that we would never take the word of a disturbing news story without discussing it face to face. That way, we thought, no outside forces could ever jeopardize our friendship.

What I resented most about the stories was the way we were constantly being compared, as if we were in a race to see which one of us would prevail. The more I had to tell myself the stories were meaningless, the more my insecurity grew.

There was no denying that my role on the show had become entrenched in the "Sock it to me" rut to the exclusion of my other abilities. I had already started to confront this grim fact the day some practical joker had showered me with bread crumbs while I sat eating lunch at the Carriage House. And that was just the beginning. Having total strangers sneak up and splash me with water in restaurants had become a semi-regular occurrence that terrified me.

The joke gradually deteriorated into gratuitous violence. When Dan and Dick said, "Tonight the spotlight falls on our own Judy Carne," they meant *just* that: A prop spotlight was sent crashing down on my head. One example that sticks in my mind involved my walking into an Automat and opening the window for the "tomato surprise." A hand came out and ground a juicy tomato into my face. Very funny.

I was always ready to do anything for a laugh, but after a while I lost my sense of humor about it. The worst part was not knowing what to do. My confidence had eroded to the point where I wasn't able to assert myself and say, "No, I won't do this anymore." I kept thinking, Were all my years of hard work and training spent for this? To have a *tomato crushed into my face*?

I was given my own private dressing room on the other side of the studio, but this just made things worse. I felt lonely, and separated from the others. I missed the camaraderie of being with "the girls." I sat in my dressing room with no one to talk to about the pressures that had been welling up inside me.

By mid-season I was overcome by these anxieties. Each day it became harder for me to apply my makeup properly, because of a rather disturbing development: I began to have difficulty distinguishing my features in the mirror. At first my face appeared blurred, and even after rubbing my eyes and looking again, I saw only the same cloudy image in the mirror. I prayed that it was just a temporary problem with my eyesight, or perhaps simple exhaustion, but as time went on it got worse. It reached the point that when I looked into the mirror, I saw nothing but a blank oval shape with no features on it. I had never experienced anything remotely like it, and I thought I was losing my mind.

I had to speak to someone. I knew Goldie was involved with psychotherapy, so I asked her if she could come to my dressing room when she had a chance, because I needed to talk.

"I'm frightened about something, Goldie," I told her, "and I think you're the only one who'll understand."

"Sure, Judy, what is it?"

"I know this may sound silly," I began, "but I've been deeply . . . disturbed lately. Goldie, you're going to think I'm crazy, but . . . I can't focus on myself in the mirror. I look in the mirror and my face is a blank. Do you think I'm going *mad*?"

She reached out and hugged me. "Of course not, Judy," she said. "You're not the first person this has ever happened to, you know." She sat me down, took my hand, and looked into my eyes. "I really think that if you talked to someone about this—perhaps a doctor, who could explain to you what you're going through—it might help."

"But I'm afraid to, Goldie. . . . What will people *think*?"

This was my conditioned response, having been brought up in England to believe that only certified lunatics went to psychiatrists.

"This is not the time to worry about what *other* people think," she said firmly. "If you want, I can call my analyst and you can just go have a chat with him, to see what it's like."

Goldie's response was wonderful, and I decided to take her advice by making an appointment. But when I arrived at the doctor's office in Century City, across town from Burbank, I was still a bit skeptical—therapy had become such a trendy, Hollywood thing to do. I sat in my car thinking everything over, hearing Goldie's words in my mind: "Just have a *chat* with him, Judy. . . ."

When I finally got the nerve to go in, I found him to be warm and soft-spoken, as Goldie had described. I told him about my alarming experiences in front of the mirror, and it didn't take him long to spot my classic symptoms and diagnose what he called an "identity crisis." Those words helped me put things in perspective. It was such a productive chat that I decided to see the doctor on a regular basis. He recommended four sessions a week, and soon my features came back into focus. But I still felt I had a long way to go.

I was grateful to Goldie for being there at a time when I desperately needed someone to point me in the right direction. It wasn't long before I was able to pay back the favor by being there when it was her turn to need support.

It started when I heard a commotion coming over my dressing room speaker, monitoring the activities on the set. A production assistant came to say that George needed to see me, *fast*. I rushed out to see Goldie trembling up on the trapdoor platform, tears streaming down her face. She looked as though she were facing the gallows.

"Listen, Judy," George said, taking me aside, "we're trying to get her to go through the damned trapdoor. She's having a *breakdown* about the whole thing and I don't know what to say to her. Why don't you give her a pep talk, or something . . . I don't have *time* for this."

It was cruel of George to be so insistent about something that obviously terrified her, and it was humiliating for her to be standing there, scared to death in front of everybody. Without hesitating I climbed up onto the platform.

"Hey, Goldie, the stunt runt's here to tell you that you're going to be okay, I promise. There are mattresses down there, and if you just keep your knees bent and your arms in, you'll be fine!"

"I know it looks silly to you, Judy," she said with a sniffle. "You do it all the time. But I'm *petrified*. . . ."

"Tell you what, Goldie, just do it this once. I'll be down there. I'll *catch* you if necessary." Then I took her by the shoulders and looked straight into her moist blue eyes.

"Goldie," I whispered, "don't you dare give him a chance to make you look like an asshole. He'll never let you live it down."

With this, her expression changed completely. I could see that my point had sunk in. She set her jaw, dried her eyes, and stepped straight out onto the trapdoor.

"I'll do it, George," she said, gritting her teeth, "if you promise me that it's the one and only time."

George agreed, desperate to finish shooting the bit. I went down by the mattresses, so when the trapdoor opened and Goldie fell through, she bounced into my arms. We hugged, and she thanked me. "Listen, Goldie, you've been there for me," I told her. "Helping you through a bleedin' trapdoor is the *least* I can do!"

We had all been pushed in ways such as this, but as a group we finally had our revenge—the notorious "paint party."

George thought the idea was brilliant: He had us dress in smocks, gave us brushes and paint, and stood us by a huge white canvas, on which we were supposed to "create." He barked orders at us, gesturing with his arms like an orchestra conductor.

"It should be fun. I want it to be a wild kind of a happening, all right? We've got one shot at it, so when I start to count, get to your positions, and *paint!*"

Peter Lawford was the guest that week. He just leaned up against a ladder in disbelief, staring at George, who continued to shout as the cameras started to roll.

"Let's go . . . it must be *spontaneous!*" Instead of promoting spontaneity, he made us feel like rats in a maze, goading us with cries of "C'mon, get with it! Make it happen! *Funnier!*"

We went through with the sketch, painting whatever came to mind on the canvas, until finally our frustrations built up and drove us over the edge. We started to splatter each other with paint. Then George shouted one order too many. We looked at him with fire in our eyes.

When he saw our crazed looks and the dripping brushes in our hands, he turned and ran for the door. "Splatter Schlatter!" someone cried, and we went after him like an angry mob. "Splatter Schlatter! Splatter Schlatter!" We chased him down the corridor, launching blobs of paint as we ran. We were by now totally out of control. Our only concern was giving C.F.G. a dose of his own medicine.

We chased him up a flight of stairs and he ducked into the control booth, where he thought he was safe. But he was wrong. We barged straight in with our pails of paint swinging wildly, cornering him for the kill. He cowered beneath a control panel, pleading with us not to ruin his beautiful cashmere sweater, but we showed no mercy. We slapped brushful after brushful of paint on him, screaming, "Here's your spontaneity, George! Is it *funny* enough for you?"

He was a gruesome sight when we finished. The control booth, covered with splotches of paint, looked as though Jackson Pollock had been there.

When the NBC officials saw the scene the next day, George had a lot of explaining to do. We had a lot of laughs imagining what kind of excuses he'd give them. To this day George still says of the paint party, "You guys ruined a perfectly good sweater!"

At home at Laurelcrest I had some memorable parties of my own. By now Dean Goodhill was living with me, and we loved to cook for small gatherings. As my circle of friends increased, these dinner parties became more frequent. I decided to throw a major bash on New Year's Eve, to usher in 1969 with style.

I invited a wide cross section of my friends, resulting in an eclectic group of about seventy-five of the most chic hippies in Hollywood. I'd had an elaborate burglar alarm system installed since the robbery, and the guests had to announce themselves through my front-gate speaker, which Dean and I monitored from inside. Safety and discretion were a big priority with this crowd, which included rock n' rollers such as John and Michelle Phillips of the Mamas and the Papas, along with Cass, who arrived with Jim Morrison of the Doors. Harry Nilsson showed up during the course of the evening, as did Graham Nash, Paul Williams, and Three Dog Night. There was Phil Proctor of the Firesign Theater, and Flip Wilson arrived with Mary Wilson of the Supremes.

Each member of this crowd came with a small entourage, which included their musicians, managers, and assorted poets, painters, and hipsters in general. As they arrived I was given handmade gifts like beaded necklaces, shawls, peace symbols, ankhs, and a wide assortment of hash pipes.

The attire at the party was a mixture of antique-style clothing and sixties psychedelia: leather patchwork, tie-dye, and cosmic capes. With the assembled musical talent, it was difficult figuring out what records to play, so I settled on a healthy mix of the Beatles, Stones, Hendrix, and Motown.

I took great pleasure in preparing a massive buffet of fresh-dressed crab, spicy chicken wings, home-baked ham, exotic salads, and organic vegetarian dishes. Alice B. Toklas cookies were a popular item. In case anyone were to munch on one unexpectedly, I kept the Toklas cookbook by the plate as a subtle reminder.

I stocked the bar with tequila, but very little else on the hard booze spectrum. When Jim Morrison asked for Scotch, everyone was stunned; drinking Scotch was as common with this crowd as lighting up a joint would have been at Dean Martin's house.

The atmosphere was loose, with no rules or restrictions. Everyone brought the drug of their choice and shared. Every place in the house had a different type of gathering. On the sundeck a group discussed hallucinogens and pondered the philosophy of Timothy Leary, while a couple got it on in the nearby hammock.

In the living room dancing broke out whenever the mood struck, accompanied by singing, clapping, and tambourines. A poet stood up and recited, and a woman sat breast-feeding her infant.

At one point during the party Dean worriedly informed me that someone apparently had fallen off the balcony. When we went to investigate, we discovered that the fortunate fellow, too stoned to realize what was happening, had broken his fall by landing in the foliage of an oak tree. He dropped miraculously onto a mattress in my tree house, to the amazement of the tripsters sitting there. "Far out, man," they said, thinking his entrance to be a hallucination.

As midnight approached the question arose of what to play to celebrate the New Year. Guy Lombardo didn't make it with this crowd.

I was sorting through my records to solve the dilemma when Jim Morrison floated by, wearing a beautiful creme silk shirt open to the waist, brown leather pants, and a studded belt that hugged his hips. He had a provocative, come-hither look. "You know what'd be groovy?" he whispered in my ear. " 'Grapevine'."

"Great," I said, "I'll put it on." Marvin Gaye's "I Heard It Through the Grapevine" was one of the hottest records of 1968.

"I want everybody to gather around for this," Morrison said, waving to the other guests in the living room.

"Hey, everybody!" I announced. "It's almost midnight. We're playing Marvin Gaye, so let's gather around in a circle. . . ."

As the clock struck twelve everyone cheered, and with our arms around each other, we danced in a circle, Greek style. We sang along with the music, spurred on by our spiritual leader, Jim Morrison.

The year 1969 had arrived, the beginning of the end of the revolutionary sixties. It would be a pivotal year for me, as I faced—at thirty years of age—career decisions that would have a major effect on the course of my life.

I made a New Year's resolution to become more involved with my finances. One bit of advice I got was to put $20,000 into orange groves south of L.A. It seemed like an astute investment, since oranges were never likely to go out of favor.

I decided to visit my fruitful real estate—to "groove on my groves," as it were—and chose a sunny day to drive to Riverside, where they were supposedly located. After hours of searching, quizzing pedestrians and gas station attendants, I realized that my "orange groves" were in fact nothing but empty crabgrass lots.

My heart sank at the thought of losing $20,000. What would my dad say? I could hear his voice repeat his favorite description of me: "Joyce, you're just *an idiot with a pen!*"

It was time to take better charge. I needed a personal manager to guide me through this crucial phase of my career, someone to do for me what Goldie's manager was doing for her. I had to capitalize on the impact of "Laugh-In" and strike while the iron was hot.

Dean introduced me to Garry Thomas, who was managing one of my favorite singer/songwriters at that time. I was immediately impressed by Garry; he was in his late thirties, articulate, and wore three-piece suits. He'd been a lawyer for many years, found it boring, then branched out into management.

He wanted to create a "family atmosphere" for his stable of performers, and promised to devote himself to my career, to see that no stone was left unturned. "We'll take care of everything for you, Judy—all you've got to do is *perform.*"

It was a smooth pitch. I signed on the dotted line, giving him fifteen percent of my earnings. Suddenly I found myself doing a commercial for Chunky chocolate.

Cuckoo, Laugh-In World

The company offered to pay me $35,000 for an afternoon's work. It was easy money to be sure, but my mind flashed back to Art Simon advising Goldie to turn down Coca-Cola to "save herself" for movies. But Garry was so enthusiastic, I didn't want to be negative this early in our relationship. I stood on top of a gargantuan Chunky bar in a miniskirt and sang, "Chun-key, Choc-late!" After three takes it was over—$11,666.66 per take. It was hard for me to grasp.

Garry wasted no time in reshuffling my affairs and insisted I sign with the William Morris Agency, where I was assured of being considered for all the major motion pictures.

It was decided that I would return to England to do "The Kraft Music Hall," an NBC summer series hosted by the multilingual singing duo Sandler and Young. I was to be a regular along with Norman Wisdom, one of England's most beloved entertainers.

An English director named Gerry O'Hara inquired about my availability for a movie he had written, *All the Right Noises*. It was a love story based on the early life of his friend, the extraordinary filmmaker Nick Roeg.

I'd known Nick since working with his sister Nicolette in my very first show. He suggested to producer Si Litvinoff that I play the part of his wife because I bore a striking resemblance to her. Nick would be played by Tom Bell, one of England's "angry young men," and Olivia Hussey, who'd been enchanting in Zeffirelli's *Romeo and Juliet*, would play a young girl with whom he had an affair.

I was excited by this offer. It seemed like the opportunity I'd been waiting for: to play a dramatic role with substance and prove myself as an actress. It was arranged that my scenes be shot on Saturdays and Sundays, so as not to conflict with the "Kraft Music Hall" schedule, and Dean was hired as a photographer for the film, which meant we would be together for the busy months ahead.

On the way to London I stopped off in New York City for business meetings and press interviews, one of which was with the *New York Times* at the prestigious "21" Club.

I arrived for the interview wearing a stylish pants suit. When the maitre d' saw me, he informed me that the club had a rule: no pants for women, so I couldn't be seated. I explained to him that I had an important interview with the *New York Times* but the maitre d' held his ground, offering no leniency and suggesting no compromise.

I noticed the coat-check counter and got an idea: if they didn't want me to wear my pants, I would simply have to *check* them. To everyone's amazement, I slipped them off and handed them to the coat-check girl, leaving my tunic top barely covering my derriere. The maitre d' just gaped as I marched past him to join the reporters for my interview.

After lunch a group of photographers was assembled, eagerly waiting for me to reclaim my pants. The incident became a cause célèbre in the press, and *Time* magazine even ran the story in its fashion section. Shortly thereafter the "21" Club announced a change in policy—ladies would be permitted to wear pants.

Everywhere I went, women congratulated me on my act of defiance. I was proud that for once my rebellious nature had achieved something constructive.

In London Dean and I leased a flat in Knightsbridge, and we visited my mum and dad at Carne Lodge as much as we could.

Monday through Friday I worked on "The Kraft Music Hall" at ATV studios in Elstree, performing musical numbers and comedy sketches with weekly guests such as Sid Caesar, Kaye Ballard, Petula Clark, Ella Fitzgerald, and Billy Eckstine.

I was singing a ballad one day, walking around the stage wearing a beautiful jersey silk top. In the middle of the song the director yelled to cut tape. There was a brief huddle in the control room, and then he came down to talk to me.

"Judy, you're not wearing a bra."

"I know."

"Well, they're *moving* . . ."

I looked at my chest and said, "They *will* do that, you know!"

"I'm sorry, but we can't have that. You'll have to wear a bra."

This posed a problem, since I didn't own one. A wardrobe lady was instructed to tape me up with an adhesive first-aid bandage. It prevented me from jiggling, all right, but stung like hell when she later removed it.

This kind of thing wasn't a problem on the weekends, filming *All the Right Noises*—especially when Tom Bell and I had to do a love scene in the nude. The sequence posed a different set of problems, however: We shot the interiors in a deserted London factory that made a spacious but unheated film studio, and the crew all wore down parkas, while we had to make do with merely an electric blanket.

I was apprehensive about doing the scene to begin with, but there was an added pressure: *Dean* would be shooting pictures of it all. The lighting was subtle, however, and when I saw that Tom was just as nervous as I was, we had a good laugh and did it in one take.

Dean wasn't bothered by the scene. In fact, Nick Roeg was so impressed by Dean's work that he hired him for his next film, *Walkabout,* which would be made that fall in Australia.

An unusual job awaited me upon my return to America. On Sunday, July 20, 1969, the Apollo 11 astronauts would step onto the surface of the moon. I was asked to perform a special song for the occasion, live on "The Ed Sullivan Show."

The song—"American Moon"—was an elaborate production number by Bob Crewe, who'd written hits for Frankie Valli, like "Can't Take My Eyes Off You." I would be backed by two dozen tap dancers in shimmering red, white, and blue outfits; *my* costume had extra sequins, with an Uncle Sam top hat. The number screamed of Americana, with military dance steps, salutes, and flag waving throughout.

Sunday was spent going over the camera blocking and doing a runthrough. As the Eagle touched down in the Sea of Tranquility at around 5 P.M., I hovered around a television set in the green room, along with some of the other guests on the show: Carlos Santana and his band (making their first appearance on network television), and Tony Bennett, with Count Basie's band. The first step on the moon was scheduled for around 10 P.M. We were told that between 70 and 100 million people would be watching us, as the nation waited for the historic moment.

The mood backstage was exciting. As we took our places behind the curtain, I could hear Ed Sullivan's introduction.

"And now, ladies and gentlemen, on our shew tonight, we've got a reely, reely big musical salute to our boys on the moon. Here to sing it for us now is Judy *Crane!*"

The curtain opened, and I stood there—frozen in front of the entire nation—having just been introduced as someone *else.* I opened my mouth and sang:

There's an American flag on the moon tonight
Waving red and blue and white,
There's an American flag waving on the moon,
Waving on the moon tonight!

There's an American flag, if you please,
Refer to it now as American cheese,
There's an American flag waving on the moon,
Waving on the moon tonight!

After a half dozen more of these choruses an exuberant cheer went up as we formed a giant flag for the gloriously patriotic finale. It was an emotional moment. I felt bound together with the audience and the viewers in celebration of such an extraordinary human achievement.

Back in L.A. my relationship with Dean entered a crucial phase. We had contemplated marriage for months, and it was time to decide. Dean was the first man I'd loved since Burt, and I felt cared for by him and his family. They were a warm, close-knit group, who stringently followed the Judaic prayers and rituals. If we were to be married, I was expected to convert to Judaism. This I was willing to do, because I found the rituals at the Goodhill home to be spiritually rewarding.

Dean and I had a number of informal chats with his rabbi. On one of these visits the rabbi asked Dean, "Tell me, if Judy does not convert to Judaism, would you still marry her?"

"No, Rabbi, I wouldn't," he said instinctively.

I was stunned. Dean looked at me and turned pale. Tears welled up in my eyes and I got up to leave. He tried to stop me, but the rabbi called him back. "No, Dean, let her go," I could hear him say as I left the temple. "She must do what she feels is right."

Dean was just saying what was expected of him; I knew that he sincerely loved me, but his response at that moment revealed a flaw in our relationship.

It was a sensitive matter, so we decided to hold off on our wedding plans. When it came time for Dean to go to Australia, he was torn; *Walkabout* was a fantastic opportunity, but he didn't want to leave me. I urged him to go, and although it signaled the end of our relationship, it was a turning point for him. Under Nick Roeg's guidance he went from being a photographer to cinematographer, and is now a director.

With Dean gone, my life was full of soul searching and solitude. Just when an acute case of loneliness set in, I had a lovely surprise: Stirling Moss was in town. He had come to L.A. on business and was visiting his pals in the process. His timing was perfect.

When he arrived at my house, I proudly showed off my sleek new Corvette that Chevrolet had loaned me for a year as a gift for attending their Soap Box Derby. I told him they'd provided an unlimited insurance policy for me and anyone I allowed to drive it. They didn't want to take any chances with the "Sock it to me" girl behind the wheel.

Upon hearing this, Stirling suggested we take a spin around a race track he knew of, just south of L.A. The place was deserted, except for a few bored track attendants who perked up when they saw us arrive. Stirling borrowed a couple of helmets and strapped me into the passenger seat. I was about to experience the thrill of a Stirling Moss "test drive."

We took off around the track and he gradually pushed the car faster, until the needle of the speedometer could go no farther: 140 mph. Stirling wanted to see how the car would respond when pushed to its limit. He went through a series of swerves, spins, quick stops and starts. He approved of the Corvette and thought it was a good sports car for me—"manageable and reliable."

I was on a cloud from the adventure of it all as we returned and left the Corvette steaming in my garage. Then we went over to his hotel, where he had another surprise for me—we would be dining with his old friend Steve McQueen.

Steve greeted me warmly and we reminisced about the fun we used to have in London, when my roommate, Janet Rowsell, and I would cheer Moss and McQueen from the pit. He'd remained close friends with Stirling over the years, and Steve still visited England for racing events as often as he could.

After dinner Stirling retired early to rest up for a slew of meetings the next morning. I hugged him and thanked him for an unforgettable day. I could always count on Stirling for that.

When Steve gave me a lift home, I experienced my *second* joyride of the day. He drove a Lotus, a street version of the car that Stirling raced. As we sped off into the hills, Steve masterfully negotiated the sharp curves on Laurel Canyon. He wasn't showing off; this was the way he drove because this was the way he *was*—swift and direct.

I invited him in for a nightcap, but he was worried about leaving his Lotus on the street, vulnerable to cars coming around the hairpin turn by my front gate.

"Any room in your garage?" he asked.

"Sure, love . . . hang on, I'll open it up for you."

"You sure I'll fit?"

"I should bloody well *hope* so—it's a two-car garage, I'll have you know!" He nestled his Lotus snugly by my Corvette.

We sat and talked, sipping Irish coffee and listening to music. When I went to flip over the record, I sensed Steve behind me, then felt his hand softly touch my shoulder. I turned around and looked into his steel blue eyes.

"I've always dug you," he said. "You're kinda like me . . . you don't want to conform. People like us get into a lot of trouble."

"No shit!"

"I can *talk* to you. It's not always easy for me to do that. . . ."

"I'm glad. Talking is so important . . . it's great when the person you love is your best friend, someone to whom you can tell it *all*. My marriage had that potential, but it never had a chance to develop."

"Mine did . . . but there are problems now."

I'd heard rumors about his separation from his wife, Neil. He said I reminded him of her, a free-spirited Peter Pan. Steve had a rugged charm similar to Burt's.

We stood there staring into each other's eyes for a few moments, and then it felt as if a valve had been released. We embraced and dropped to the floor, landing softly on the cushions and fusing ourselves together. It happened magically and spontaneously, and since we knew it might never happen again, our lovemaking at that moment was vital to us. We fulfilled a mutual longing that had built up over the years, an attraction that evolved from a tender friendship and didn't demand more than we were prepared to give.

I returned to "Laugh-In" with renewed confidence and optimism, but it wasn't long before they eluded me once again.

Cuckoo, Laugh-In World

Having been the number-one show on television the previous season, we now had the pressure of having to live up to that success. We were made to repeat the gimmicks we were known for ad nauseam, leaving no room for growth. For me this meant another season of "Sock it to me."

When they finally decided to phase it out, there was little for me to do in its place. I hungered to do something I could sink my teeth into, but I only got an occasional bucket of water.

Everyone had their own way of coping with the pressure. Goldie took up needlepoint and sat engrossed in patterns she was working on. Arte got into it, too, and they became fanatics, advancing into petit point. I couldn't divert my anxieties that way, and as the later scripts included me less and less, I retreated to my dressing room to sit, engulfed by feelings of uselessness and futility.

Someone who really cared about our morale was David Panich, one of the most brilliant—and eccentric—of our writers. "Hey, Judy, I know you're not doing much on this week's show," he'd say, genuinely concerned. "Don't worry—we're working on some great things for you to do next week."

Panich often looked haggard, with dark circles under his eyes; he seemed to have been sleeping in his clothes. Henry and I heard him describe the conditions in the Toluca Capri Motel, where the writers were isolated away from the rest of us.

"If C.F.G. doesn't let us out soon," he said, "there's going to be a *death* in there!"

A few days later we heard that the manager of the motel had complained that the writers had been scrawling graffiti on the walls of their rooms. Fearing eviction, Ed Friendly dispatched a crew to repaint the defaced motel rooms.

That night, after the other writers had left, Panich remained. The next morning they discovered him asleep on the floor. Every inch of the wall was covered with fine print that read: *I must not write on the walls*. He'd stayed up all night printing the phrase literally *thousands* of times.

I also took pen in hand to deal with my anxieties—I started keeping a daily journal. The idea had been suggested by a friend, Henry Jaglom, a writer who'd worked on the movie *Easy Rider*. We met at a party given by the film's producers, Bert Schneider and Bob Rafelson, whom I'd known at Screen Gems when they were making "The Monkees" next door to "Love on a Rooftop."

Jaglom was bright, amusing, and aggressively introspective. He had a way of leading me into realizations about myself that I'd never been able to express, and he encouraged me to write those things down.

"Think of the journal as a place to centralize your life, Judy, to give your mind a home," Henry told me. "It will become something from which you can derive strength and comfort." He gave me a spiral notebook, and I decided to give it a go, by scribbling thoughts and meanderings as often as I could.

> *October 27:* Hello, dear book, nice to know you in your smart brown cover. . . .
> Unbelievable time with Jaglom last night. He filmed my exit from his house, down the stairs and into the street, the sunlight pouring on my red velvet coat. He was in a brown jersey/silk robe, a flowing Mother-Earth vision with a movie camera whirring away, photographing the entrances and exits from his life.

The journal became my friend, my analyst, my conscience. After filling the notebook, I graduated to leather-bound books in which I diligently continued to write.

> *November 3:* Saw "Laugh-In" tonight. I'm depressed about my work on the show . . . I do so little. Tension reigns on the set.

On days when our morale was low, I would be close to tears, Henry would hang his head, Goldie and Arte would retreat to their needlepoint, Alan would pace nervously, while Ruth remained silent. Jo Anne Worley was the one who kept us together by suddenly bursting out with an outrageous comment that would unify us. Jo Anne was our emotional Rock of Gibraltar.

I was the first one to freak out. The breaking point came one day when I tried to suggest an idea to George. The Judy Doll gags were wearing thin, so I thought it might be amusing if we put her into the cocktail party, where she could spout the typically programmed remarks that people say. I was sure the writers could come up with some good variations on this premise. When I mentioned the idea to George, he was indignant.

Cuckoo, Laugh-In World

"Look, Judy, don't try to tell *me* what's funny," he said harshly. "I make forty million people laugh each week, and you think you can tell *me* what's funny?"

I was crushed. In the early days, George had said, "Hey, gang, tell me what's funny. I want *all* your ideas." We gave them to him and now "Laugh-In" was a hit.

I felt like a tube of toothpaste, squeezed until nothing was left for me to give, discarded when empty. I was the "Sock it to me" girl and nothing more.

"You've got all you can get out of 'Laugh-In,'" said Garry, my manager. "It's time for you to make it on your own."

Inquiries had come in from prospective Broadway shows, and there were Las Vegas offers for a nightclub act. Leaving the number-one show on television at the height of its popularity was risky, however, so I was reluctant to take such a bold step.

When George lashed out at me that day, I realized Garry was right. I asked him to tell George of my unhappiness, to see if anything could be done to improve my contribution to the show. When George failed to offer any solution, Garry told him I wouldn't renew my contract.

George blamed me for being the one to "break up the family"— even though he'd always reminded us that we were dispensable. From then on I was virtually written out of my remaining shows.

On my final day at work I answered a knock on my dressing room door to find Ruth and Goldie with a candlelit cake, Jo Anne and Henry with bottles of wine, Alan with cold cuts and rolls, and Arte bringing up the rear with cups, paper plates, and a corkscrew. Billy Barnes, Hugh Lambert, and Gary Necessary all stopped by, and Gary Owens arrived after his radio show to join the festivities.

I was given good-luck cards, flowers, and presents. Goldie made me a petit point herbal cushion, and the other gifts ranged from a book on how to "grow your own" to an X-rated talking doll. There was much laughter and merriment, until the tender moment when Arte raised his glass to propose a toast.

"Hey, Judes . . . we're really going to miss you," he said, and the others echoed him. My eyes watered at the thought of breaking away from my extended family, these unique people with whom I'd spent the last three years, pouring our souls into the show and uniting in the joy of bringing laughter into people's lives. The room was quiet for a moment, as the melancholy undertone of the occasion hit us.

"Okay, gang, enough with the schmaltz," Jo Anne broke in. "Let's make with the champagne!"

Laughter resounded once again, and soon we were back on the set, getting ready to shoot what would be my final joke wall sequence. As the others hammed it up behind the wall, I waited dolefully for my cue, and popped out to deliver my last laugh on "Laugh-In."

9. Broadway, Vegas, and the Land Down Under

"**H**ey, Judy, sock it *to* me!" shouted cab drivers as I walked down the New York City streets. Passersby stopped and stared, and strangers followed me for blocks, hiding behind lamp posts when I turned to look. The recognition was flattering, but worrisome. I never knew when fans would get the urge to throw something at me—popcorn, peanuts, beer, anything they could get their hands on. I began to feel like a walking target. I'd hear "Sock it to me!" and duck.

Cabaret had just ended its smash Broadway run when I accepted Lee Guber's offer to star in the production at his theater in the round in Westbury, Long Island. It was a good place for Broadway producers to see me work before a live audience. I thoroughly identified with Sally Bowles, the frenetic and free-spirited English cabaret singer that Christopher Isherwood wrote about in his original short story *I Am a Camera*. I'd yearned to play her ever since hearing about the Broadway stage adaptation starring Julie Harris.

> *November 9:* Dream Flash: I was doing *Cabaret* and I couldn't make it. . . . I arrived at the theater and had to squeeze through crowds of people to get in. I got ready with great difficulty, then couldn't make entrances, for one reason or another. I then went

onstage to find it tipped at an angle toward the pit. I couldn't walk. I just slid into the footlights . . . then I woke up.

Fortunately, the real performers were nothing like this nightmare. The audiences were responsive, especially when I drank Sally's cure for a hangover: a raw egg with a dash of Worcestershire sauce. The hidden glass method, normally used to avoid drinking the vile concoction, would be too obvious in theater in the round, so I decided to swallow the damn thing and play it up for full effect. I'd give the egg a whisk with my cigarette holder, and slowly raise the glass to my lips as the crowd moaned in disgust. When I sent it down the hatch in one gulp, they went wild.

The audiences were almost *too* enthusiastic. I got my first taste of the "Sock it to me" syndrome that would plague me for years to come:

> *November 21:* It's amazing . . . people are touching me, saying "Sock it to me!" and cracking up with laughter as I walk down the aisles to enter stage for a serious scene. This will happen all the time . . . it's unbelievable, and it's a drag.

During the run, various Broadway producers were in to see the show and a number of upcoming projects were discussed. I accepted the most impressive offer—the lead in a revival of *The Boy Friend.*

> *December 5:* Mum and Dad's four dreams for me:
> 1.) That I star in a West End show
> 2.) That I star on Broadway
> 3.) That I appear in a command performance for the Queen
> 4.) That I'm the subject of a "This Is Your Life"
> I just called to tell them to make their plane reservations. I'm going to fulfill one-fourth of their dreams in April.

My tour guide around New York City was Bob Crewe, who'd written "American Moon," the song I'd sung on "The Ed Sullivan Show" the night of the moon landing. Crewe knew that Christmas had always been a miserable time for me, so he lined up a nonstop itinerary of sightseeing, theatergoing, nightclub hopping, and *endless* partying.

> *December 20:* Did "The David Frost Show." Good vibes from him and Dyan Cannon. Then Crewe took me to a cocktail party for Mayor John Lindsay, attended by a lot of rich, bored folk . . .

Broadway, Vegas, and the Land Down Under

Crewe insisted we catch a fantastic new singer named Bette Midler, who was gaining a reputation from appearances at the Continental Baths, a gay bathhouse on the upper West Side. I wanted to avoid being recognized, so Crewe dared me to dress as a man. This was easily accomplished, as I already owned a lot of boyish clothes. With no makeup, dark glasses, and a cap, I looked like the Artful Dodger.

"Just don't *speak!*" Crewe implored me as we walked down the staircase to the dimly lit club. Inside, the attire of the men ranged from towels to tuxedos. There was a swimming pool at one end of the room, next to a door which led to the "steam room," and the activity continued in full view as the show started on a makeshift stage.

Bette Midler *was* fantastic. She belted out song after song, quipped with the audience, and strutted around in her heels with the same outrageous style and charisma she's known for today. The audience cheered her every move.

After a while I had to go to the toilet, so I took my chances and slipped into the men's room. The bright lights betrayed me. A guy caught a glimpse of me as I rearranged my hair underneath my cap.

"It's okay," he whispered. "I *know* who you are . . . in fact, I think it's *far out!*" The news of my presence spread through the club like wildfire, and when I returned to my seat, the house lights came up.

"We have an unusual guest in our midst tonight," a voice said over a loudspeaker. Crewe and I looked at each other in panic, ready to make a fast exit if necessary. "You all know her from television, a very funny lady—Judy Carne!"

I got a wild ovation for the ridiculous trouble I'd gone through to avoid being noticed.

> *December 22:* I found out yesterday I have $75,000 in cash in the bank. That's nice . . . I've earned it and feel good about that. But what does it all mean, really? It means I can go buy a few things. So what? I'm alone. Thirty years old. No children. Is that enviable?

On Christmas Eve Crewe took me to the townhouse of Francesco Scavullo, one of the world's top fashion photographers, for a party in honor of film director Luchino Visconti. He was there with his new protégé, actor Helmut Berger.

I was introduced to Scavullo, who was dressed in black from head to toe, and had an elfin face and delicate hands. As I scanned his breathtaking photographs adorning the walls, I noticed a young man across the room, staring at me. He looked like an Italian movie star, dark and handsome, with a gorgeous smile and full, sensuous lips. He was dressed—*groomed* is more accurate—exquisitely, and he leaned against the wall, smiling at me. I soon found myself engrossed in conversation with him. He was outspoken about his thoughts on psychoanalysis, something we had in common. We didn't leave each other's company for the rest of the evening.

> *December 25, 10 A.M.:* Spent the evening at Scavullo's, at a party where I met Robert Bergmann. We chatted. Attractive, wealthy background, super aware, and sensitive. I related to him in the strongest way.

Later that morning the phone rang in my suite. It was Bergmann. He was downstairs in the lobby with a book on psychoanalysis he thought I might find interesting. I was startled, but invited him up. Over coffee I felt the same kind of magnetic attraction toward him that I'd felt the night before. We went out for lunch and I learned—or *thought* I learned—a great deal more about him.

Bergmann was twenty-three, articulate, and well informed on a variety of subjects. He said he'd attended Harvard, that he was currently between jobs, and that he sometimes worked for his father, who produced television commercials. He professed to being a good photographer, among other things, and since I was enchanted by his charm, I had no reason to doubt him.

Meanwhile, to polish my stage skills for Broadway, I had signed to do *Dames at Sea* in Palm Beach, Florida, after Christmas.

> *December 27:* En route to Palm Beach. I'm thinking of Burt. I guess it's being near his hometown. The last time I came here, we were married. . . .
>
> I feel protected by Robert, cared for, treasured, and willing to give unlimited amounts of love to him, but I have to do my work now. Turn the key in my back and I do my thing.

The producers of *The Boy Friend* flew down to Palm Beach along with the director, a pudgy man named Gus Schirmer. They came to watch me work in *Dames at Sea* and to address the issue of what part I was to play in *The Boy Friend*. I told them I wanted to play Maisie, the "personality" girl. Schirmer was opposed.

"No, no, Judy," he insisted, "you *must* play Polly. That's the *leading* role."

"But I don't care. Maisie does the tap dancing and has the funny lines. It's *made* for me!" Having done the show before, I knew what I was talking about, but I listened as both Schirmer and even Garry—my own bloody *manager*—tried to talk me out of it.

"It's predictable for you to play Maisie," Schirmer argued, "but it's totally *un*predictable for you to play Polly!"

I was a sucker for that line. If I thought anything was unusual or challenging for me, I wanted to try it.

"Polly is a classical role," he went on. "Only a highly trained, experienced actress like you can do it justice. The critics will *love* you for it!"

We agreed to think it over and decide when I returned to New York the following week.

> *Friday the 13th of February:* Robert was lovely last night on the phone. He suggested we live together in New York, but that scares me a bit. One must have freedom, after all. . . .

When I arrived in New York, Bergmann had already gone ahead and found us a beautiful brownstone on East Thirty-first Street. We were settled in within the week, and then my script for *The Boy Friend* arrived. It was for the part of Polly. Despite the stand I had taken about playing Maisie, the issue was apparently a fait accompli.

I went to see Gus Schirmer at his home, a luxurious townhouse full of theatrical decor—framed *Playbills*, sheet music, and photographs everywhere. When I brought up the casting issue, he was evasive.

"Now, Judy, we've got these wonderful costumes for you, darling. They're fabulous, simply marvelous. Come and look at these sketches . . . aren't they *stunning?*"

"Yes they are, Gus, but that's not why I've come to see you—"

"And you'll be glad to know we've already signed a lovely young actress named Sandy Duncan to play Maisie. She'll be great with you."

Sandy Duncan? This was the first time I'd heard her name mentioned. Schirmer ended with a big finish: "Believe me, I've been in this business for many, many years—you'll be the *darling* of the critics! The *toast* of Broadway!"

I knew when I was licked. I later found out why Gus Schirmer had insisted I play Polly rather than Maisie: He was Sandy Duncan's manager and she'd been signed to play Maisie from the outset.

Sandy was a gifted performer, but I had been used in a backstage power play to which my own manager had been oblivious.

> *February 16:* Dream Flash: It was about Goldie. She came out winning all the time on every level of work. I guess I do feel subconscious competition with her . . . I don't know why, other than the movie she's gotten and the fact that we are linked together all the time. Very interesting.

This dream was prompted by hearing that Goldie had landed the role in *Cactus Flower* for which she later won an Oscar as Best Supporting Actress. By "saving" herself for the movies, she made an auspicious transition from "Laugh-In."

> *February 18:* Heard today that the business office bought me an apartment building in L.A. I'm thrilled. My first big investment. It's $250,000. I'm having to put $35,000 down. It's very complicated, but exciting. I feel all my hard work is paying off. I'm listening to "Love, Peace, and Happiness" by the Chambers Brothers . . . I just love it.

I got in touch with Suzan Kroul, one of my first friends in America. She was working in New York as a legal secretary and unhappy with her job, so she became my girl Friday.

Suzan and I had been roommates since before I met Burt. She'd seen me through the tribulations of my marriage and cared about my well-being. She said she'd heard some disturbing gossip about Bergmann, that he was a gigolo. I was upset that she would believe such a vicious rumor, but she mistrusted him from that day on and was vehemently opposed to my living with him.

I was in no position to be objective. I was engrossed in my Broadway opening and felt an enormous pressure to prove myself. I felt insecure and uprooted in New York, and vulnerable enough to give Bergmann my full trust.

"I'll take care of you, Judy," he said to me.

"I know you will," I replied, thinking he was just being romantic.

"No, I mean . . . I won't let them *know*."

"Let *who* know *what*?"

172

"Come on, Judy, you and I know that you've been under a lot of pressure . . . I'm the only one who understands. I'll protect you."

I had no idea what he meant until certain events made me think that perhaps there *was* something wrong with me. I began to lose my cash, or so it seemed. Bergmann would ask me for a few dollars and I'd look in my purse, only to find that it was empty.

"*That's* odd . . . I'm sure I had a hundred dollars this morning."

"Judy, how could you have lost it so easily? I'm worried about you . . . you're losing your memory."

I defended myself by pointing out that I'd been learning lines and songs, rehearsing day and night.

"You don't even know where your cash is going. I shudder to think how much you've lost this week alone!"

I became confused. I *was* under a lot of strain, after all. I began to fear being apart from him, afraid that others would find out I was losing my mind. When he suggested we undergo therapy, I readily agreed.

February 22: Robert took me to see Roger Parnell, founder of a new therapy called Dynametaphysics. Fantastic self-improvement thing. I enrolled for fifty hours, starting tomorrow. . . .

Roger Parnell's "office" was on the top floor of a four-story walk-up, in a seedy part of Greenwich Village. I never saw another "patient" on the premises. There were no diplomas hanging on the wall, just a collection of charts, along with a handful of pamphlets on his coffee table.

A heavyset man in his late fifties, Parnell had graying temples that gave him a slightly professorial look. He was a good talker, with the air of someone who knew a lot about therapy. He claimed to have written books on the subject, outlining a plan of living, like Scientology and est. But Roger Parnell had no books and no devoted masses; he just had those pamphlets, and me, and Bergmann, convincing me that Dynametaphysics was the answer to all my problems.

February 23: Had a session today. I was asked questions like "What can you depend on?" I said things like "my sense of humor," "my talent," "my love for Robert."

February 26: Getting into Dynametaphysics. One session last night—two hours, one today—three hours, one tomorrow—three hours. I must say, they're marvelous. . . .

Parnell always brought the conversation around to my relationship with Bergmann. He said I was being unusually reluctant to devote myself to him, yet at the same time too possessive, because I got upset when he returned home at dawn with vague excuses about where he'd been.

March 4: Had a three-hour session of Dynametaphysics today . . . I realized my possessiveness is out of line.

Roger says Robert's in bad shape. He says he needs supporting, more sessions, and my help financially and otherwise. . . .

These marathon sessions were very expensive, especially since I was also footing the bill for the many sessions Bergmann claimed he was having with Parnell.

April 3: Garry suggested I do "I Wonder Who's Kissing Him Now" on "The Tonight Show." I'm excited about that . . . I see myself rapping about freedom, no wars, no bras, free love, then going over with just a spotlight and singing that song ever so sweetly in a see-through dress. . . .

In those days "The Tonight Show" was based in New York City. In the green room before the show I met one of the other guests, a gracefully aging blue-eyed matinee idol. He was friendly and boisterous and I could see from his "mod" way of dress that he was trying hard to stay "hip." He let me in on a secret—the ring on his finger contained not a stone, but a tiny supply of cocaine. He put it up to my nose and told me to sniff.

"It's Peruvian flake," he said proudly as I inhaled it.

"That I *believe*," I said, my eyes watering from the sting.

As we watched Johnny's monologue, the drug started taking effect. Ah, yes, I thought, this feels good. I'm going to go out there and be sensational. Far out.

My song went well, but when I started talking with Johnny, I suddenly lost my train of thought in the middle of a story.

"I'm sorry, but what was I just talking about?" I asked.

Carson just stared at me and said, "I don't know, Judy. *You* were telling the story. . . ." He got the laugh and I felt like a fool.

I didn't get to finish the story, and they went to a commercial break, during which I was moved down the panel next to the man with the unusual ring. I remembered the end of my story but it was much too late. Judes, I thought, *that'll* teach you to accept candy from strangers.

That Sunday night, after I appeared on "The Ed Sullivan Show" to promote the opening of *The Boy Friend,* Bergmann took me for a stroll through Central Park, to the majestic Bethesda fountain. He sat me down by the water's edge.

"I once saw a couple married right here," he told me.

"Oh really? How nice . . ."

"Don't you think it's a *great* place for a wedding?"

"Yes, I imagine so . . ."

He kept pointing out how nice the fountain was and I kept agreeing, until I finally realized he was asking me to *marry* him.

"*We* should get married right here," he said.

We'd only known each other a couple of months, and although he'd rhapsodized about having children and carrying on the "Bergmann dynasty," I'd never taken him seriously. Nevertheless, it *was* a romantic notion. I found myself standing up on the fountain, *very* stoned, saying, "What a wonderful idea! Why *not*?"

I didn't realize that he meant we should be married *immediately.*

"No one will know about it," he promised. "It will be a secret wedding . . . right here at dawn. The beginning of a new day, the start of our new life together. No one will find out."

I was bewitched by this vision of our wedding. Preoccupied with my opening on Broadway, I found myself believing that marriage might provide the balance I needed in my life. We set a date: May third.

The next day Bergmann called the press and informed them of our "private" wedding. Then he called the producers of *The Boy Friend,* to let them know their leading lady intended to be married in Central Park at dawn soon after opening night. They'd always been wary of Bergmann but now they loved him. The event would be great publicity for the show.

When my parents arrived that week for the opening, they were somewhat surprised to learn of my sudden wedding plans. They weren't very impressed with Bergmann but they didn't pass judgment. They were there to watch their daughter fulfill one of their dreams.

April 16: I've neglected you badly, dear book, but I've had an opening on Broadway. A successful one, by all accounts. I was fussed over, pampered, and presented with everything. When I got home, I didn't know what it all meant . . . I lost my identity completely . . . withdrew, recovered a little, then carried on. I must—my folks are here. I adore them and worry if they're okay.

It's career peak time, whatever *that* means. I'm surrounded by love, yet I still feel lonely . . . what is happening?

April 19: Earl Wilson popped into my dressing room to interview me, quite unexpectedly. He was asking about the wedding plans . . . I'm now afraid it's becoming a publicity shambles.

New York *Post,* April 20, 1970:

IT HAPPENED LAST NIGHT
by Earl Wilson

Judy Carne is getting married at dawn at Central Park's Bethesda fountain, on May 3rd, to TV commercial producer Robert Bergmann, 23, who is eight years her junior. . . .

Her husband to be, six feet tall with an Omar Sharif mustache, said they believe in marriage "but not for the wrong reasons, like fear of a commitment, or of being alone—all those things." He likes dawn. . . . "The start of a new day, of a new life."

Judy, hearing sunrise was so early, exclaimed: "Oh wow! Maybe just a few minutes *after* dawn." Regardless, they should be starting their wedding night by 7 in the morning.

April 27: It's my birthday. Mum and Dad leave tomorrow. They must get back to their shop . . . they'll miss the wedding, but that's okay. Dad said, "You're not really going through with it, are you, Joyce?" I let it go at that. . . .

Last night I forgot Whitney and left him in my dressing room all night. Poor little dog, I don't know how I did that. My mind is out to lunch, full of details, plans . . . generally off the wall.

May 3: I was married today. A real happening. It began last night—after my second show we took some mescaline and saw the Grateful Dead at Fillmore East . . . later the cars arrived. In one limo my darling and I sat with six pretty children, a black bodyguard, and the Reverend. Far out. . . .

Arrived at Central Park at dawn . . . it was misty, dewy, chilly, and inspiring. We walked over the hill with friends, relatives, hangers on, and children. . . . Pushing, shoving, flashing cameras and shouting. Happy onlookers. Tired eyes and joyful strides. . . .

. . . I am floating down the hill toward the fountain, still high from the mescaline . . . I am at the fountain and Bergmann is at my side . . . the minister is saying we'd better get a move on . . . it's very crowded, tighter and tighter, we're being pressed together and toward the water in the fountain.

The minister is starting to talk . . . my body is only vaguely responding to orders. I am not conscious enough of my predicament to do anything about it. I am experiencing astral projection: I look down at myself and I see myself surrounded by hundreds and hundreds of people, press, photographers—I am out of myself. I am asking myself what the hell I am doing here.

The minister is almost seven feet tall . . . towering over us, lending a freakish quality to an already unbelievable situation. He starts the service but it doesn't sound quite right. He is changing the words: "And Judy, will you take Robert Bergmann—who *Could Be Happy with You* in your *Room in Bloomsbury,* because *It's Never Too Late to Fall in Love*—until death do you part?"

I am bewildered. My marriage vow is full of song titles from *The Boy Friend.* I am about to say "I do," when I hear a photographer behind me shout "Got any Tri-X, Fred?"

"I do." I look around me at the sea of faces and there is not one person I recognize.

I am now married. . . .

May 9: Tonight I made a speech before the show for the students who were killed at Kent State. I tried to do it simply, in good taste. Ran into Shelley Winters at Sardi's, who said that some actresses were booed for doing it in other shows . . . ah, well, people *are* strange.

May 23: Gwen Verdon was in to see the show and came backstage afterward, full of praise that I'd played Polly so legitimately. She'd been curious to see how I would do such a classic piece and was impressed . . . a great ego boost.

May 27: I've had a Vegas offer. Two weeks at Caesar's Palace, September third, with Tony Newley. I'm knocked out. $15,000 a week, which is unheard of for a new act. The idea of going on stage—*just being me*—turns me on.

The booking seemed perfect for me. I looked forward to seeing Tone again and felt that I was likely to appeal to his audience.

Three months was not a lot of time to organize an act. I needed costumes, a musical director, a choreographer, and a *lot* of rehearsal.

I knew Don Feld, the Oscar-winning designer for *They Shoot Horses, Don't They?,* who offered to do my costumes for a fraction of what he normally charged. He even threw in a special padded bra that Jane Fonda had worn in that picture, a nippled device that gave my low-cut gowns some *oomph.*

During rehearsals for *The Boy Friend* I'd made friends with the pianist, Randy Edelman, a bespectacled young man with long, curly hair who was moonlighting from his job as a song plugger for MGM Records. He was a talented composer and arranger at the age of only twenty-three, and I loved hearing him play his songs during the breaks. He was a perfect choice to be my musical director.

One afternoon Randy took me to an acoustically tiled listening room at MGM studios to discuss what material would be right for me. He knew my tastes were eclectic, so we lay on the shag carpet with the lights off, listening for hours to everything under the sun at full volume on the state-of-the-art sound system. When we were finished, we had dozens of possibilities.

In only a few weeks Randy came up with full arrangements for an English music-hall medley, some Beatles songs and a medley merging Laura Nyro's "Save the Country" with "Abraham, Martin and John," a somber tribute to America's slain political leaders. Randy even wrote a perfect song for me, called "Give a Little Laughter."

I recruited one of the principal dancers from *The Boy Friend,* Tony Stevens, who recommended choreographer Eddie Gaspar, who'd just done Juliet Prowse's act. Eddie's assistant, Frank De Sal, also joined the act, and they put me through my paces. After months of doing Polly's delicate dance steps night after night, I felt like an uncaged animal.

Working on my act was a welcome therapeutic diversion from the mounting anxiety of my marriage. Bergmann was up to his old tricks again. In the middle of an interview I was giving at Sardi's, Bergmann walked in and interrupted with a strange announcement.

"I've just been rolled in Harlem."

"What?"

"I was out at the track and I won an incredible amount of money, but then some guys followed me home and took it all. That's why I came here, to find you and get cab fare home."

He was wearing a perfectly pressed suit, with a silk shirt and cuff links. I could see myself in his shoes. The reporters were looking at each other in amazement. Suzan, who was with me, glared at Bergmann and hissed, "Not *now!*"

She knew it was a hoax. "Did you notice his watch?" she later said to me. "He was 'rolled' in Harlem but he's still wearing his Cartier watch? *Right* . . ."

Although I'd always defended him, I was finally becoming disillusioned with Robert A. Bergmann.

June 8: I mistrust Robert . . . I don't think he's telling me the truth all the time—only when it suits him.

I do not respect his work scene. He must validate himself by contributing to our family: the two of us.

I should have realized that the key to Bergmann's strange behavior was that he lacked an identity of his own. "Mr. Carne" was a title he craved, which was why he had insisted we be married. He lived *through* me; his conversations were always about me and my work and what he could do for me. This obsession was unhealthy—even dangerous—and I finally woke up to the sad fact that the marriage had been a disastrous mistake.

June 25: My God, Whitney was stolen out of the car. I feel sick . . . that dear little dog I loved and adored. This has held us together, momentarily. "I won't leave you while this is going on," Robert said.

I'd left Whitney locked in the car while we were seeing a movie on the upper East Side. He was gone when we returned. Strangely enough, the car showed no sign of forced entry.

I was so upset, I asked "The Tonight Show" if I could make a short appeal. They were agreeable but they warned me of a precedent: Dustin Hoffman had recently offered a reward for his missing dog on the show. He got it back, in the mail. Cut into pieces.

I decided to place ads in the newspapers instead.

The following week I returned home after the show to find Bergmann waiting for me with a smile on his face.

"Someone called while you were out. They've got Whitney!"

I was overjoyed. "How *wonderful*! Where?"

"In Harlem." (Harlem *again*.)

I asked him if I could go get him.

"Oh, *you* can't go," he said. "It's too dangerous. I'll do it for you. I'll get him back, but they want some money."

"How much?"

"They might settle for five hundred but you'd better give me a thousand, just in case. . . ."

At that point I didn't care anymore. The next day I gave Bergmann the money to retrieve my dog in Harlem. He went about it with gusto, talking about the "drop site" and the "ransom."

When he returned he had Whitney, who looked well-fed and brushed, with a bow in his hair. Bergmann said they'd wanted the full thousand dollars.

> *July 10:* Robert is still living at Thirty-first Street and I'm now in the Algonquin Hotel. I need to live without hysteria and panic . . . right now I'm ordering Whitney a chicken sandwich from room service.
>
> Where did the relationship go? I mean, it was only *May third* we were married. Once communication is lost, there is nothing. As I left, his last words were, "I hope you survive it all. . . ."

The Boy Friend finally limped to a close later that month. I *wasn't* the darling of the cuties; and I *wasn't* the toast of Broadway.

> *August 4:* Fears:
> 1. Lack of financial security
> 2. Having a child
> 3. Raising a child in this strange world of problems and uncertainties that I don't seem to be able to handle too well

"Cuckoo, *Laugh-In* World"—Dan Rowan and Dick Martin sit below *(clockwise, from me)*: Dave Madden, Chelsea Brown, Dick Whittington, Goldie Hawn, Arte Johnson, Alan Sues, Jo Anne Worley, Ruth Buzzi, and Henry Gibson. *(Roy Cummings)*

Reading *The Odyssey:* "It may be an epic to you, but it's a *saga to me!*" Splash! (*Dean Goodhill*)

With Goldie in my dressing room, after opening night at
Caesar's Palace, Las Vegas, September 1970
(*Las Vegas News Bureau*)

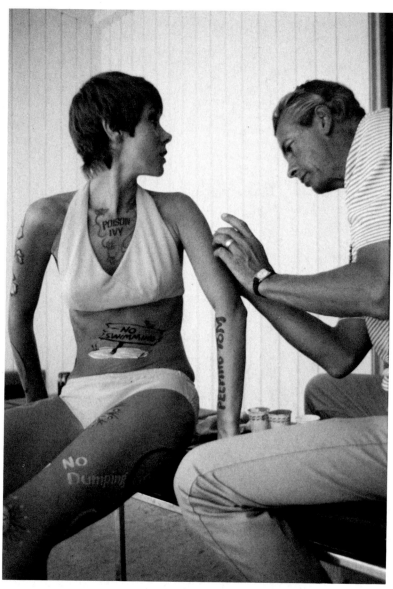

Art Trugman turning me into a human canvas. Notice how my navel has been disguised. *(Dean Goodhill/Gamma, Ltd.)*

The "Sock It to Me" session for *Reprise,* with Sammy Davis, Jr., spring 1968 *(Dean Goodhill/Gamma, Ltd.)*

Henry Gibson giving Sally Field and me some words of inspiration *(Roy Cummings)*

Peter Deuel and me with Mum and Dad at Finocchio's, in San Francisco, 1967 *(Judy Carne Collection)*

Back home at Carne Lodge in the "halo." The body cast reached down to my hip.
(photo copyright © by Ben Martin/PEOPLE Magazine)

Overleaf: During a break on the set of *All the Right Noises,* 1969
(Dean Goodhill)

4. Loneliness in later life
5. Losing the love of the one I love
6. Depending on someone else for everything
7. Losing sight of who I am
Sometimes I wonder what *not* being confused is like.

August 28: Robert is suing me for divorce. After four months of marriage he's asking for half of everything I have, plus alimony. How can that be, with a perfectly healthy young man?
Another chapter of my life: a Broadway show, a marriage, and now a legal hassle with Robert. It's been very heavy, but I'm off on a new venture on the road. . . . It's frightening, but exciting in a strange, panicked way. Try to be happy, Judes. . . .

To warm up for Las Vegas we tried out the act in El Paso, Texas, near the Mexican border. The entourage was quite flamboyant, consisting of Suzan as road manager, Randy as musical director, four male dancers, a guitarist, costume trunks, and Whitney. When we arrived, the locals thought we were from Mars.

The La Fiesta club was actually located in Juarez, Mexico, so each night we crossed the Rio Grande to go to work. The opening act was a cockfight, a gruesome event that worked the raucous crowd into a frenzy as they gambled, got drunk, and watched two roosters peck each other to death. After the dollars and pesos changed hands, the blood was mopped up off the stage and a voice came over the loudspeaker: "Ladies and gennelmen, it's *cho-time!* La Fiesta eez proud to present—Miss Yudi Carne!"

During the show the patrons felt the need to throw things at me: tacos, matches, anything that was handy. During one number I walked into the audience and people stuck out their feet to trip me. It was a bad case of culture shock. On Broadway I was used to having the audience's undivided attention. Suddenly I was hearing drunks shouting, "Sock it to 'em, señorita!"

During another warm-up in Dayton, my manager Garry called to say there'd been a scheduling conflict. Instead of being paired with Tony Newley, I'd open for Mr. Show Business himself, Milton Berle. This was disappointing news. I was afraid that my act wouldn't appeal to his audience, and my career couldn't afford a disastrous nightclub act. I thought, If I blow this one, I've *had* it.

I was encouraged to see my face on billboards everywhere as we arrived in Las Vegas. The Caesar's Palace staff gave me a lovely welcome, settled us into a plush suite, and that night we all went to see Connie Stevens close in the room we'd be playing. Her show was superb, and later she gave me tips on what to expect from the crowds.

When Randy and I showed up the next day for band call, the stage manager asked, "Miss Carne, is your conductor ready?"

"Yes, we're ready."

"Well, where *is* he?"

"This is Mr. Edelman," I said, pointing at Randy, who stood there grinning with his long hair and glasses, wearing shorts and a torn T-shirt that said SUCK.

The manager froze in disbelief, and it took awhile for the seasoned Las Vegas musicians to adjust to Randy. When he handed out the parts, they gave him strange looks, almost hostile vibes. As soon as they started the overture, Randy stopped them with the tap-tap-tap of his baton.

"Second trumpet, that's an E flat. Third trombone, you're sharp, and strings, hold back a little, it's much too loud. . . ."

By the end of the rehearsal he'd gained their respect, and they gave him their all. Hearing my arrangements played for the first time by over fifty musicians was exhilarating.

Waiting to go on that night, I peered at the audience through a spyhole in the wings. Thick cigar smoke permeated the room, which was filled with overweight older men and mink-stoled women with teased hair, their tables littered with highballs and champagne bottles.

Also in the audience was Goldie Hawn. She was planning a nightclub act of her own and had come to lend her support.

I came out to a tremendous ovation, but after each number the amount of applause gradually diminished. The audience was waiting for jokes, or a bucket of water. Instead I was singing and dancing, and they weren't very interested. They were in Las Vegas to drink, gamble, and forget.

During my finale Milton Berle snuck down into the audience and started hamming it up, causing a commotion. As I belted out my very last note, he yelled, "Isn't she *terrific,* folks? Give her a hand!" The spotlight went to him, and I was left to die onstage in the dark.

Goldie came backstage for the usual pictures and congratulations, but when we were alone, I told her how worried I was.

"Goldie, let's face it—I *died* out there. They wanted 'Sock it to me' time, and I couldn't give it to them."

"I feel for you, Judy," she said. "I'm sure I'll have the same problem. That's why I've postponed my act. I can't just stand there and say, 'I forgot the question.' "

September 19: Flip Wilson came to visit. We all went to Boulder Dam . . . beautiful desert country. Had a lovely time. Flip was so easy to be with. I dig him: no bullshit.

September 23: Awoke to an excellent review in *Variety*, which cheered me up. Flip took us to see Ike and Tina Turner's show: fabulous. A real turn-on. . . .

In between shows one night the headwaiter came to my dressing room with a sack of gambling chips. "Here, Miss Carne, these are for you to play with," he said.

"Thank you, but I don't know how to gamble," I said politely.

He was shocked. "Oh, we'll be happy to teach you."

"No, you don't understand . . . I hate to *lose!*"

We found other forms of recreation. Late one night Suzan, De Sal, and I were in a particularly giddy mood after being insulted by Don Rickles at the Sahara. ("Judy Carne, folks, this chick is *kinky*; she's got a guy in her dressing room who paints her tokus!") As we were returning to the hotel, I took one look at the majestic fountain in front of Caesar's Palace and had an idea.

"Wait right here," I told the others.

Up in my suite was a half-gallon bottle of bubble bath I'd purchased that day. I grabbed it and brought it back downstairs.

"You're not *serious*," said Suzan.

It was now 5 A.M., and anyone still awake was in a casino. I put a smidgeon of the bubble bath into the water and then ran to the bushes to watch. Nothing happened.

I dashed out again, this time emptying the entire bottle next to the water spout. Seconds later it started.

The bubbles shot up, sending a geyser of suds gushing twenty feet into the air. It was a breathtaking sight. Huge bubbles rose into the air like helium balloons. Those that fell back into the water doubled and rose again.

The suds started overflowing onto the pavement, and for a few cataclysmic moments, it looked as though they were going to take over the entire hotel. There would be hell to pay if we were caught, so we ran to the back entrance and nonchalantly entered the casino.

Upstairs we concocted our alibis. De Sal went back down to have a look. He reported that the hotel entrance was roped off and security guards were shouting for cleanup crews.

The next day the fountain was turned off and the cleanup was still going on. I was terrified that we'd be found out. "Maybe they'll have a *contract* put out on me!" I said to Suzan in a panic.

"No way! You'll apologize, and they'll get great publicity out of it. Just think of the headlines: 'Sock It To Me Girl' *Socks It* to Caesar's Palace!"

My problem was that I wasn't socking it to the *audiences*. I felt out of place in Las Vegas, where twice a night I suffered a slow and painful death onstage. I overreacted and slipped into an identity crisis. Then something inside me snapped. One night, in between shows, I swallowed a handful of barbiturates. A silent scream.

When I started to slip away, Suzan realized what I'd done and called a doctor. Then she and Randy poured coffee down my throat and walked me around.

"Please . . . let me lie down for a moment," I'd beg, which only made them walk me around some more. If they'd let me sleep, I might never have awakened. I felt as though a large magnet were pulling me down to the end of a long tunnel. To keep me awake, Suzan slapped my cheeks and put me into a cold shower every fifteen minutes.

A Las Vegas doctor arrived. He said I shouldn't have my stomach pumped if I planned to attempt a second show. He gave me a shot of Ritalin—"Garland's Up," they used to call it. Soon I was walking up and down the hotel corridor like a foal taking its first steps.

I was given my thirty-minute call as I struggled to put on my makeup with blurred vision. The doctor returned to give me another booster of Ritalin just before the overture. The first number was "If My Friends Could See Me Now." Thank God they couldn't.

I wasn't aware enough to be nervous. Randy whispered encouragement from the piano, and De Sal and Tony handled me with kid gloves. My head was spinning and my sense of balance was off. I was on automatic pilot. It wasn't until I heard Milton Berle's voice and the audience's applause that I knew it was over. I'd made it.

I was a mess when I came off, so Suzan took me directly to the sauna to let it *all* sweat out. Then it was back upstairs, where I slept for fifteen hours.

On closing night I knew I was expected to tip the stagehands, but I didn't know how much was appropriate. So I asked Milton Berle.

"Lemme tell ya, kid," he said, as I stood there with a pad and pencil. "Give the stage manager two hundred bucks, the lighting man a hundred bucks, and then there's the crew. . . ." He went on to list over five hundred dollars in tips. Unfamiliar with the procedure, I tipped as he said. I later found out that Berle had doubled the amount and told everyone *I* was tipping for *him*!

October 8: Washington, D.C.: I'm in Arlington Cemetery, just wandering around. Opened last night at the Shoreham Hotel. A drunk lady called the guys "faggots." Now the hotel wants us to use the service elevator and enter the club via the kitchen. . . .

October 22: Opening night in Reno. I'm on with Bobby Goldsboro, another mismatch for me. Someone overheard me saying "fuck" in the coffee shop, so they've confined us to our rooms. . . .

Wherever we went, we managed to get into trouble because of a fundamental mistake: We traveled as though we were a rock band, yet we were playing to straight, middle-American audiences in conservative establishments. I wasn't earning the kind of money that rock bands make, either. I returned home after Reno to a rude financial awakening: Everything I'd earned had gone for salaries and expenses. I had nothing to show for it. The bill for my costumes alone came to $10,000. Then came an American Airlines bill for $20,000.

I was outraged. A proper budget had not been prepared, and the itinerary was planned so poorly that we'd crossed the country four times, which was grossly uneconomical.

It was time to find a new direction.

November 10: Back in L.A., went to see Henry and Lois Gibson. Lois and I have come up with a good idea for a series for me called "Poor Judy." The female reporter idea—the escapades of a young, hip, modern-day reporter.

I pitched the idea of "Poor Judy" to Sidney Sheldon over lunch at Screen Gems and he was so enthusiastic, he assigned a writer to develop a pilot. In the meantime I had some upcoming bookings for the act, and I needed new management, *fast.*

I asked the advice of Roy Silver, who'd managed Bill Cosby. I knew Roy socially. He was somewhat of a gourmet cook and invited me to his house for dinner.

"Roy, I need help with my career," I told him as he prepared the meal. "Where do I go from here?"

"Judy, you've got to understand something," he said, preoccupied with his cooking. "No one's *excited* about you anymore. You just gotta hang in there."

Hang in *where*? I thought. Roy's vibe was so negative, he didn't even suggest someone who might be able to help me.

My next meeting was with a powerful Hollywood agent who was just as blunt. "Judy, you're not hot right now. The 'Sock it to me' thing is over with, and you're . . . well, *cold.*"

On hearing this, I could only go for the joke. "If I'm so bloody cold, how about putting me up for some Frigidaire commercials?"

He looked at me and shrugged. "Judy, you've got to face facts. You're yesterday's news."

I was so devastated by these words, I left his office and drove aimlessly around Hollywood for hours, in tears.

November 28: My whole career and life in general is going down the drain. I keep repeating, "My light's out, my light's out."

December 6: Went to dinner at Goldie's. It's good to see her. We had a nice long chat . . . she was very supportive. It's a shame we're always being compared.

December 9: Met with Cass, and Flip showed up. We had a good day. It's times like this I need these friends.

Had dinner with Shelley Berger, from Jerry Weintraub's management firm. Shelley's an ex-actor who understands . . . it could be a new beginning.

Broadway, Vegas, and the Land Down Under

Super-manager Jerry Weintraub took an interest in me when he heard I was booked into the Persian Room of New York's Plaza Hotel. It was a first-class booking on the nightclub circuit, and success there was essential if I was to prove myself as a cabaret performer. I signed with Weintraub's company just before flying to New York for my opening.

> *January 11:* Went with Randy to see Jackie DeShannon at the Copa. It was divine. We said hello backstage. Jackie was very warm and friendly . . . she and Randy really hit it off.
> Later we went to a club in the Village to hear another singer. Caught the last set of the Lady's act. She's fascinating. Honest, self-involved . . . I was strangely nervous speaking to her. Some sort of fantasy seems apparent. . . .

"The Lady"—as I referred to her in my journal—was a beautiful, sophisticated nightclub singer and the first person I'd been attracted to since my separation from Bergmann.

That night was also important for Randy; in Jackie DeShannon (whose hits included "What the World Needs Now"), he found his future wife.

> *January 15:* Opened last night, the best show I've ever done. I got my first standing ovation. It was fantastic. At last an audience that understood my thing . . . I felt totally rewarded. The Lady was sitting out front. I was aware of her all the time . . . she looked fabulous.
> The after-party was a bore . . . then it seemed the Lady and I had to be alone. We locked ourselves in the kitchen to touch, she very drunk, me very stoned. We ended up in her suite. . . .

The Lady enchanted me with her velvety voice, lithe figure, and strength of character. I'd always admired her work but never dreamed I'd find myself in a close encounter with her. My journal describes the unfolding relationship.

> *January 16:* Waiting to prerecord my number for "The Ed Sullivan Show," I must recap: The Lady and I lay on the carpet for hours, in a trance. Her sweetness and shy qualities knocked me out. The exchange was truly beautiful . . . fell asleep around 6 A.M. to find it suddenly noon.
> Awoke feeling joyful. In between shows I did an interview with John Wilson of the *New York Times.*

LAUGHING ON THE OUTSIDE, CRYING ON THE INSIDE

The New York Times, January 18, 1971:

JUDY CARNE, AT CLUB, SINGS IT TO THEM
by John S. Wilson

A reputation based on the ability to take a bucket of water in the face poses problems for a performer who wishes to capitalize on this fame. When Judy Carne moved out of her 'sock-it-to-me' role on television's *Laugh-In* to play the lead in the Broadway revival of *The Boy Friend* last season, there was no question about what she could do because the role was established. . . . But a nightclub act, something the pixie-faced English performer had never attempted until three months ago, could not be so clearly defined.

"A lot of people expect me to do comedy, because of the water," she explained. "But I can't stand that aggressive joke syndrome. I have no hit records to sing. I have no 'bag.' So I put together the things I do best—singing and dancing. My personality is my 'bag' . . . all I have is vitality and personality."

And those she has aplenty. Miss Carne has brought to the Persian Room a compact, polished, razzle-dazzle of song and dance that, once it gets its steam up, moves at a joyous, buoyant pace.

She is an excellent singer with a voice that has powerful resources . . . can take on intimate shadings on *Close to You,* or go boisterous with some give and take with pianist Randy Edelman on *Give a Little Laughter.* She is a sufficiently capable dancer to use a tap-dance specialty as her finale. She can dip into jaunty English music-hall material with authority. And she has charm. A warm, unaffected, but direct manner of reaching out to an audience.

All these elements are fused and balanced, each supplementing the other to produce an unusually rounded performance, something one rarely gets on a nightclub floor from people who are leaning on hit records.

January 19: I've had a lovely day . . . awoke to an excellent review in the *New York Times.* What a lift. The Lady and I read it at breakfast, and spent the day together. . . .

John S. Wilson's review was extremely rewarding. At last I'd found a responsive audience. Unfortunately, a few nights later some members of the audience got a little *too* responsive, as another Wilson, named Earl, reported in the New York *Post,* January 21, 1971:

JUDY CARNE IN A PLAZA BRAWL-IN
by Earl Wilson

Judy Carne's act broke up the Persian Room. Really.

The "Sock It To Me" girl had just finished singing a number last night, when an exuberant customer rose with a glass of water in his hand and shouted, "Yer doin' just *great,* Goldie!"

Miss Carne took exception to this, even though she's friendly with Oscar winner Goldie Hawn, her former colleague on *Laugh-In.*

"Hey, that's really uncalled for," she told him.

With the glass of water still aloft, the man started making remarks about Judy's navel, which was quite visible, thanks to her white pants outfit. Words followed words, and, according to Judy, "He threw his glass of water on me. I then threw water on him, and while I stood there, dripping, my conductor, Randy Edelman, came down and got water thrown on *him.*"

The water-throwing phase of the battle tapered off, but then some customers exchanged insults in the men's room, and hostilities opened afresh back in the Persian Room. The belligerents began pouring water over each other, and a waiter banged one participant over the head with a tray. At least 20 men were brawling when police began arriving at about 10 P.M.

But don't tune off yet, folks. It was just the beginning. Because a free-for-all fight broke out with customers taking sides, waiters, captains and hotel security officers joining in, blood flowing, and numerous police arriving to haul three men off to the 54th St. station, charged with harassment and disorderly conduct.

The six stitches taken in the head of Gregory Penny, 24, a contractor from the Bronx, at St. Clare's Hospital, proved that nightclub fighting is not dead in New York.

In the alcoholic mist hanging over the battle royal, it wasn't clear who brought the blood, nor whether the man with the glass of water was in the fight or merely the cause of it. One thing certain was that John, the usually faultlessly-dressed maitre d', was a much mussed-up host when it was over.

"John told me, before the show started, that it might be kind of rough," Judy Carne said. "He told me that a lot of men were coming over from the Boat Show."

189

The reference to Goldie Hawn "wasn't cute," and the further reference to her own navel was "ugly and hostile."

"I got emotional," she said. "After that, it was just splash, splash, splash . . . definitely a *sock it to me* evening!"

I was about to begin my last number when I first noticed the inebriated conventioneer get up with his glass of water. After we exchanged words, he doused me and I saw red. Like an angry bull I went for the pitcher and drenched him with it. After Randy came to my rescue, he whispered, "It's okay, Judes, carry on . . . you can do it."

He went back to the piano and began to play a vamp as I tried to pull myself together to sing, ironically, "I'm All Smiles." With my hair soaking wet and my makeup smudged, I tearfully started in singing, "I'm all smiles, darling . . . you'd be too. . . ."

As soon as I'd sung my last note, I ran offstage. Then a royal free-for-all punchout began. The last thing I remember seeing, as I peered out through the portals of the kitchen door, was a waiter hitting some poor bloke over the head with his tray. De Sal rushed back to see if I was okay and took me up to my suite, where Suzan tried to console me. "Don't worry, we'll turn this negative action into a positive one," she said. "We'll call the *press!*"

We didn't even have to. Before I'd even dried my tears, Earl Wilson telephoned from the hotel lobby; he'd just *happened* to be in the audience that night, so he came up for an interview. Phone calls from other reporters finally ceased at around four in the morning.

The next day I went on "The Dick Cavett Show." The incident generated so much publicity that the Persian Room was packed for the rest of my engagement.

January 26: The Lady gave me a small gold whistle that I love. On the card she wrote, "If you need me, just whistle—put your lips together and *blow.*" I love the Lady, our closeness is incredible. I never tire of her. . . .

I have a month off. I may travel with her to Puerto Rico for her booking. This thought pleases me: God knows I need a break from the bizarrety of recent weeks.

February 12: Arrived in Puerto Rico with the Lady, two dogs, endless luggage, and, to top it off, a life-sized Raggedy Ann doll that the Lady bought me. Tried to arrive incognito but I was recognized the minute we got off the plane. "Mira, mira! Sock-ee-to-me! Sock-ee-to-me!" they shouted.

Us sneaking into Puerto Rico—what a laugh!

February 24: Recap: It's Mardi Gras here in New Orleans, so yesterday the Lady and I sat on a balcony watching the parade, sipping mint juleps, listening to jazz bands pass by. Flowers were thrown to us, then a beautiful young boy with long hair threw me some beads with a joint attached . . . he said, "Say it, Judy, say it!"

Soon a small crowd was chanting in rhythm, "Say it, say it, say it, Judy! Say it, Judy! Say it, Judy!" I got all weird . . . begged off, but more started to chant. When I finally said it, they went wild. Joints, rolling papers, and roach clips rained up at us, then *bonk,* a lump of hash hit my head.

Last night the Lady opened. Fantastic. The loving of the night was extremely free and exciting. It was more satisfying than I can ever remember, just a *total* thing.

Today's review of the Lady's art: "Judy Carne sitting ringside, smiling, mouthing the words to the songs."

February 27: Had a long chat with Jerry Weintraub about my future. He's worried about my relationship with the Lady—he says the gossip is detrimental to my career. It would be fine if I were *just* a nightclub performer, but I have to contend with TV sponsors, a different ballgame. I feel down and problemed about it all.

March 1: En route back home to L.A. I miss the Lady already.

Dream Flash: I was dying from a shot in the heart, but I couldn't seem to let go. People were saying "It's hopeless to try to save her!" but I wouldn't die. It made me sweat, and I woke up.

March 3: I got a job within an hour of flying in. Rushed over to Universal for fitting in western gear for "Alias Smith and Jones," with Peter Deuel. . . .

On my first morning of work I was sitting in a makeup chair on the Universal back lot when suddenly a pair of hands covered my eyes.

"It's the big whale, come to *spout* on you again!" said Peter. He lifted me high in the air and we hugged joyously.

It was divine to be working together again, as we laughed about old times. But soon Peter admitted he was unhappy about the mediocrity of the show. At first I thought he was overreacting, but as the week wore on, I began to see what he meant.

March 6: On the set of "Alias S & J" the director came up to me right before a take and said, "I'll give you the name of a doctor in Santa Monica who can fix those crow's-feet around your eyes. . . ."

I was taken aback. I was just about to go on *camera.* It was one of the most insensitive remarks I've ever heard.

Every hour a trolley carrying a tour group drove by the set, with a guide barking through a megaphone: "And here, folks, is an episode in the making of 'Alias Smith and Jones,' starring Ben Murphy and Peter Deuel. Today they are joined by guest star Judy Carne, the 'Sock it to me' girl!"

Each time this happened, the director told us to freeze in our places, and we'd have to wait until the trolley was well out of sight before we could resume acting. I'd look at Peter and see him shaking his head in frustration.

Peter came over to my house that weekend and told me he was seriously depressed. He described feelings that were all too familiar to me, like lost confidence and lack of purpose. I insisted he take a drive with me to a special place. I wouldn't tell him where; I simply played some Ravi Shankar music in the car to relax him.

I drove to the Self-Realization Foundation near Malibu Beach, a beautiful shrine of Indian mystics with a tranquil lake, exotic gardens, and hypnotic sitar music emanating from speakers around the grounds. I'd been going there for years. "Every now and then," I told Peter, "when I feel incomplete and insecure, I come here to clear my head."

As we wandered around, he was wide-eyed, like a child, watching the ducks float gracefully along the lake. "It's so beautiful here," he said, smiling, "it makes me feel like a *jerk* to be depressed."

By the end of the day we'd talked out our anxieties and Peter was sounding positive. I was glad that our visit to SRF had cheered him up. But still, I noticed a sad, faraway look in his eyes. When we said good-bye that day, I left with a strange feeling of concern for his emotional well-being.

March 3: Burt was on Dick Cavett. I was tempted to stay up and watch, but I couldn't handle it. I'd like to see him, talk to him for a while . . . I wonder what he's like now. It's a long time ago, I've been through many changes. Has he gone through the same?

March 16: Recap: Party all day at my house. . . . About 65 people were in and out. Flip was into heavy raps, Peter Deuel was super fun, Sally Kellerman brought Bob Altman, Lou Adler, and some of the cast of "Brewster McCloud"—interesting. Burt Schneider showed, also Bob Rafelson. I met Barry K., Jr., son of the famous actor. Intriguing . . . we got on well together.

Cass arrived later, with Bruce Johnston of the Beach Boys. Bruce played beautiful piano and we had a super sing-along ranging from old Beach Boys hits to even a few *Boy Friend* songs, with Cass. Rod Stewart joined us. A divinely degenerate little Englishman . . . very interesting. It ended at 5 A.M.

March 17: Barry K., Jr., called. I had a feeling he would after our encounter at the party. How strange, being born into Hollywood royalty. . . .

Barry K., Jr., was lean and handsome, with short curly hair and huge green eyes, like a cat. He was second-generation Hollywood but surprisingly unaffected by his father's notorious reputation as a rogue. Barry had a secure, independent quality about him, which fascinated me. He spent most of his time at his desert retreat in Joshua Tree, and he invited me to come out for a weekend "happening" he was planning in June. I couldn't wait.

March 29: Party at Bumble's for a lot of English folk. Saw Vidal Sassoon and we chatted endlessly. He says he's grateful to me, referring to our relationship of many moons ago. I was so moved, hearing that. He is the same lovely person he was, not operating on an ego level. . . .

April 27: It's my birthday. Found out that CBS is interested in "Poor Judy." Sidney Sheldon told me a pilot will be made in the summer. Feel overjoyed. The future looks bright.

It finally looked as though I had a shot at doing my own sitcom, the direction I'd been hoping for. Until then, however, I had to continue touring with the act.

May 20: I'm in Sparks, near Reno, Nevada. A little plastic blip of a place surrounded by mountains of true beauty. Someone came along and built a monstrosity between the hills.

JUDY CARNE, *PLUS* BERTHA AND TINA, THE AMAZING ELEPHANTS! screamed the billboard in Sparks, Nevada. During the first rehearsal the stage manager took me aside.

"Miss Carne, we'll need about fifteen minutes after Bertha and Tina come off before you can go on."

"Oh?"

"We've gotta clean the you-know-what off the stage. . . ."

Later, backstage, I happened to glance into an open dressing room to see an extraordinary sight: There sat Bertha the elephant, covered with feathers and jewelry, with her massive foot on a stool as her trainer painted her giant nails with a brush from a huge bottle of elephant nail polish. Only in America.

June 19: I'm at Barry K. Jr.'s desert haven in Joshua Tree. I sit here, having taken sun, climbed rocks, sat naked in caves. . . . Yes, it has been a glorious day.

"Timothy Leary was married right here," Barry told me after my arrival at Joshua Tree. It had been a major event in the psychedelic community. Leary and his bride had wandered around the desert in white robes, looking for a magic spot where it "felt" right to be married.

Barry led me up a steep climb to a special, secluded place where a small group of people were gathered in a primitive meditation hut. Barry and his friends had built the structure, which had a fireplace in the center and an open skylight for gazing at the stars.

Later Barry took me to explore the desert. The beauty of the rocks and the cacti was awesome, and I felt as though I were on another planet. Suddenly a storm loomed over us, and we were drenched with rain. Barry and I just stood and looked at each other in the downpour, then slowly peeled off our clothes like layers of dead skin. We cavorted naked in the desert, feeling the raindrops melt into our bodies. Yes it *was* a glorious day.

June 25: I feel inspired by Barry. He makes me really think, examine myself and everything around me. He fascinates me.

He came over, cooked me an omelet, and left. I sat in the same position for ages after he left, just staring, until I felt his presence had really gone. . . . I feel there's something to be learned from him about self-love and self-preservation.

It could be endless in its development. He calls me his "consultant," which is a lovely way to put it.

Now that Barry was in my life, I was happy to hear that my divorce from Bergmann had been finalized. He needed money, so instead of holding out for alimony, he'd agreed on a settlement of $25,000. To be rid of Bergmann, it seemed a bargain.

July 9: Here I am, sitting in court, waiting to get a divorce. The words of the day are "Never again." What one is subjected to, in and out of marriage, is just the worst. This is my second time around, with the same words and the same answers, just different names. Dumb, Judes, really dumb.

Flash: In court just now, when asked my name, I had to look at the petition. It sounded so foreign to me: Joyce Audrey Bergmann? Who the hell is that? The judge smiles, the lawyer smiles. The ex-wife holds back a laugh.

A mad episode, but it's over. There's a new beginning. Past is past, more wisdom backlogged.

My nightclub act had yet to turn a profit, so for one last try I was booked into one of the major hotels in Sydney, Australia, halfway around the globe.

July 22: I've lost a day. I'm in Sydney. Arrived in cosmic clad and did an enormous press conference with four TV cameras rolling. It was fun, totally impromptu. Then to the hotel for two newspaper interviews.

Robert-the-Bergmann called and said he'd had a dream in which I was in a car crash and I had to be *pieced back together again.* He called from the other side of the world to tell me this, mind you.

August 2: I can't believe it . . . last night I was thrown out of a restaurant for wearing hot pants. Cameramen were in today to put me on the news. That's a statement in itself—that it's on the *news.*

August 4: The continuing drama of being here: I got all pulled together to do the show, and we found out the room is closed. I can't find the owner, the manager, or *anyone* in a position of authority. We sat there, numbed. . . . All dressed up with no place to go, sitting outside in the lobby.

I feel I'm being used as a pawn in a scheme I don't know about. No one has any answers. Went to sleep upset, confused, and angry.

August 6: Still no news. Spoke to Weintraub's office and was advised to be ready to do my shows every night, even though there are none. "Fulfill your contract, whatever happens," he said. My money was safe, provided I did what I was told. So I get ready for the show every night, and we sit in the lobby. I call the manager and the hotel owner every hour—no answer. They're all avoiding me. . . .

When I returned to L.A., I found out what had happened. The club had apparently been in financial trouble for some time, so when they discovered a loophole in my contract, they jumped at the chance to kill two birds with one stone: They wouldn't have to pay me and they wouldn't have to keep the club open.

The loophole they found was a telling example of how badly my affairs had been managed. I had a corporation—as many entertainers do—but I was not properly listed as a *director* of my own corporation.

August 20: I'm $5000 out on the Australia deal from salaries and expenses. I have to sit back and question a) my judgment of people I chose to represent me, and b) my attitude of "whatever you think is right, I'll do my job and you do yours and it will all work out." Well, it sucks. Nobody comes through. What a drag.

September 8: I'm in a period of artistic frustration. I feel underestimated, unappreciated. I need to work on something I can get behind. Sometimes it's hard to hang on, with all the knocks that keep on coming, but I do bounce back. I seem to be in a state of permanent bounce. Maybe that's the key to my whole personality: Permanent Bounce.

10. Judes the Obscure

In September my parents arrived in time to watch me make two unique television appearances: a "Laugh-In" reunion, celebrating its one-hundredth show, and "The Tonight Show"—guest-hosted by Burt Reynolds.

> *September 16:* Did "Laugh-In" today. The famous read-through was the same as always: lots of tension. I get wet three times in the script. Same jokes. I do the Judy Doll and Robot Theater, but there is nothing new.
>
> Hang on, Judes . . . use it and make it work.

It came as no surprise that I would get a bucket of water again. The setup was Dan and Dick, presenting me with a welcome-back gift—a light socket. My fatal words were, of course, "You're just giving a *socket to me*?" Splash.

It was wonderful seeing the other original cast members who returned—Jo Anne Worley, Henry Gibson, and Arte Johnson. Only Goldie was absent. No one seemed to know why she chose not to return, and we all missed her.

> *September 22:* It's late at night and I'm here on the set of "Laugh-In" watching John Wayne recite Henry Gibson poems.

197

That, in itself, is a trip. My dad got a kick out of Wayne, saying, "I'm so used to beating up people in black hats, I don't trust myself around nuns!"

It's been a hard day's shoot, and I've been working like a frog. I've made the best of it, though, even the dousings. While my good old mum and dad are here, togetherness is imperative.

That weekend I took my parents to visit Mama Cass. She was suffering from a bad case of asthma and had to stay in bed, so while my parents took sun and had a swim in her pool, I kept her company.

Cass's bedroom was quite a scene. She loved disorder and couldn't find anything if it was tidy. She sat on a myriad of pillows in her huge, ornate four-poster bed, dressed in an antique lace nightie and surrounded by flowers and chocolates. Beside the bed was an oxygen canister, for use in the event of an asthma attack.

Cass and I shared a special friendship. We wanted to trade places: She wanted to act, and I wanted to be a rock star. We dreamed of doing a sitcom together someday, playing nutty neighbors or roommates—a show that would incorporate music and comedy. We envisioned ourselves as the female Laurel and Hardy of the Flower Power generation.

> *September 25:* At Cass's house today my folks were funny. We turned on with some Moroccan Joy and Mum actually took a few puffs on the joint. "Blimey, I think it's overrated!" she said. We cheered Cass up.
>
> Just heard that Burt wants me for "The Tonight Show" in New York. I'm very tempted, but I haven't made up my mind yet. . . .

When I first got the call to appear on "The Tonight Show," I was surprised. I wasn't promoting anything in particular.

"What's the occasion?" I asked.

"Burt Reynolds is hosting," I was told. Burt had just caused a sensation by posing for his infamous nude centerfold in *Cosmopolitan.*

"Are you . . . *sure* you know who you're talking to?" I said, thinking there was some mistake. "I'm his ex-wife, you know."

"Oh, yes, we know. Burt's *asked* for you."

"Well, if *he's* game, so am I," I told them. The next week I flew to New York with my parents for the taping.

In my dressing room before the show, the director, Fred de Cordova, came to ask me if I'd like to discuss anything with Burt before we went on the air.

"I know how important this night is for Burt," I said. "I'll leave it to him. If he'd like to see me, fine. If not, that's fine too."

De Cordova came back a few minutes later and said, "Burt says he will see you out there—on the air."

I was terrified and excited at the same time. I hadn't seen Burt since our divorce six years earlier. Okay, I thought, it's just another show—even though it *is* your ex-husband. As I stood backstage nervously waiting to go on, I heard Burt start my introduction.

"Right now, folks, we're going to do something unusual. I'm going to bring out a talented lady you all know very well. She happens to be my ex-wife." He went on to give me such a lovely buildup, I felt a lump in my throat. "Here she is—Judy Carne!"

I strode out and was mesmerized by the sight of him, looking even more attractive than I'd remembered. After a lengthy embrace we sat down, and the vibe between us was electric.

"God, you look good," I said.

"I'm sorry to say, so do you," he replied.

The audience giggled.

"So how the heck *are* you?" I asked.

"Oh, terrific . . . I just sit home with my Burt and Judy towels." Laughter.

"When was the last time we saw each other?" he asked.

"Let's see . . . I think it was when you threw me against the fireplace!" I said. The audience howled.

"Have you seen my centerfold?" he asked.

"Of course, Burt, who hasn't? I think it's terrific. But it's missing your best feature—your *arse!*" *Big* laugh.

"It's true," I said to the audience, "he has the most *divine* little arse! In fact, Burt, I've been getting all these phone calls, since I'm the only one who *legitimately* knows what's underneath your hand in the picture."

"Arm," he said firmly.

"Hand."

"Arm!"

"Hand!"

The audience was screaming with laughter, but the director seemed worried, so he signaled Burt to go to a commercial, not realizing we were just putting each other on.

"Are you . . . *seeing* anyone?" Burt asked me when we returned.

"Yes, I am."

"A younger guy, I suppose?"

"Well, yes, actually. I hear you've gone older," I said, referring to Dinah Shore. The audience laughed, but Burt didn't.

"Not older," he said, "just *classier.*" The audience applauded, and I knew I'd made a boo-boo.

"I'm sorry, that wasn't nice," I said, tearing up. "I really admire her . . . I was just going for the joke."

"We know that and we still love you," said Burt. "Don't you still love her?" They applauded, and I was out of the woods.

Burt described the show in an interview for *Playboy*:

> . . . Judy and I were on for more than half an hour together, and it was explosive, frightening, and beautiful. She cried, and laughed, and made *me* laugh, and it was just fabulous.
>
> The audience loved her and wanted us to get back together . . . a lot had happened to me in the six years since we'd been divorced. I'd grown up, I'd gotten a lot of confidence, and I'd become an adult, so I told her all that, and said, "You know, whatever problems we had, the divorce was my fault."
>
> She said, "No, it was my fault," and all of a sudden, we were going back and forth about whose fault our divorce was. We forgot where we were, and it was *very* funny.

After the show everyone gathered at Sardi's. Burt and I didn't get a chance to be alone at first. He finally pulled a chair next to me and asked, "So . . . are you okay?"

"I *think* so. Tell me, Burt . . . why did you want me on the show?"

"I knew you'd say the first thing that popped into your head, and that it would probably be funny. I was right."

As we talked, he told me about Dinah. "She's been great for me . . . I've really grown. We have quiet evenings with friends, like Jimmy Stewart and his wife." Our lives had taken such different directions, but still, I felt a special bond between us.

As he left, Burt said to my dad, "I'd better go now, Harold, before I fall in love with your daughter all over again. . . ."

Judes the Obscure

* * *

Everyone was talking about our appearance on "The Tonight Show." The response was so encouraging, I hoped perhaps Burt would get in touch and suggest a project for us to do together—something we'd always talked about when we were married. Surely our chemistry could be used for more than just a talk show. But it was not to be.

October 28: I'm on location for *Dead Men Tell No Tales,* on skid row in San Pedro. Bums everywhere, which is a drag . . . we shot endless car chases, watching traffic and acting. Then a box lunch, and now I've been waiting two hours to be dismissed. Thank God for my dear book. At times like this, I really appreciate you.

November 10: Up at six. A full day's work on "Love, American Style." I start *Cade's County* with Glenn Ford tomorrow. Mum is thrilled I'm working with him. He's always been one of her idols.

November 20: On location for "Cade's County." It's going well, but the director is a bring-down. Before every single take he yells, "Okay now, Judy, be *perky!*" God.

Although I was grateful to be working, it seemed like such an anticlimax after the momentum I'd built up. I'd attained major recognition on a hit TV show, starred on Broadway, and headlined in Las Vegas, but none of these had propelled me to a higher level.

January 1, 1972: I sit in Barry K.'s study, looking through the latticed windows at the first sunshine we've seen in days. Things look good—a new journal, and a new year, a feeling of beginning.

My New Year's optimism was shattered that day by a phone call from Henry Gibson, telling me that Peter Deuel had been found dead from a self-inflicted gunshot wound, beneath the Christmas tree in his Hollywood Hills home. I was devastated—we'd only recently worked together. "Judy, he wanted to be buried at SRF," Henry told me.

I wept, recalling the time I'd first taken him to the Self Realization Foundation. I knew he'd been depressed about his work; his standards were so high that any form of mediocrity gave him an overwhelming feeling of futility. He'd point to his lines in the script and say, "It's all so *meaningless.*"

Peter carried the weight of the world on his shoulders. He was deeply affected by news stories involving any form of tragedy or suffering. He was always asking, "What can *we* do?"

Peter had helped me through a difficult time in my life. My only consolation was that I'd helped him find a moment of peace that day at SRF. Hollywood lost a brilliant actor and I lost a loyal friend. I shall never forget him.

> *January 10:* I just saw "Love, American Style." I hated it, and me, and the whole level of work. Last night I was on "Cade's County." I'm depressed by it all. How wonderful it would be to work on something I'm *proud* of. . . .

That week my agent told me that Screen Gems had canceled all plans for "Poor Judy." They'd rejected the pilot after having changed the concept into an ersatz *Perils of Pauline* set in the 1920s. But the bad news didn't end there.

> *January 15:* I found out that I am $80,000 in debt. $65,000 must go to the government for back taxes. I have no work and no prospects, so I may have to sell my house. . . .

"It's *deductible,* Judy," was all I'd heard from my business advisers over the last three years. An IRS audit revealed that this was not the case, and I dreaded the thought of selling my beloved Laurelcrest. Just when it seemed things couldn't get any worse, they did: I discovered I was allergic to my birth control pills.

> *January 28:* I had an IUD put in and it was agony. They gave me a shot of Demerol and then some Newmorphin, a painkiller, which was *amazing.* The doctor gave me fifty of them.

Barry's family doctor prescribed the Newmorphin for the discomfort of adapting to a new IUD, but it had a disastrous psychological effect on me. At first everything seemed divine, and my problems just faded away. Then the medicine ran out.

> *February 16:* I've hit a terrible low. I can't sleep. Can't stop crying. I feel stifled as an actress. . . . Every now and then I think maybe I couldn't deliver, even if I got a job. How much rejection can one take? Why am I feeling so self-destructive?

Judes the Obscure

I didn't realize that I was experiencing a form of withdrawal from Newmorphin. I felt an emotional hunger, a feeling of longing, and thought, If I could just feel like I did last week, after one of those pills . . .

Thanks to an abrupt change of scene, I was able to snap out of this listless gloom. Barry was hired as special photographer for a film being made in Mexico by the avant-garde Chilean director, Alejandro Joderofski, so I joined him for the adventure.

March 4: Mexico City. The people in this movie are from A to Z, all colors and types: an older gay cat just finding out about himself . . . a tall, omnipresent black girl carrying her hostilities wrapped up in a big warm smile . . . an older businessman just learning about spiritual contact . . . a bland-looking no-spark American boy with a ranch in Big Sur, who will never be the same again . . . a perfectly-boned young Mexican girl, sensitive and devilish at the same time. And so it goes, a bizarre scene, all of them different. Not dull, for sure.

In his films—such as the cult classic *El Topo*—Joderofski was noted for combining skilled actors with odd characters such as these, many of whom he had discovered. During the first week of filming, Barry and I met one of his finds, a young beauty named Toni Starr. She looked no older than eighteen and bore a striking resemblance to Rita Hayworth but with long blond hair, large blue eyes, and a peach-colored complexion. Her hands were unusually large, however, and I had a feeling that beneath this beauty was not a woman, but a young man.

Barry and I were fascinated, so we befriended her. She was in the process of a gender change and was taking female hormones to eliminate facial hair and enlarge her breasts. She looked fantastic in a backless dress.

Growing up in a small southern town, Tony spent his childhood in the shadow of three breathtakingly beautiful sisters. His effeminate nature was a great source of embarrassment to the family, so his parents kept him out of school. When relatives came to visit, he was locked in his room. He rarely left the house and lived a Cinderella-like existence, spending lonely hours sewing clothes for his sisters.

At sixteen, filled with the shame of this rejection, Tony ran away to New York City and joined a renowned troupe of outrageous female impersonators. That is where Tony became Toni, and where Joderofski found her and cast her in his movie.

While we were in Mexico I accepted an offer to do *Cabaret* that summer in dinner theater. It was always a gutsy pleasure playing Sally Bowles, but I didn't want to go on the road alone. I knew Toni didn't have a job after the movie, so I asked her to be my girl Friday. She was an expert on makeup and fashions of all periods, and I knew she could help me capture the right look for Sally.

We flew to Toronto for the opening of an eight-week run, during which Toni was invaluable to me, keeping my wardrobe and cosmetics organized to perfection. She altered my clothes and costumes, and could transform scraps of fabric into beautiful creations overnight.

One afternoon, as we ran errands in the car, I gave her a pad and pen and asked her to jot down a memo for me. She was evasive, but seemed to write as I dictated the note. When I saw the note later, it was just a bunch of squiggles. I thought it was a joke, so I confronted Toni about it.

"I'm sorry, Judy, but . . . I can't write," she admitted.

"Neither can I," I said. "I'm terrible at letters."

"No. I mean I can't *write*," she repeated.

"Oh . . . you mean like *not able?*" She nodded. "Well, how about *reading?*" I asked.

"I can't read, either." Because her parents had kept her out of school, she'd never learned. She'd been afraid to tell me.

"Listen, Toni, don't worry. I'll help you. C'mon, it'll be a laugh . . . I'll show you how!"

No one had ever said that to her before. We began with addresses and restaurant menus, and soon she was taking great pride in reading me newspaper headlines in my dressing room before the show.

Toward the end of our run in Toronto, I took a bad fall during the finale. I was thrown into the arms of two downstage dancers. They lost their grip on my slippery satin costume and I dove head first onto a front table, scattering drinks, plates, and silverware on a party of six as I landed.

As I lay there in agony, the audience stood up and cheered. They thought it was a stunt, and chanted "Sock it to me! Sock it to me!" I slithered off the table onto the floor and crawled out of sight.

The M.C. assured the audience that I was okay, and the show resumed. I limped out in slippers and sang the finale in place. When it was over, my ankle was the size of a football.

There was no understudy for my part, so the doctor taped me up and I performed from a wheelchair for the rest of the week. Each night an announcement was made before the opening curtain: "Ladies and gentlemen, due to an injury sustained by Miss Carne, she will not be able to dance tonight." The audience gasped. "She will, however, perform the rest of the show as usual."

They cheered as I entered in a wheelchair, which Toni had cleverly disguised with fabric and flowers. From time to time the dancers picked me up and put me on a chair, then on a table, then up on the piano, as I threw in impromptu lines to explain these moves.

When we opened in Chicago the following month, the understudy shortage caused a problem once again. Two chorus girls came down with the flu, but we had only one girl to replace them.

A cast meeting was called. I suggested Toni, since she had a good voice and already knew the songs, but some of the cast members were leery about turning *Cabaret* into a drag show.

"She won't fit the clothes," they said.

"So she'll *alter* them," I replied. "What alternative *is* there?" We took a vote and it was unanimous. She would go on.

Toni was ecstatic. Her dream of being a real chorus girl in a real musical was coming true. The other girls made a fuss over her, insisting she make up with them in their dressing room. By curtain time she looked devastating.

Right before Toni's number, "Two Ladies," we gathered backstage to cheer her on. The number went well until the end, when Toni had to sing a short passage alone. She panicked and forgot to use a falsetto, which dropped her voice down two octaves. The audience didn't seem to notice, but the next day I opened a Chicago newspaper and read the headline: IN CABARET, NOT ALL THE GIRLS ARE LADIES. The article mentioned Toni by name and revealed that she worked for me and shared my dressing room.

It was a press agent's nightmare. Bruisers and hecklers started showing up by the truckload, jeering and shouting catcalls at Toni during the show. But that wasn't the only unpleasantness. The local restaurants suddenly refused us service, and our landlord tried to evict us. The treatment bore a chilling resemblance to the oppression we were portraying each night in *Cabaret*.

When we returned to L.A., Toni had a sex-change operation and moved to Lake Tahoe to work as a showgirl. There she met and married a wealthy dentist—a happy ending, to be sure.

It wasn't a happy ending for me, however. My agent was furious about the incident, and chided me for my "outrageous behavior."

"Judy, just what are you trying to *pull?*" he demanded.

"Pull?" What an odd expression, I thought.

"It's all over the industry that you went on the road with a drag queen. C'mon, Judy, this isn't Greenwich Village, it's Hollywood. You're committing career suicide!"

I didn't know how to respond to this. I was a magnet for trouble, never looking for it, always finding it. It seemed as though "Sock it to me" was becoming a self-fulfilling prophecy.

I found trouble again on my next, and last, "Hollywood Squares" appearance. I'd been doing the show for years. It was a thousand dollars for a night's work, in which they taped five shows. I wasn't placed in a strategically popular square that night, and so, for the first three shows, I was asked no questions. When we broke for dinner, I made the mistake of having an extra cocktail out of boredom. By the time we returned to finish taping, it was midnight and I was exhausted.

The fourth show went by, and again not *one* question came my way. I dutifully waved during the music and credits, changed clothes, and sat down for the "Friday" show. The heat from the lights made me feel groggy, and I began to droop. I rested my chin on one hand and tried to concentrate on the host, Peter Marshall, but it was hopeless. My eyes closed and I was out.

Suddenly sirens screamed and lights flashed. I jumped up to discover that I was the "Secret Square." I thought, who am I? Judy Carne, right. Sock it to me.

"I'm sorry, Judy, did we wake you?" Peter Marshall asked.

"Well, actually . . . *yes,* to be quite honest!"

The audience howled with laughter, but the producer was furious. Out of the corner of my eye I could see him signal the cameras away from me. I knew right then that my "Hollywood Squares" days were over. Sure enough they never asked me back, and offers stopped coming in from other game shows as well. I guess I was on the shitlist.

October 18, 1973: I feel the urge to write, after months of self-doubt. . . . I feel insecure about myself the soul, and myself the actress. Worst of all, I'm losing my sense of humor about everything.
I can't find the "Up" button of life. . . .

As unemployment set in, I became dangerously self-destructive. I woke up each morning feeling empty and lacking in purpose. I had no children or husband to look after. I only had the company of some of Hollywood's most sophisticated drug connoisseurs, growers, and pharmacists. They loved to display their wares and discuss drug use as if it were a high art.

One evening after a dinner party at my house, one couple stayed late—a noted screenwriter and his lovely wife. They wished to show their appreciation for my hospitality by offering me a few lines of dark powder which they produced from a small vial. It was heroin.

I was frightened. I'd always thought of heroin as "the killer drug," and I was determined to avoid it. I'd been told that the high was similar to that of the Newmorphin pills I'd been prescribed. The couple assured me that an occasional snort was not enough to get me hooked, so I cautiously inhaled the small line they'd prepared for me.

The emotional warmth generated by a snort of heroin was overwhelming. One small line of brown powder changed anxiety into calm, insecurity into confidence, and depression into euphoria. After one snort, all was right with the world.

I developed a taste for the drug that night. It was readily available, having achieved an exotic, almost glamorous status in the Hollywood drug culture. For months I straddled the treacherous line of addiction. Whenever I felt the monkey trying to perch on my back, I'd head for the sanctity of Barry's house at Joshua Tree to clean out. I was convinced I could stop at any time.

I broke this escalating pattern of abuse that summer, by going on the dinner theater circuit in George Axelrod's comedy, *Goodbye, Charlie.* The play opened in Denver, a scenic, healthy city, far removed from Hollywood and its temptations. In July we moved to

Minneapolis. There I heard the awful news that Cass Elliot had died in Harry Nilsson's London flat.

Cass had just finished a triumphant two-week engagement at the Palladium, and as she celebrated on that last night, her heart simply gave out. An autopsy revealed no trace of drugs or alcohol. The heart attack was attributed to the fact that she'd lost seventy pounds on a crash diet, and her body couldn't take it. It was cruel irony, and more proof, as far as I was concerned, that life was simply theater of the absurd.

In my case it was *dinner* theater of the absurd. I was alone in a Minneapolis motel, grief stricken by the loss of yet another of my soulmates. Our dreams of working together someday would never be realized. Although Cass's great musical talent was preserved on records, the world would never get a chance to see her tremendous comedic gift.

More bad news greeted me upon my return to L.A.: I would have to sell my house unless I immediately met the government's demand for $65,000 in back taxes. I went into a deep depression and wondered if perhaps I was destined to end up like Cass, or Peter Deuel.

As I pondered my fate, I was contacted by Bob Guccione of *Penthouse* magazine. He wanted to see me about a special project he "couldn't discuss over the phone," so I agreed to meet him at a restaurant on Sunset Boulevard. He had a deep tan and his open collar revealed a collection of gold neck chains.

"I suppose you're wondering why I wanted to meet with you *personally*," he said.

"I take it you're branching out into movies or television?"

"Well, yes, but frankly, I wanted to talk to you for a different reason. You like . . . women, don't you?"

"Of course."

"I mean, you enjoy . . . *close* relationships with women, don't you?"

"Let's just say I appreciate women very much."

"How'd you like to see it in photographs?"

"You mean . . . *sexually*?"

"Yes. I'd like to shoot it personally."

"Why?"

"For my magazine."

"What for?"

"Fifty thousand dollars."

"Fifty thou—" I immediately thought of those back taxes. "Well . . . what would I have to *do* in these pictures?"

"Be passionate with another woman."

"*How* passionate?"

"You're a very free lady, Judy . . . just be free."

"You don't understand. I'm known from TV. What'll people *think*?"

"They'll go *crazy*."

I'm sure the layout would have made Burt's nude centerfold in *Cosmopolitan* look like *Better Homes and Gardens*, but the idea of posing with one of his buxom "Pets" was a turn-off. *My* idea of sensuality has always involved lithe, graceful figures.

"Look, Bob, things may not be going well for me right now, but if I appear in *Penthouse* with my head buried in a huge set of tits, I can kiss my acting career good-bye. No thanks."

And so I put my house up for sale instead.

Soon after Laurelcrest went on the market, I got a part in a Spelling/Goldberg TV movie, *Only with Married Men,* playing the wife of Dom DeLuise, one of Burt's closest friends.

Dom was an incurable giggler, which made things difficult when the time came for our scene in bed together. I felt something poke me underneath the covers as we embraced—he'd stuffed a banana into his pajama bottoms. Just before we had to kiss, he filled his mouth with Jell-O. "Your ex-husband said this would turn you on," he grunted, as it oozed down his chin. "You know Burt's next door, don't you?"

"No, really?" I asked. "Doing what?"

"Are you ready for this? A *musical!*"

"I don't believe it. Singing?"

"Singing," Dom whispered, "and even . . . I'll say it fast: *dancing!*"

He fanned himself with a handkerchief as we hooted at the thought. Burt was working on Peter Bogdanovich's *At Long Last Love.*

"We've *got* to pop in on him!" Dom insisted.

"Shouldn't we let him know we're coming?"

"Of course not. We'll surprise him. I can't *wait* to see his face!"

To get to Burt's soundstage on the Fox lot, we had to walk past the original set of *Hello, Dolly,* a big attraction on the studio tour.

"I wanted that part so bad!" Dom shouted, shaking his fist. "They didn't want to take a *chance,* so they went with Streisand. *Fools!*"

We arrived to find Burt dressed in tails, practicing a dance step with his co-star, Cybill Shepherd. They were resplendent in a magnificent Art Deco ballroom with multiple chandeliers and a gleaming floor.

"Fred! Ginger's here!" I shouted.

"We've come to save you!" Dom chimed in.

Burt went deadpan, as if he'd just seen a ghost. Then he grinned and came over to give us each a bear hug. He took us to his plush, spacious trailer, with a saloon-style bar and country music blaring.

"This is a *villa,*" said Dom. "My trailer is a cardboard box!"

"Them's the breaks," said Burt.

"You know you look like a complete idiot on that set, don't you?" Dom shot back.

"Yes, but it takes *balls* to go out there and do it!"

The laughter was nonstop throughout the short visit, as Burt and Dom outdid each other, each line funnier than the last. Seeing Burt again brought back the memory of the day we first viewed Laurelcrest and decided to make it our dream home. Now, twelve years later, I was losing that home.

> *April 12, 1975:* "I was a born adventurer, an entertainer, who couldn't avoid outrage and uproar." That was said by Laurence Harvey, who died last year.
>
> I sit here in the hills, wasting away, hungering for highs.

Broke, out of work, and lonely, I reached out again to heroin for relief. It was more available than ever, now that Johnny Briefcase was on the scene.

He was the archetypal Hollywood dealer. Handsome, charismatic, and always impeccably dressed, J.B. drove a Porsche and had a disarming smile that instilled in his rich and famous clients a feeling of well-being—just like the high-quality drugs he carried in the snakeskin attaché case that had earned him his nickname.

Judes the Obscure

Johnny Briefcase had been a promising rock musician before he forsook his talents to sell drugs to his many friends in the music industry. His girlfriend, Crystal, ran a hair salon in Westwood, where he laundered his profits and discreetly conducted business from a back office.

Crystal was English, and fun, so we soon became friends. I often stopped by to visit her, since she always invited me into the back room to sample J.B.'s latest wares.

One afternoon Johnny Briefcase arrived at the salon from the airport with rock musician Gregg Allman, who'd just flown in from his home in Georgia. Although weary, Gregg looked splendid, resembling a foppish cowboy in a Renaissance jacket and Stetson hat, his blue eyes and long blond hair framing an angelic face. I'd always been a fan of the Allman Brothers and was excited to hear that he was in town for an important gig at the Troubadour—his first major appearance since his brother Duane was killed in a motorcycle accident.

Gregg and J.B. needed a place to relax for a while, so I invited them back to my house. J.B. opened his briefcase and laid out a generous amount of heroin that kept us high for the rest of the afternoon and evening. Long after Johnny Briefcase had left to attend to other business, we were still feeling the effects. Gregg even picked up a guitar and played some of his new songs. He was so comfortable, he remained on the couch until the following morning, when I gently woke him with some breakfast. He thanked me profusely, quickly devoured it, and went on his merry way.

I later found out that Gregg had been fighting a heroin addiction since the tragic breakup of his band. He was receiving daily methadone treatments at a Century City clinic.

When Barry and I went to Gregg's opening at the Troubadour, the club was jammed to capacity. At a nearby table I spotted Cher, whom I hadn't seen since "Laugh-In." I'd heard she was launching her own series, having just divorced Sonny Bono.

"My friends brought me here," said Cher. "I don't know much about this guy, Gregg, but he seems pretty far out." She was already intrigued by him.

The music was fantastic. Gregg led the band into some of their classics, as well as his new songs. The audience stood and cheered throughout. After the set Gregg came over to our table, and Cher pulled her chair closer to me.

"What do you know about him, Judy?" she whispered.

"Well, he's warm and soft . . . very low-key," I told her.

As they were introduced, I could tell that Gregg was equally infatuated with Cher, so I suggested to everyone that we gather at my house. Cher gladly accepted a ride in Gregg's sports car and they followed us home.

By the time we arrived, they were in a world of their own. I put on some music and a joint was passed around while Gregg and Cher sat in a corner, talking softly and rarely taking their eyes off each other. Later I was alone with Cher as she freshened up in my bathroom.

"Tell me, Judy, what *else* do you know about Gregg?" she asked, brushing her lovely waist-length hair, just a bit longer than his. Cher never used drugs and seemed unaware of Gregg's problem. I didn't think it my job to tell her.

"Cher, he's a super guy and a great musician," I said. "But watch it—with all that hair, if you two get carried away in bed, you're liable to strangle each other!"

A few weeks later Gregg moved into Cher's Beverly Hills mansion. It was such a whirlwind romance that by the end of June they were married, and Cher revealed she was expecting a child.

When I next saw Cher, she was alone. Her pregnancy was just beginning to show, and although she looked radiant, she told me of her fears. "The doctors say the baby will be healthy, Judy, but I'm worried. . . . Gregg was addicted when I conceived."

"From what I've heard, Cher, it's only a problem if the *mother* is addicted," I said, trying to reassure her. "Don't worry—your baby can't help but be a superstar."

But Cher still had a lot to worry about. Gregg was spending too much time with Johnny Briefcase, and they often came to my house. Cher called one day when they were there. She'd been crying.

"Judy, I'm looking for Gregg. Do you know where he is?"

Gregg was on the couch, in no shape to talk, so J.B. motioned for me to tell her they'd left.

"Uh . . . he's not here, Cher," I lied, "but if I see him, I'll have him call you."

"Judy, when he goes out, his eyes are clear, his hair flows in the breeze, and his stride is confident. That's the person I love. But when he comes back, his eyes have no pupils, his hair is dirty, and his clothes are rumpled. I don't know him."

I felt terrible. Cher truly loved him and I couldn't blame her for thinking I was a bad influence. I'd convinced myself that I was helping Gregg by giving him a safe place to hang out, thereby protecting him from "unsavory" characters, but this was just a way of rationalizing my own growing addiction.

I didn't see either of them again after that day, but a few months later I was happy to hear that Cher had given birth to a healthy blond and blue-eyed boy, Elijah Blue.

> *August 12, 1975:* Depression reigns. . . . I'm missing a certain strength inside.
> Tears come easily. God, when will it end? I'll do anything to change this space. I'm trying to clean up, but it's a living nightmare. I loathe the people around me, my "friends," but I know I must change them myself. No one can do it for me. My true friends are bored with my scene; it's been going on so long, we're *all* bored with it. I must deal with it now. It's essential.
> If only I had the incentive of a job, to shift emphasis. . . .

That incentive came with an offer to appear in the Theater Guild's national tour of *Absurd Person Singular,* the Broadway comedy by English playwright Alan Ayckbourn. The tour began in October, so I had less than two months to solve my drug problem. It was time to seek professional help.

My doctor recommended a hospital in Westwood noted for discretion in its treatment of people in show business. There I was given a series of medications and psychiatric consultations that nipped my addiction in the bud. After a few weeks my system was clean, and I was released to begin preparing for *Absurd Person Singular.*

The touring company boasted an impressive cast. Sheila MacRae, who'd been in the original Broadway production, played the wife of Patrick MacNee, of "Avengers" fame. I played the batty suburban wife of Michael Callan, an old friend who'd starred in the Screen Gems sitcom "Occasional Wife." Betsy von Furstenburg, a veteran of TV soap operas, played the sophisticated but suicidal wife of English actor David Watson.

The cast got along splendidly, except for Betsy von Furstenburg, who treated everyone coldly and had the sense of humor of a toad. After our opening in Chicago the tension finally came to a head one night during the last act. As I cleared the dinner table during one of Betsy's speeches, a lighting fixture above the stage dislodged and came crashing down near my feet. The audience gasped. I made a face and shrugged, which drew a laugh.

Betsy glared at me and I feared she thought I'd deliberately distracted the audience. In the next scene, as I carried in a drinks tray, she grabbed a glass and threw the drink in my face, knocking my wig sideways and ruining my makeup. The audience laughed, assuming it was part of the script, but I went into shock. My "Sock it to me" days had *long* since been over.

The rest of the cast was equally aghast. There was an awkward silence. I was furious but I knew it would have been unprofessional to retaliate, so I restrained myself and delivered the next line.

Later, during a speech of mine, Betsy scraped a knife back and forth against metal, producing a sound worse than fingernails against a chalkboard. It wasn't quite loud enough for the audience to hear, but loud enough to make me wince as I tried to speak. Then she dropped the knife with a loud clang.

I was fed up. In the last scene, which involved the six of us playing a parlor game, I was supposed to hand Betsy an orange for her to hold between her knees. Instead, I reached for a pitcher of water and doused her. Again the audience roared, thinking it was planned, and the curtain came down to end the play.

Betsy and I lunged at each other and started grappling. Then the curtain rose for our curtain call. We quickly separated, smiled, and took our bows, but as soon as it came back down we were at it again. We repeated this procedure for three more curtain calls, until the cast finally had to pull us apart after the last curtain. "I'm going to *report* that bitch!" I heard Betsy scream as we were led away to our dressing rooms.

She did just that and it became a major incident. She sent an angry letter to Actor's Equity and a copy to *Variety,* which they printed. It was all very one-sided: Betsy von Furstenburg, the noble lady of the theater with a "von" in her name, was *far* more credible than Judy Carne, the outrageous "Sock it to me" girl. Even though the cast backed my story, I was reprimanded by Actor's Equity and warned that, if it happened again, my membership would be suspended. I later got a few congratulatory letters from actors who had worked with Miss von F., but my rebuttal letter to *Variety* was useless. The damage was done.

The gossip mongers had another morsel of dirt to circulate: I was a "troublemaker," prone to *cat fights*!

Barry and I spent Christmas knowing our relationship had disintegrated. He'd taken literally the motto "tune in, turn on, drop out" and was spending all of his time on a newly acquired farm near L.A. He was trying to escape the shadow of his father's reputation by pursuing the bucolic life of a farmer. He wanted me to quit show business and adopt his reclusive life-style, but it was an offer he knew I couldn't accept.

When Barry moved out to his farm for good, I felt more lonely than ever and soon found myself visiting Crystal's salon again. She was delighted to see me. Before long I saw that familiar Porsche pull up in front of the shop. Johnny Briefcase hopped out, grinning from ear to ear. He threw his arms around me, told me how much he'd missed me, and insisted we celebrate. Within minutes I was snorting heroin on the marble table in his office, welcoming the high like a long-lost friend. I quickly slid back into daily use and in a matter of weeks was readdicted.

This time, however, my sickness took on an uglier dimension. I was needing to snort more and more, and it had become a severe financial drain.

"You know, Judy, you won't need nearly as much if you *shoot* it," Crystal told me one day at my house. "Mainlining. It's far more economical—*and* a better high."

I was appalled. "Oh, no, I couldn't do that. I'm terrified of needles. I have a hard enough time giving myself *vitamin* shots."

Ever since childhood doctors had given me monthly shots of vitamin B-12 and B-complex, to combat my anemia. It kept my resistance up and stimulated my appetite. When I first went on the road, my doctor taught me how to inject myself: I'd pinch my derriere, slap it hard, and pop in the needle. I had a prescription for syringes, and Crystal knew that.

"*I'll* do it for you, love," she said. "I promise it won't hurt. C'mon, you don't know what you're missing till you give it a go."

She put a few small granules into a teaspoon.

"*That* tiny bit? I won't even feel it."

"Just you wait. This will keep you high all *day*."

The process began: She added a few drops of water to the teaspoon and lit a match beneath it, dissolving the granules into a brown liquid. Then she added a small cotton ball, to trap impurities as she drew the liquid into the needle from the cotton.

She tied a scarf around my arm and told me to clench my fist. I turned my head away, afraid to look, and felt the needle's sting. In seconds a burning sensation flashed through my body, a rush, a quiver, followed by calm, *incredible* calm, a deadening of nerve ends. All pain was gone. Crystal was right—I stayed high all day.

When I awoke, I was disgusted with myself, but nevertheless I found myself inviting Crystal over to do it for me again. And again. Sometimes I even stopped at her salon for an injection. When I finally got the nerve to put the needle into my arm by myself, it was the beginning of the end.

> *February 16, 1976:* Richard Pryor once said: "The only thing a junkie worries about is running out." I'm understanding that more and more. . . . I'm in despair again, not only about work prospects and bad habits, but because I have no money. I don't know what to do . . . once more, death seems warm company.

Morbid thoughts were commonplace. Showing my house to potential buyers was depressing, since signs of neglect were everywhere. Paint was peeling, weeds were popping up through cracks in the stone steps, and the foliage had grown so far out of control that it looked as though it were actually choking the house.

I found a new accountant to oversee the sale. After reviewing my tax returns, he was astonished. I wasn't aware of just how dire my financial affairs were. Not only had there been no tax planning, but my options hadn't been fully considered. I was eligible for loans from my unions and a payment schedule could have been arranged to allow me to keep my house. It was too late for that now.

> My house has just been sold, sadly. But I must be positive . . .
> I have a new nest to build, a fresh beginning.

Judes the Obscure

I rented a one-bedroom apartment on Hilldale Avenue south of Sunset Strip, and faced the nostalgic task of moving out of Laurelcrest. In the garage I discovered my MRS. BURT REYNOLDS director's chair. While moving out a china cabinet, I noticed a touching personal message on the back: "To Burt and Judy on your wedding day, may you have a happy life together, from Milburn Stone and Amanda Blake." I quietly wept as I took one last look at the memory-filled living room.

I lost the will to write in my journals anymore, and the entries were few and far between. There was nothing to write *about*; I'd just sit and stare at the blank pages for long periods of time and then pathetically scrawl *Help*.

> *May 21, 1976:* For the past two months I have been living a nightmare. . . . I've been obsessed with death, even desired it at times. At this rate I am slowly killing myself anyway. . . .
>
> Tonight I feel I am moving up and out. I realize that from this low place, if I am careful and stay aware of my actions, I can come out of the depths and stay there. I must. I'm being given a chance.

A kind and loyal woman who believed in my ability reached out to help. Ruth Webb, a key agent for the dinner theater circuit, offered me a chance to star in Jean Kerr's comedy *Mary, Mary*.

By now my habit had reached the point where I needed an extended cure. I went to a clinic in Century City that Gregg Allman had told me about and met with a psychiatrist who explained the program: For three weeks I would be given a daily glass of orange juice containing decreasing amounts of methadone. Three days a week I would have therapy sessions.

That was the good news. The bad news was that it cost five hundred dollars just to enter the program, and the daily treatments would run into the thousands. I simply couldn't afford it.

I had nowhere to turn. I couldn't bear the thought of asking my dad, and I knew there was no chance of getting a bank loan in my predicament. The only person I could think of who was in a position to help me was Burt.

I called his lawyer and said that something had come up, "a matter so personal, I can only discuss it with Burt." I was told to visit Burt at his house at 2 P.M. that Friday.

217

When the day came, I was ridden with anxiety about what to say and how Burt would respond. I put far too much emphasis on it all, fantasizing that he'd take me under his wing and guide me through my rehabilitation. Perhaps we'd even live happily ever after.

I drove up to his gate exactly on time, rang the buzzer, and was startled to hear Burt's voice over the speaker.

"Yeah? Who is it?"

"It's me, Judy . . ."

The gates parted electronically, and I drove down the lengthy driveway to his sprawling Spanish mansion, set in the trees. I parked in front of the house, which looked deserted, as though it were closed down. The front door slowly opened, and there he stood.

"How's that for timing?" I said nervously. "Dead on two o'clock."

"That was never one of your faults," he said, dressed in a suit. I noticed luggage lined up in the hallway.

"I've got to catch a flight this afternoon," he explained, leading me to his den. "If you'd been late, you might have missed me."

He went over to the saloon-style bar and poured us drinks.

"Burt, I'll get to the point," I began. "You know I wouldn't bother you with my troubles unless I was desperate, but I've had to sell Laurelcrest, and I'm deeply in debt. Worst of all . . . I've got a drug problem."

He stared at me and said nothing.

"I tried to get over it once before, but failed. This time I'm determined. I want to enter a clinic, but it costs five hundred dollars just to enroll, and I just don't have the money."

I wanted to assure him it was legitimate, so I gave him a card with the name and phone number of the clinic. "You can check, if you want to. They'll tell you how I'm doing."

"It's okay. I believe you." He produced a money clip from his pocket and counted out five crisp hundred dollar bills onto the bar.

I was stunned. The last thing I'd expected was to get *cash*. I'd wrongly envisioned that he'd want to get involved, perhaps by sending a check to the clinic directly. I didn't want a handout, I just wanted some *caring*.

"Burt, I feel bad about this . . . I shouldn't have come," I said, hanging my head. "I'd better go, I don't want to make you late."

I stared at the money for a moment, wanting so much to leave it there, but I couldn't. I needed it too desperately. He walked me to my car, and I thanked him again.

"I'm going to do it, Burt. *Really* I am . . ."

"I hope you do," was all he said, and we parted. I couldn't blame him for not wanting to get involved in my problems. As I drove away, disappointment overwhelmed me. The money would only cover the entrance fee to the clinic; I still wouldn't be able to afford the treatments. My body started to ache. Instead of driving home, I impulsively drove right to Crystal's boutique, where I used Burt's money to make my troubles disappear the *easy* way. . . .

June 12, 1976: The tears a lonely one can cry,
aiming another shot, fastened to die,
desire Transcendence
Artificially coming,
Hot veins burning
'tis only illusions.

I'd reached the level of addiction at which I needed an injection before I could function at all. I didn't have the confidence to walk onstage without it, so when the time came to go on the road with *Mary, Mary,* I had no choice but to maintain my habit. I gave Johnny Briefcase the money to send me weekly "care packages."

I felt it only fair to tell my co-star, David Watson, about my problem, since we'd become good friends on the *Absurd Person Singular* tour. He knew that I meant it when I promised I'd never let him down during a performance.

"Judy Carne and David Watson are an electrifying combination," wrote one critic after our opening in Oklahoma City. Said another, "Both English born and bred, Carne and Watson turn this American play into a Noel Coward drawing room comedy . . . a rewarding evening."

Everything was going smoothly until, three weeks into our run, my package failed to arrive. I called Johnny Briefcase in L.A., but his phone was disconnected. I started to panic at the thought of going through withdrawal while having to do a show every night.

Fortunately, I'd met a resourceful young woman named Leslie Sherwood, who handled public relations for the theater. She made sure that David and I weren't too bored or lonely during our stay and had arranged a constant stream of places to go and people to meet.

Leslie had become a trusted confidant, so I reached out to her for help. She enlisted the aid of one of her friends, a doctor who was sympathetic. He agreed to help me by prescribing the necessary medication to get me through the run of the show, on the condition that I would seek professional help when it was over. He wrote a prescription for Dilaudid—synthetic morphine.

There was an unforeseen side effect to this temporary solution: the strength and purity of Dilaudid raised my tolerance dramatically. I recorded a day's intake in my journal:

> *August 25, 1976:* A list of medicines:
> One D at 11 A.M.
> Two D's at 2:40 P.M.
> Half a Valium, 6:22 P.M.
> Two D's, 7:46 P.M.
> One Valium, 1:35 A.M.

I wasn't living, I was merely existing. Each day was an emotional pendulum that never came to rest. My most lucid moments were onstage, absorbed in the part of Mary, puffing furiously on cigarettes and gesturing à la Bette Davis.

The last stop on our tour was six weeks at the Pheasant Run Playhouse in the Chicago suburb of St. Charles. I'd been prescribed just enough Dilaudid to get me through the rehearsals and opening of the show, after which I'd promised to enter a Chicago outpatient clinic recommended by the doctor. Leslie was concerned about my welfare, so she came along as my girl Friday.

The opening night reviews in Chicago were all positive. That was gratifying, but my supply of Dilaudid was nearly depleted. The sand in my hourglass was quickly running out.

By the time I managed to contact the director of the clinic, Dr. Stephen Jacobs, it was the morning of a matinee day. I was already feeling early signs of withdrawal. When we arrived at Dr. Jacobs's office, I was shivering and barely able to talk.

"Please . . . you must believe me . . . I *want* to be helped," I kept repeating. He left his office and returned with some methadone in a glass of juice, which I eagerly swallowed. Soon I dried my tears and pulled myself together. I was a new person.

Dr. Jacobs set up a daily schedule of methadone and psychiatric therapy. His reassuring attitude convinced me that I had taken the first major step toward getting well.

I returned to the theater feeling uplifted and sailed through the matinee. At dinner I had the healthiest appetite I'd enjoyed in a long time. But later, as I put on makeup in my dressing room, my hands started to tremble. I began to feel tight and my shoulders hunched. Please, it can't be, I thought . . . not *again.*

I made it through the first act, but by intermission I was sweating profusely. David made me a cup of tea, and I prayed to God that I would just make it through the show.

During the last act my shaking was so noticeable that I had to improvise, "Look, you've got me so upset, I'm even *shaking!*" When the final curtain came down, I couldn't even take my bow.

David quickly threw his jacket around me. "Judy's got the flu," he told the concerned stage manager.

"I'll call the house doctor, then."

"No, no, that's okay," said David. "It's already been arranged."

He steered me to my dressing room, where I collapsed on the floor. Leslie was on the phone to Dr. Jacobs. "Judy's into total *withdrawal,*" she said frantically.

"I know, I was about to call you," the doctor told her. "I've just seen the results of her blood test. Judy's problem is more serious than I thought. Get her over here right away, I'll be waiting for you."

They wrapped me in a blanket and carried me out to the car. I was delirious when we arrived and only remember being taken into an elevator, a cup at my lips, and the doctor saying, "Drink this, Judy, you're going to be okay . . . just drink this. . . ."

As I came to, I could see David and Leslie smiling at me. I was bundled up on the couch in Dr. Jacobs's office.

"For a little lady, Judy, you've got the tolerance of a *horse,*" he said. "At five-feet-three-inches and one hundred pounds, it doesn't seem possible, but you need one hundred milligrams of methadone a day. We're going to give it to you for the rest of your engagement, with the strict understanding that you will then go directly into a hospital for further help."

I told him I wanted nothing more than to do *just* that.

Later that week I received an added incentive: Rick Allen, who managed the Burt Reynolds Dinner Theater, came to see the show and told me that Burt wanted it for his theater in January. I was encouraged by Burt's vote of confidence. It was now or never.

Dr. Jacobs helped me make the final step toward recovery—detoxification. When *Mary, Mary* ended in December, we discussed where to accomplish this. He knew I couldn't afford an expensive clinic.

"I know of a state hospital in Oklahoma, headed by a woman psychiatrist who has worked wonders for people with your problem. This hospital is primarily for the disturbed and mentally ill, and it may be rough in those surroundings, but I think this woman is the best there is."

I happily agreed. Spending Christmas in a lunatic asylum sounded no worse than the living hell I would return to in L.A.

"Can I register under an alias?" I asked him.

"Not really . . . it's a government hospital, so you'll need proper identification."

I told him that my green card bore the name Judy Carne Reynolds.

"That's perfect," he said. "I'll arrange for you to be admitted under the name J. C. Reynolds."

When I said good-bye to David Watson, I promised I'd be well when he next saw me. I *had* to be. In two weeks we would be in Florida, opening in *Mary, Mary* at the Burt Reynolds Dinner Theater.

As soon as we arrived in Oklahoma City, Leslie drove me straight to Lomax State Hospital, which was not far from her home. As we entered through the barbed-wire gates, it had the austere look of a prison, with gray walls, and bars over the windows. I was shaking with fear, so Leslie took my arm and led me in to be admitted.

"Your name?"

"Judy . . . Judy . . ."

"She's J. C. Reynolds," Leslie blurted out. Somehow I couldn't bring myself to say that name.

"Any personal effects?" In the car were my suitcases, my dog Whitney, and my show trunk strapped to the roof.

"I have some luggage outside," I said.

"Well, you won't be needing much in *here,* honey."

I put together a bag of essential clothes and toiletries and then said good-bye to Leslie. "Try not to worry, Judy," she said. "I'll take good care of Whitney, and I'll visit you each day." It was my only comforting thought.

The head nurse gave me an identification bracelet and collected my watch and valuables—including my lighter, nail scissors, and razor.

"These will be kept by us for your own protection," she said. "If you need them, you must ask an orderly, who will supervise your use of them." I was then told to take my clothes to the laundry room to be stamped with my name, before reporting to Dr. Purdy's office.

Dr. Purdy was a gray-haired woman in her fifties. She spoke in gentle tones, like a kindly aunt. "Dr. Jacobs has informed me who you are and the history of your problem," she began. "We're not able to give you any special treatment here. You're a patient, just like everyone else. You may find it difficult dealing with the other patients, but just try to concentrate on what you're here for."

Since I had only ten days in which to shed my dependence on methadone, my reduction rate would be much faster than what was usually attempted. "It will be painful, I know," said Dr. Purdy. "I'll see you every day, and talk you through it. Just take heart in the knowledge that, when you leave here, you'll be *cured,* and you'll have done it in the face of adversity. I think you'll find this achievement to be a great source of strength to you in the future. Good luck, Judy."

The nurse returned to show me to my ward—a large, run-down room with ten beds, each with its own small night table and clothes cupboard. The communal bathroom lacked mirrors, and had a row of stalls without doors.

"When your name is called, report for your medication over there," she said, pointing to the nurse's station. "And over here is the day room. I'll introduce you to some of the others." We walked into a noisy room full of women, some huddled around a television set, others playing cards, others just aimlessly pacing.

"Girls, this is Judy," she announced. Only a few turned their heads to look. A pudgy, elderly woman rushed toward me and began pulling at my clothes. "Ooohh! Lovely!" she cried, with a glazed look in her eyes.

"Now, now, Edna, mind your manners," the nurse told her. "I want you all to make Judy feel at home."

I sat down apprehensively and buried my head in a magazine.

"That's *my* comic book," said Edna, grinning at me. "You can have it . . . *if* you'll be my friend."

Before I could respond, a piercing scream came from across the room. A woman was writhing on the floor. Two orderlies rushed in, restrained her, then put a tongue depressor down her throat. After a fierce struggle, her body went limp and they released her. Then she calmly returned to her chair and resumed her knitting.

I was still trembling at this sight when Edna tapped my shoulder and whispered, "Look out . . . here comes Baby Jane."

An old woman approached, wearing a doll-like dress, with heavy makeup and a bow in her hair. *Whatever Happened to Baby Jane* was obvious—she was here at Lomax State Hospital.

"Would you like to play Ping-Pong?" she asked in a child's voice.

"Well . . . all right," I said, not wanting to offend her. She led me to the table, handed me a paddle, and said, "You serve first."

"But where's the *ball*?"

"We don't need a ball, silly. We can play *without* one!" she said, pantomiming a fancy shot. As I wondered whether I should return her imaginary ball, a loud bell sounded.

"Dinner time!" cried Baby Jane, and everyone scurried out of the room. I followed them into the cafeteria, and noticed the male patients filing in on the other side of the room, jockeying for position as they joined the line.

A foul-smelling man shuffled in behind me, eyeing my movements. Each time I put food on my tray, he removed it and placed it onto his, until I finally let him go ahead of me, his tray overflowing. The only way I could cope was by thinking of it as just another scene in this theater of the absurd.

After dinner I went back to the ward and found my clothes in a pile on my bed. Everything—even my underwear—was stamped J. C. REYNOLDS in black ink. I lay down on the lumpy mattress, looked up at the barred windows, and wept.

December 25, 1976: Well, dear book, it's Christmas and I'm in a nut house. I've been here three days, and at times I don't know whether to laugh or cry. So I do both.

The weirdness never stops: Bessie, with belly out, tits hanging, and ragged slippers, asked for a drag of my cigarette. When I gave it to her, she ground it into her *arm*. My, my . . .

Wanda, with red hair, red nails, and bloodshot eyes, is Lucille Ball gone wrong . . . today she accused me of stealing her husband. "I know your type!" she shouted as the orderlies took her away.

Judes the Obscure

Word has slipped out that I'm on TV. Poor Edna has been glued to the set all day, waiting for me to come on. . . .

God, I'm ready for the sequel to *Cuckoo's Nest.*

The days crawled by. I sat and watched the clock, counting the minutes until my sessions with Dr. Purdy. One afternoon Leslie brought Whitney with her. Since dogs weren't allowed inside the hospital, we had to meet outside by the fence. Whitney was so excited to see me, he was jumping up and down, trying to scale it one minute, then burrow underneath it the next. I could only poke my fingers through the wire to touch his nose, a simple pleasure that never felt so good.

> *December 28, 1976:* I'm weak from the reduction of methadone, but coping. If I lie down and think about it, I feel like I'm dying, so I walk around instead. I must keep myself distracted. . . .
>
> Good session with the lady doc. I realize that unlike the others in this place, I've done this to myself, and only I have the power to undo it. Hang on, Judes . . . won't be long now.

I was reduced from one hundred milligrams of methadone a day to none in only eight days, leaving an extra two days for observation. The drastic withdrawal put my body through painful changes, as the narcotic shroud around my nervous system gradually was stripped away, layer by layer. On December thirty-first, I was ready to be released.

Dr. Purdy was beaming. "Judy, I want you to know that your progress is not only remarkable, but in my experience it's *miraculous.* I have men in another ward being reduced at a fraction of your rate, screaming out in agony and begging for more methadone. How do you do it?"

"I have a goal, Doctor. I've got to be well to go to Florida for my play. I want Burt to see that I've pulled myself together."

When Leslie arrived to pick me up, I said good-bye to everyone: Baby Jane, Bessie, Wanda, and poor Edna, who was still at the TV set, waiting for me to appear. Then I said good-bye to Dr. Purdy.

"Call if you need to, Judy, and write if you can. But I must say, I hope I never see you again—except when you're working. *That* will be my reward."

"Mine too."

That night, after a wonderful home-cooked New Year's Eve dinner with Leslie and her family, I quietly celebrated my reentry into the world by taking a long, hot bath.

I was filled with pride and a sense of accomplishment as I boarded the plane for Florida the next day. Although I couldn't tell Burt about my ordeal, I felt sure he would notice my newfound confidence.

I was welcomed at the airport by Rick Allen and Mary Greene, Burt's secretary, who explained my itinerary in the limousine ride to the hotel. "Burt's going to stop by in a couple of hours," said Rick. "In the meantime, Mary will get you settled into your suite. It's a special apartment they provide for Burt, *gratis.*"

The entire hotel had a "Burt Reynolds" motif. Pictures of horses, guns, and rifles were everywhere, and the "BR" Cocktail Lounge was saloon-styled, with paintings, sketches, and photos of him.

Before he left, Rick handed me a set of car keys. "Burt thought you might like to drive this while you're here." He pointed toward a gleaming rose-colored 1956 T-Bird convertible with white-walled tires. I choked up. Burt knew I loved that car—he'd often talked about buying me one when we were married.

Mary then showed me to my luxurious suite.

"By the way, Judy, don't be alarmed if Burt looks a bit pale or thin," she said. "He hasn't been well lately."

"Is it anything serious?"

"They don't *think* so, but . . . I just thought I'd mention it."

She left me to unpack and I started searching for just the right thing to wear, eager to look my best. Then I tried each chair in the room, wondering what kind of pose would be most effective for Burt's dramatic entrance. Perhaps I should be sitting, poring over my script . . . no, I'll stand by the curtains, admiring the view, and then slowly turn.

As I pondered this dilemma, the phone rang. It was Mary, in the lobby with Rick and Burt. They were on their way up. I took one last look at myself in the mirror and then struck a casual pose by the sofa just as their knock came.

"Come on in," I said. Mary and Rick entered, leaving Burt in the doorway with a grin on his face. "You look great," he said.

"Not bad for an old broad, don'tcha think?" I said. As we hugged, I could feel his bones. He looked gaunt and lacked that familiar spark. Something was definitely wrong.

"You'll love it here," he said. "They're going to take real good care of you." As we sat and chatted, Rick got a call summoning him back to the theater and Mary left, saying she'd return shortly.

"Well . . . alone at last," I said.

"Are you comfortable? Do you have everything you need?"

"Yes, I do. It's so wonderful of you, Burt, especially the car. You remembered . . ."

"Aw, shucks, it's nothin'," he said. "Listen, you've got to come out to the ranch to see Burt and Fern while you're here. I want you to see my horses."

"I'd love to." Suddenly Burt wheezed. Then his breathing became erratic, and he began gasping for air. He was hyperventilating.

"Burt, what's wrong?"

He backed away from me. "Can't . . . breathe," he said, retreating into the bedroom and curling up on the bed. I asked if there was anything I could do, but he shook his head and held out his arm to keep me away. "Just call Mary . . . *quick.*"

I dialed the front desk. They located her immediately. I then knelt by the bed in tears, feeling utterly helpless as I watched Burt in such agony.

Mary arrived quickly with his medicine. Then she led me into the living room. "He'll be okay now, Judy. The doctors don't know what's wrong with him yet, but he's had some tests. . . ."

Just then Burt emerged from the bedroom. "Mary, you'd better take me home," he said weakly. "Don't worry, Judy, I'm okay . . . I'll see you out at the ranch." He managed a wink and then he was gone.

I was stunned, and sat down to try to compose myself. What was happening? I'd just come *out* of a hospital, yet Burt looked as though he was on his way *in.* . . .

When we began rehearsals the next day, I was reunited with David Watson, the one person who knew how I'd *really* spent my Christmas. He was delighted to see me looking well, and our rapport on-stage was better than ever.

A few days before opening night Mary arranged my visit to Burt's ranch. Getting there was no problem, since every roadsign and billboard pointed the way to the B-R RANCH. Burt was playing with his dogs in front of the main house when I pulled up in the T-Bird.

"You want a ride, handsome?" I said.

"Sure, I'm just goin' up the road a piece."

"Well, hop in . . ."

He took me on a quick tour, starting with the stables where he kept a dozen Appaloosas, ending at the old general store/souvenir shop where tourists could buy feed, grain, and Burt Reynolds memorabilia.

Burt's parents were waiting for us back at the house. They were the same as ever, Fern offering home-baked treats, and Burt, Sr., in his rocking chair, asking after my parents. As the four of us sat there talking, it felt as though time had stood still.

Before leaving, I asked Burt about his health. "I was really worried the other night. Is everything all right?"

"Yeah. I'm going to be okay. They've found out what it is: *hypoglycemia*. A case of low blood sugar. I'll be fine."

"Will I see you on opening night?"

"Unfortunately, no . . . I have to leave for L.A. tomorrow to start work on a new project. But I know you'll be great." That project was *Smokey and the Bandit.*

At first I was crushed that he wouldn't get to see me perform. I wanted him to be proud of me. But as I drove away from his ranch that day, I was able to put it into perspective and see that at every low point in my life since we were divorced, I'd fantasized about being with Burt again. When all else failed, I always said to myself, "If only I were with Burt, I'd have a child and a good life."

I finally realized that the reality of Burt and me being together again could never live up to the fantasy.

11. Here Comes the Judge

My life was a vacuum when I returned to L.A. I was determined to avoid the drug crowd, and was out of touch with my closest friends, since I'd been afraid to let them see me when I was sick. Making new friends was difficult, since my reputation preceded me wherever I went.

April 1, 1977: I suddenly feel the need to write. I've been wanting this feeling for some time. I'm spending time with my ex-husband, Robert-the-Bergmann, remembering all the good and none of the bad. He called two nights ago and we've been in contact ever since. It's been six years and we've both grown . . . we've rapped out the old shit and it feels good. I'm very lonely, so it's comforting. I can't go back to my old habits. I'm living moment to moment right now. . . .

His phone call came from out of the blue, and as always, his timing was impeccable—I was lonely and more vulnerable than ever.

"Where are you?" I said.

"I'm just around the corner, but relax, I'm not going to hassle you. Everything's fine, I just want to see you for a few minutes. I have something for you. I promise you, it's not trouble."

Minutes later he was at my front door wearing a Cardin suit, silk shirt, and Cartier watch. With short hair and no mustache he looked younger and more attractive than ever. Outside, a BMW full of Louis Vuitton luggage completed his new image.

"Things have improved," he said. "I've just returned from Milan on a modeling assignment." He showed me a portfolio of layouts he'd done for *Vogue* and *Bazaar,* and said he'd also been back to Harvard for graduate school. Then he gave me a present—an antique cameo ring identical to one stolen from me when we were married. He said he'd found it after a diligent search of New York jewelers. I was charmed.

He used the phone to call a friend who was putting him up.

"What?" I overheard him say. "You don't have any room for me? That's okay. I'll try to find a hotel or something. . . ."

He looked dejected. "I can't stay there tonight. Do you know anywhere around here I could get a room for the night?"

Bergmann still knew how to push the right emotional buttons in me. Before I knew it, his Vuitton luggage was in my living room. "The bad things that happened between us won't happen again," he said. "We've both learned from it." In only a few hours he'd talked his way back into my life.

> *April 25:* Robert has his own survival problems; he's trying to help me with mine. I see him very differently from when we were married. . . . I feel my light coming back on.

The familiarity of being with Bergmann felt comfortable. We helped each other by going on a self-improvement program, attending group therapy sessions and exercise classes, all of which Bergmann paid for with a seemingly unending supply of traveler's checks.

> *August 15:* Ruth Webb has booked me to replace Virginia Mayo in a tour of *Move Over, Mrs. Markham,* the Cooney and Chapman comedy. . . . I'm young for the part, but at least it's a *job.*

I joined the play in Indianapolis and Leslie Sherwood flew up from Oklahoma to work for me again. In November we moved to Cincinnati, and Bergmann came to visit, since the theater gave me a two-bedroom apartment for the engagement.

He had some "college buddies" in the area with whom he would disappear for long periods of time, returning early in the morning. I didn't see very much of him; he always seemed to be going out on mysterious "errands."

Near the end of the run, I returned one night to find Bergmann passed out on the couch. Next to him, on the coffee table, was an open bottle of Quaaludes. The prescription bore the name of the house doctor at the Beef N' Boards Dinner Theater, a respected Cincinnati physician who'd prescribed my usual sleep medication. I knew this because the same doctor had recently renewed my prescription for Dalmane—a mild sleep medication that my regular physician prescribed.

"How did you get this?" I shouted, trying to wake him. He mumbled something about a prescription pad and then dropped back off to sleep.

When I woke up the next day, Bergmann and his luggage were gone. He left a note saying he'd taken a flight back to L.A. for a modeling assignment. I didn't know it yet, but the most harrowing and tumultuous period of my life had just begun.

During the last act of the play that night, I noticed some unfamiliar men milling around in the wings. After delivering my last line, I exited the stage and was confronted by two of them.

"Police officers, Miss Carne. We have a warrant for your arrest."

The audience burst into applause. I was handcuffed and my rights were shouted to me over the noise, while the rest of the cast waited onstage for my curtain call, unaware of what was happening. That bow never came. Instead I was taken to my dressing room where a stout, round-faced man with greasy hair flashed a badge.

"We're from RENU, the Regional Enforcement Narcotics Unit," he said. "You're being arrested for a felony—using a forged prescription to obtain narcotics." I stood there in shock as one of them frisked me and another searched the room.

"Before we take you to the station, we've got a warrant to search your apartment. As soon as you change into your street clothes, we'll be on our way." My handcuffs were removed, but the officers remained in the room. I was wearing only a caftan, with nothing on underneath.

"Are you just going to *stand* there?" I asked.

"We're not allowed to leave you alone."

"Could you turn your backs, then?"

"We're not allowed to let you out of our sight."

"Would *closing your eyes* be out of the question?"

They didn't budge, so I turned my back to slip on my jeans, pulled the caftan over my head, and grabbed the first shirt I could find. Through the mirror I could see them staring at me.

Leslie was detained outside, to prevent us from communicating. They put me into a squad car and drove to the apartment, and she followed us in my car with Whitney, who was cowering with fright.

The search began calmly and systematically as I watched, handcuffed, in the living room. Gradually they became more frantic, overturning sofas, dumping out drawers, and removing pictures from the wall. "Don't worry. We'll find what we're looking for," one of the cops said. He was red-faced and beginning to sweat.

After ransacking the place, they took me to a precinct across town for questioning. I was led into a bleak room with an old table and chairs, and a lamp hanging from the ceiling. It was an honest-to-God we-have-ways-of-making-you-talk room.

"You know, they can lock you up for a long time for this," one of them said, dunking a doughnut into his coffee.

"I don't know what you're talking about. . . ."

"I'm talkin' about a *felony,* Carne!" he shouted. "We want some answers. Where were you yesterday afternoon?"

"At my apartment."

"Who was with you?"

"My secretary, Leslie Sherwood."

With each question he pounded his fist into the palm of his hand. Then he grabbed the back of my neck and swung the lamp into my face. "Lemme see your eyes . . . *they'll* tell me what you're on."

You bastard, I thought, I've just been through all that. My eyes are *clear.* He released me with a shove.

"We're moving her," he said, storming out of the room.

"Hey, take it easy," one of the cops said, trying to console me. "He *gets* like this. . . ."

By 1 A.M. Leslie had awakened a lawyer and a bondsman, who were ready to bail me out. The problem was *locating* me. No police station seemed to know where I was. "She's in transit," was all they'd say. During the night I was taken to three separate precincts and questioned without the benefit of counsel. They were intent on breaking me down.

"You like cocaine, don't you?" one of them asked, pacing behind me. "*All* you people in show business like cocaine, don't you?"

I shook my head.

"Don't lie to me!" he shouted. *Wham!* I felt a fist slam into my lower back. My head snapped back and I fell down onto the floor.

"You people think you're better than everyone else," he said, pointing his finger at me. "You think you can do anything you goddamn please. Well, this time you're not going to get away with it!"

I was finally booked and fingerprinted at 4:45 A.M., after five hours of questioning. When the Men from RENU left, I was approached by a policewoman the size of a telephone booth, who took me into a cold examination room and ordered me to undress.

"But I've *already* been searched," I protested.

"Just keep your mouth shut and do as I say," she snarled. After an agonizing and humiliating internal exam, she gave me a blanket, led me to a dark cell, and slammed the door. A body moved in the top bunk bed and a dark face with huge eyes peered out from under the blanket.

"Got any cigarettes?" asked a husky voice.

"No, I'm sorry, they questioned me for hours. I'm out."

I thought perhaps I'd found someone sympathetic to talk to, but instead a hand reached down and snatched my blanket. "You wouldn't be fool 'nuff to tell, now, wouldja, *sister*?"

I lay there shivering, watching for dawn to break through a tiny window near the ceiling, wondering what was happening to me and cursing the day Bergmann was born.

"C'mon, get dressed, you two are due in court," a policewoman announced at 8 A.M. I was handcuffed to my cellmate, a behemoth black woman, and taken outside to the paddy wagon. There we were chained to five men who had been arrested with her. They were all charged with armed robbery.

We squatted on benches in the wagon, with bars separating us from the driver. During the drive the other prisoners noticed my gold watch and started grabbing at my wrist. A struggle ensued, and the driver ignored my shouts for help, but luckily we soon came to a stop and the doors flew open.

"Everybody out!" a cop ordered, herding us into a holding tank inside the courthouse.

"Miss Carne! Miss Carne!" I heard someone shout. A man with a briefcase was motioning to me through the bars.

"Miss Carne, I'm George Clark, your attorney. Miss Sherwood is outside, waiting for you."

"Thank God. Please, you've got to help me. . . ."

"Don't worry, we'll have you out of here as soon as possible. Once we see the judge and post bail, you'll be on your way home."

The judge scheduled my arraignment for the following week, and set bail at $5000—a large amount, he admitted, because the police told him I was leaving town and "might just jump bail."

Reporters, photographers, and a television crew were gathered to document my haggard exit from the courthouse. I then had to face another ordeal: it was Saturday—matinee day—and both shows were sold out. If I didn't perform, the manager could refuse to pay me for breach of contract.

The Cincinnati *Enquirer,* Sunday, November 13, 1977:

BEEF N' BOARDS STAR CARNE NABBED ON DRUG CHARGE
Judy Carne, television's "Sock It To Me" girl, was hit with drug charges by Harrison, Ohio, police, who arrested her early Saturday at the Beef N' Boards Dinner Theater after her performance in *Move Over, Mrs. Markham.* . . .

"Everything's going to be fine," Miss Carne said before performing her last two shows in the play here. "It's all been a mistake. I'm sure the charges will be dropped. I'm going to go out there and be funnier than ever."

By curtain time news of my arrest had already been on radio and television. The audiences sat stone-faced, almost defying me to entertain them as I struggled through the shows on automatic pilot. When it was over, my troubles were just beginning.

I was told to stay in Cincinnati for my arraignment, but we had to vacate the apartment, so Leslie went on ahead to Salt Lake City, where I· was due to open in *Mary, Mary.* I stayed with a friend, Madonna Crabtree, a member of Cincinnati's theater crowd. She accompanied me to court for moral support.

Here Comes the Judge

The men from RENU—clean-shaven and in their Sunday-go-to-meetin' clothes—presented the evidence against me: A woman named Barbara Brown, wearing a hat, dark glasses, and a beige raincoat, had walked into a local drugstore and filled a prescription for Quaaludes. The police were called in when the prescription was found to have been stolen from the house doctor at the Beef N' Boards. The pharmacist identified me as the suspect when the police showed him my picture in the *Move Over, Mrs. Markham* playbill.

My lawyer was not very encouraging. "I dunno, Miss Carne," he said, shaking his head. "That's a mighty serious charge."

New York *Daily News*, November 22, 1977:

JUDGE SOCKS IT TO THE 'SOCK IT TO ME' GIRL

Cincinnati (AP)—A drug case against Judy Carne was sent to a Cincinnati grand jury yesterday. . . . Cops say Judy used a false prescription to obtain Quaalude, a depressant. She faces 10 years in jail, and a $5,000 fine.

As we were leaving the courthouse, the plot thickened. The men from RENU suddenly arrested Madonna and booked her on the same charge, involving a different pharmacy. We needed a good lawyer *fast*.

Madonna's husband knew of a criminal attorney named Philip Pitzer, who had a strong reputation in the community. I was honest with him and described the scene with Bergmann that night before he left town. Pitzer was optimistic. It clearly was a case of mistaken identity.

Madonna's case was open-and-shut. They'd arrested her because she conformed to a description they had—buxom, with blond hair. But Madonna had a solid alibi: She was three months pregnant and had been attending a birthing seminar when the crime took place. (She later sued for false arrest and won $175,000 in damages, since the trauma had endangered her pregnancy.)

Pitzer said the case against me was weak. In their search of my apartment, the police hadn't found the prescription I'd allegedly filled, let alone the beige raincoat and hat I'd allegedly worn. The pharmacist was confused when the police showed him my picture, because I'd been in the same drugstore to fill my *own* prescription. Pitzer was confident I would be exonerated.

On Thanksgiving Day I left for Salt Lake City—the Mormon capital of the world. Because of my arrest people virtually boycotted *Mary, Mary.* Each night it was *granite* out there, as Lenny Bruce used to say.

To add injury to insult, I fell six feet onto a concrete floor and bruised the base of my spine when a stagehand failed to catch me as I exited a scene with a comic fall. I finished the play in agony and was so delirious when the paramedics came that I screamed at the sight of their uniforms, thinking they were police, there to arrest me again.

> *December 25, 1977:* Salt Lake City. Another Christmas to forget. . . . I sit here with back pain from my fall, feeling down and upset by the mess in Cincinnati. What next?

Two days after Christmas Pitzer called me with bad news.

"Judy, the grand jury just handed down its indictment. In addition to the prescription charge, they're charging you with possession of heroin."

"What? That can't *be* . . ."

"It's shocked everyone," he said. "I don't understand how they can suddenly claim to have found heroin, when there was no mention of it at the time of your arrest. An officer named Hensley said he found 'traces' of it that night in the apartment. The amount they're charging you with is microscopic."

I'd been through hell to kick heroin. Why was this happening to me *now*?

Philip explained that prosecutors sometimes "over-indict" when they have a weak case, in order to bargain the defendant into pleading guilty on one count in exchange for having the other dropped. He advised me not to accept any such bargain when the trial commenced in June. "Hang in there," said Philip, "we're going to get you through this."

I returned to L.A. in January and confronted Bergmann, who'd been staying in my apartment. He broke down and cried about the trouble he'd caused and vowed that he had changed his ways. He was two different people: the charming, level-headed Robert, and the erratic, belligerent Bergmann.

On the afternoon of February thirteenth he was the latter, so I finally asked him to leave. This led to a loud argument, during which

Here Comes the Judge

I managed to lock him out. A neighbor heard the commotion and called the police, who arrived to find Bergmann pounding on my front door, screaming at the top of his lungs.

When I came to the door, the policemen recognized me and their attitudes changed. They let go of Bergmann and started questioning *me*. Before I knew it, they were searching the apartment. The St. Valentine's Massacre had begun.

New York *Post,* February 14, 1978:

LAUGH-IN'S JUDY SEIZED ON DRUG RAP

Los Angeles (AP)—Judy Carne, the "Sock It To Me" girl, was arrested in her West Hollywood home for possession of dangerous drugs for sale. . . . Sheriff's deputies said they were responding to a domestic complaint when they noticed a plastic bag containing a white powdery substance resembling amphetamine sulfate.

Miss Carne, former wife of actor Burt Reynolds, was arrested and booked at the sheriff's Hollywood station.

The New York Times, February 18, 1978:

. . . A powdery substance found by the police in Judy Carne's Los Angeles apartment turned out to be a laxative instead of amphetamine, as the police suspected, so they have withdrawn all charges of possession of dangerous drugs for sale. . . .

In their zeal the arresting officers had dispensed with the formality of a search warrant, and they didn't bother to test the substance before hauling me into the precinct for booking. I called my Los Angeles lawyer, Richard Chier, who was able to settle the matter over the phone. But although charges were dropped, the damage was done. The story was front-page news all over the country.

That weekend, in desperate need of diversion, I accepted an invitation to go to Santa Monica, where an old friend, Claude Monaire, was promoting a rock concert at the Civic Auditorium. He'd arranged a hotel room for me, gratis.

I enjoyed the concert, but at the after-party people were openly taking drugs and getting rowdy, which made me uncomfortable. I retreated to my hotel room and curled up in front of the TV set.

John Belushi had just yelled *"Live! It's Saturday Night!"* in a samurai outfit when the phone rang. It was Claude, at the Santa

Monica police station. He'd been arrested for disturbing the peace after a fracas of some kind at the party and he needed his wallet from his hotel room to bail himself out. Sympathizing with his predicament, I got the bellhop to let me into his room. I grabbed the wallet and rushed downstairs to find a cab. There, in the lobby, was Bergmann.

"Don't start," I said, keeping him at arm's length.

"I came to see if you were okay. . . ."

"I'm fine, but Claude is in jail. I'm going to bail him out."

"I'll drive you." He had a blue Chevy parked outside. "I just rented it," he said proudly. It was late and there were no cabs around, so I got in and off we sped.

After driving only a few blocks, he ran a red light and a police car appeared behind us. Bergmann panicked and sped up.

"What are you doing?" I shouted.

"I don't wanna get pulled over!"

Sirens blared and another police car entered the chase from out of nowhere, forcing us off the road. A cop opened Bergmann's door and pulled him out in one swift move. Then my door flew open, and I was dragged out, thrown up against the car, and frisked.

"On your knees! Hands behind your head!"

I knelt on the pavement, felt the barrel of a gun at my temple, and heard a mortifying click. Then a flashlight was shone in my face.

"Well looky, looky, looky who we have here," the cop said. "You just can't stay out of trouble, can you, little lady?"

"Where did you two get this car?" another cop shouted.

"I just rented it," said Bergmann, kneeling next to me.

"Bullshit! We just ran a make. It's a stolen car."

"But I rented it from Avis, you can check it out."

"Oh, we intend to do a lot *more* than that." After a thorough search of the car, they found a joint in the ashtray and three codeine pills in Bergmann's jacket.

For the third time in three months I was booked and fingerprinted. This time the charges were "investigation of auto theft" and "possession of a controlled substance"—in this case, "one-fourteenth of an ounce" of marijuana. I was put into a cell for the rest of the night.

At daybreak I tried calling Richard Chier, but he was away for the weekend. I finally reached a dear friend named Frank Halatek, a scriptwriter, who put up his car as collateral for my bail. I was released at 2 P.M., after twelve hours in custody.

When Bergmann and I appeared in court the next day, a man from Avis Rent-A-Car testified that "a computer error" had caused them to report the car as stolen. The charges against us were immediately dropped, but the headlines had already blazed: SOCK-IT-TO-ME GIRL ARRESTED IN CAR THEFT, DRUGS FOUND; COPS SOCK JUDY AGAIN; CARNE ARRESTED 2ND TIME WITHIN WEEK, and on and on. . . .

Needless to say, Ruth Webb was unable to get me any more dinner-theater bookings. "Judy Carne? No, we offer *family* entertainment," managers would tell her. In a matter of days agents in all fields returned my photographs, saying they could no longer represent me.

The old show biz gag that actors use when they can't find work is, "I can't even get *arrested*." In my case, it was the only thing I *could* do.

The ordeal of the Santa Monica arrest gave Bergmann and me a common bond that brought us back together. I had no one else to turn to. With each traumatic event my health deteriorated; in addition to chronic nervous tension, I developed a kidney problem which my doctor diagnosed as the result of having been punched during my Cincinnati arrest.

On the night of March twenty-first, I felt especially ill. I was feverish, my mouth was dry, and my vision blurred. When I got into bed, I was unable to swallow my sleeping pill. It melted, leaving foam in my mouth. I called out to Bergmann, who came in and found me on the floor, trying to reach the bathroom. He called for an ambulance.

Miami *Herald,* March 22, 1978:

JUDY IS IN HOSPITAL: 'VERTIGO' OR OVERDOSE?

Los Angeles (AP)—Judy Carne was rushed to a Los Angeles hospital yesterday, foaming at the mouth, from what one hospital official politely called "vertigo" and what a sheriff's deputy labeled an apparent drug overdose. . . . Carne is facing a string of marijuana, heroin, and pill charges from practically one end of the country to the other.

The New York Times, March 23, 1978:

. . . She's been having a lot of difficulties lately, that's perhaps why, when Judy Carne was rushed to the hospital in Los Angeles, it was first reported she had suffered a drug overdose. As it turned out, the actress collapsed at her home because of a kidney ailment. . . .

According to the press, the rumor that I had "overdosed" was given to reporters by the policemen assigned to watch my apartment in an unmarked car. The news had reached my parents before I was even released from the hospital the next day.

I felt victimized by this destructive chain of events, and tried to stop the terrible momentum before it was too late.

The New York Times, April 8, 1978:

. . . [Judy Carne] has filed a false arrest suit against the City of Santa Monica, charging she has suffered worldwide damage to her reputation. . . . She was arrested twice in the past several weeks on charges of stealing a car, and dealing in and possessing dangerous drugs. The charges, felonies, were all dropped after the police admitted they had made a mistake.

All of this, said Miss Carne's attorney, "has disabled her, and she is unable to get work; even her hairdresser has told her not to come back to his shop."

My hairdresser's reaction was just one of many snubs. I couldn't get tables at my favorite restaurants, and the places where I had charge accounts suddenly wanted cash. Everywhere I went people treated me like a leper. When the police began round-the-clock surveillance, it was time to get out of town.

I had a few weeks before my trial in Cincinnati, so Bergmann's mother kindly offered us the use of her cottage in the sleepy old village of Pineville, Pennsylvania. I was afraid to go anywhere I'd be recognized, so the remoteness was a welcome retreat.

I got to thinking about my parents and the heartache they must have felt as they watched all my press clippings over the years change from positive notices to depressing accounts of my legal problems. I wrote them a long letter of apology, saying that I'd failed them and that I hoped one day I could make it up to them.

My dad replied with the most moving letter I have ever received.

"Stop doubting yourself," he wrote. "I want you to know that you have already surpassed any hopes and dreams your mother and I had for you. You've accomplished a lot. Don't blame yourself for every-

thing, for God's sake . . . that town in Ohio must have money to burn. I bet they could build something useful with the money they're wasting on this bloody trial. . . ."
New York *Post,* June 6, 1978:

CAREER DOWN THE TUBES
Judy Carne, TV's "Sock It To Me" girl, says "everything has been cancelled. Films, television, theater, commercial spots." She's on trial in Cincinnati on charges of possessing heroin and using a false prescription for Quaalude, and blames the demise of her career on a series of drug-related charges both in Ohio and on the West Coast. "We are fighting to clear her name," said her attorney, Philip Pitzer.

When I arrived in Cincinnati, the publicity was intense. Dozens of reporters were on hand to photograph my every entrance and exit from the courtroom, shoving microphones and cameras in my face. I took refuge in the ladies' room, but even there, a female reporter shoved a microphone into my stall!

The response from the public was warm and encouraging. Everywhere I went, people wished me luck and said they were praying for me. The courtroom was always filled to capacity, and many of the same faces returned each day, as though I were a friend or relative on trial.

The state's prosecutor, Fred J. Cartolano, was the first assistant to the Attorney General. He seemed to have a preference for highly publicized trials—the only other case he'd taken on that year was an obscenity trial against publisher Larry Flynt. As Pitzer had predicted, Cartolano immediately tried to bargain with me to plead guilty on the prescription charge, in exchange for a dismissal on the heroin charge. I refused.

I don't think I had a very objective view of my own trial. Bob McKay, reporter for *Cincinnati* magazine, wrote an article after it was over. He didn't take sides, but merely offered his many observations after sitting through all five days of testimony:

Miss Carne . . . is the kind of person who speaks through her body, especially in her mobile and expressive face. It is a face built for humor, made for a smile, a clown face with clown features that were not made for grief or age. When the light goes out of it, it falls apart, shattered. She wore heavy makeup to compensate . . . a mask for a troubled clown.

Enter Fred Cartolano. Judging by the bulldog leader and his spaniel-faced first lieutenant, bloodhounds must thrive as prosecutors. Jack Webb would love Mr. Cartolano. . . . Not a fashionable man, he wears solid color suits of brown and blue. His clothing, his appearance, his behavior all reflect an unmistakable, unshakable superiority.

Miss Carne's defense attorney, Philip Pitzer, is a tall, tanned dandy, with a long, dark brown mane . . . favoring dark pinstripe suits with lighter, silver-shaded ties that arched out before they plunged into his trim vest, flared trousers and suede shoes. He leaves the impression that his breath would smell like lilies and his words would be bouquets.

Pitzer worked hard to establish openings: an oath is no guarantee of the truth; mistaken identity is a common thing; and all entertainers are not hooked on drugs. He emphasized the "presumption of innocence, that priceless cloak that can be penetrated by only two things: an honest mistake, and perjury."

Cartolano clawed back by reminding the jurors that a third possibility is guilt. "Presumption has nothing to do with actual facts," he said. "If we brought Adolf Hitler or John Dillinger in here, you would presume them to be innocent."

When Cartolano was finished comparing me to Hitler and Dillinger, Pitzer was ready to challenge the evidence.

First came the heroin charge. Officer Doug Hensley testified that he found "traces" of heroin in a plastic straw, in the drawer of a bedside table. He admitted, however, that he had found it in Leslie Sherwood's room. Pitzer then reminded the jury that dozens of people had stayed in the apartment in recent months, because it was used by the theater to house transients—the actors in its productions.

Pitzer called two expert analytic chemists to prove that the substance found was not even heroin. Dr. David Cornette backed up the testimony of Dr. Joseph Edgar Roget Todd, a Ph.D. from Johns Hopkins, who explained that the amount found was so infinitesimal that the evidence was actually lost in the process of analysis. He also produced a model of a heroin molecule—which goes by the name diacetyl morphine—and told the court that it was not the substance on the police lab report.

When Dr. Todd was dismissed, the state's chemist, Dr. Walker, was called. Pitzer gave him a piece of chalk and asked him to draw a heroin molecule on the board. He wasn't able to do it.

"Would *this* refresh your memory?" Pitzer asked, handing him Dr. Todd's model.

"Yes, that's a diacetyl morphine molecule—heroin."

"But the police report shows that the substance found contained neither *di*—two—nor *acetyl*—red—components, correct?"

The chemist looked at the report and blanched. "Apparently not. . . ."

Pitzer approached the defense table as if he were through with the witness, but then he turned back for one last question.

"By the way, Dr. Walker, you know Dr. Todd, don't you?"

"Yessir, I do."

"Would you please tell the court *how* you came to know Dr. Todd?"

"He was my professor in analytic chemistry at the University of Cincinnati. . . ."

"What we have here, then, ladies and gentlemen of the jury, is a case of the *teacher* telling us that the *student* has not learned his lessons." Muffled laughter penetrated the stillness of the courtroom.

"No more questions," said Pitzer, returning to his seat.

After this hurdle I had to take the stand in my own defense, for two full days. It was a terrifying ordeal, especially when it came to questions about my arrest.

The Cincinnati *Enquirer,* June 8, 1978:

> DRUG AGENTS DENY CARNE BEATING CHARGE
> Actress Judy Carne said Wednesday she was beaten and humiliated by officers who arrested her in November at a Harrison dinner theater. . . . "I felt they had a lot of animosity towards me. I think they enjoyed the fact that I was an entertainer," she testified. . . . Each of the four agents denied her charges of brutality or of having forced her to disrobe in front of them. . . . Miss Carne, dressed in a burgundy suit and wearing a wide-brimmed hat, was unruffled while giving testimony, but she began crying softly when she returned to her seat.

Bob McKay described my testimony from his vantage point:

"I was thumped in the kidneys"; "They forced me to strip naked in front of them to change my clothes"; "I was treated very badly in jail. The woman who gave me the physical examination was very rough with me." Miss Carne pronounced these charges convincingly, like a manhandled Mary Poppins. "She's tellin' the truth," whispered a black man in the back of the courtroom. "Those guys are *madmen*. They lyin'. She's tellin' the truth."

After Miss Carne stepped down, the police officers were paraded one by one back on the stand to refute every charge she had made categorically, in a brilliant display of perfectly synchronized testimony. The lone deviation came from the Harrison police officer in on the case, who admitted that Officer Guthrie and the other men refused to leave the dressing room and refused to turn around, at which time, he testified, "Miss Carne got mad and undressed on her own."

The evidence in the trial, which Cartolano later called "adequate," was scant and vulnerable. There was no beige coat, no sunglasses, and no prescription vial. There were no fingerprints. The prosecutor tried his best to hang the defendant with her own words . . . but words, like a ten-second glance over the counter in a drugstore, are fleeting, and Barbara Brown was not described as to height, weight, age, hair color, or distinguishing features.

To this, Cartolano said: "Hey, if Raquel Welch were there, and I told you I saw her, you wouldn't say 'What did she look like?' She'd look like . . . *Raquel!*"

Each night after leaving the courtroom, I returned to a quiet motel room in the Cincinnati suburbs, where Philip would explain what was happening and prepare me for the next day. Madonna Crabtree would come by to comfort me, and my friend Frank Halatek flew in from L.A. to give me moral support and make sure I had someone to talk to.

June 8: Tomorrow I will find out my fate. I'm frightened . . . a tragi-funny thought: if the verdict is guilty, maybe I should swallow poison as I enter the jail and tell them, "I'm going to take this lying down!"

Hang on, Judes, it's going to be okay. . . .

On Friday morning the summations began. Pitzer was first.

Here Comes the Judge

"Eliminate all other facts and what you have left is the truth," he began, quoting Sherlock Holmes. "The question here is simple—do you believe Judy Carne? If you do, then nothing else matters, and you have no choice but to find her not guilty.

"We have clearly devastated and obliterated the heroin charge. As for the prescription charge, there are so many unanswered questions. First of all, who in their right mind would go to the same drugstore they normally use? It was the least likely place in the world for her to palm off a phony prescription.

"And where did the pills go? If they want to convict somebody, let's see 'em get the evidence together." Pitzer went into a lengthy rehash of all the discrepancies in the state's case. "They've got the facilities, they've got the men—why don't they *use* 'em?

"The presumption of guilt is a grim reality, folks, the kind of thing that undermines our system of jurisprudence." He walked over and put his hand on my shoulder. "Judy Carne should not be required to suffer any longer."

There was a deafening silence in the courtroom as Pitzer returned to his seat. Then it was Cartolano's turn.

"It's funny the way the bad guy is always the cop, and somebody else did it," he said, pacing in front of the jury. "But there's no stage or TV writer writing this play, so let's not talk about these smoke-screens." He stopped pacing to make his big point.

"This isn't just you or me we're talking about, this is the 'Sock it to me' girl! She has a very severe problem. This is not a stage for her, this is her *life*. A verdict of not guilty would only compound her problem. Someone must help her. That's her only chance. She's a victim of her own acts. I urge you to return a verdict of guilty, so that she can get the help she so desperately needs."

Ten years in jail wasn't exactly my idea of therapy, but there was nothing I could do anymore. Judge Thomas Heekin charged the jury, and they filed out of the courtroom just before noon.

When Philip and I reached the corridor, there was a big commotion among the press corps. Bergmann had just entered the courthouse and was being arrested by the men from RENU, who couldn't believe their eyes—there he was, just *standing* there! Pitzer had warned him not to show up at the trial, since a warrant was out for his arrest, but Bergmann had flown in anyway. The men from RENU proudly led him away in handcuffs, and as the jury decided my fate, I had to make frantic calls to Bergmann's family to arrange his bail.

On my way back into the courtroom I noticed Judge Heekin's name being scraped off the door to his chambers. It was his last case before retiring, and it reminded me of show business, the way your name is wiped off the dressing room door before you've even packed up your belongings. When we returned to the courtroom, the judge gave a little speech, commending both Cartolano and Pitzer for the way they handled their cases. He said it was the most memorable trial of his career.

The five-hour wait in the corridor seemed shorter than the few minutes it took the jury to file back into the courtroom. Everything seemed to be in slow motion, especially Judge Heekin's ominous words: "Ladies and gentlemen of the jury, have you reached a verdict?"

"We have, your honor," said the foreman, handing it to the clerk.

"On the count of possession of heroin, the jury finds the defendant, Judy Carne, *not* guilty."

Cheers broke out in the gallery, and Judge Heekin pounded his gavel. "Order! We must have order!"

"On the count of using a false prescription to obtain narcotics, the jury was not able to come to a decision."

"Do you feel that further deliberation would be productive?" the judge asked the foreman.

"No we do not, your honor."

"Then the case is dismissed." Judge Heekin struck his gavel for the last time in his career and pandemonium broke out in the courtroom. I hugged Philip and felt as though the weight of the world had just been taken off my shoulders. We emerged from the courtroom to face the television crews, who were waiting to go on the evening news, *live.*

The Cincinnati *Post,* June 9, 1978:

TEARFUL CARNE WINS ACQUITTAL

Judy Carne cried, hugged friends, addressed reporters and signed autographs for the courthouse cleaning staff, as she celebrated her acquittal in Hamilton County Common Pleas Court. . . . When the verdict was read and Judge Heekin dismissed the jurors, Miss Carne hugged the friends who have surrounded her during the trial—laughing and crying at the same time.

Cincinnati *Enquirer,* June 9, 1978:

ELATED CARNE SEES NEW LIFE AFTER VERDICT

. . . As tears flowed down her face, Miss Carne said she will use the verdict to "start a new life." She said she was anxious to resume her acting career that was disrupted when she was arrested here on November 10th. . . .

"I'm going to leave this town with a good feeling about the people here," Miss Carne noted. She said she may return here for another play someday. . . . "The next performance will be the best of my life," she exclaimed.

The celebration was short-lived, since Pitzer and I had to bail Bergmann out of jail. I didn't even want to hear an explanation about why he'd come to Cincinnati. I just wanted to get out of town as soon as possible, so we took the next plane to Philadelphia and drove to the cottage in Pineville.

Columnist Joe Adcock wrote in Philadelphia's *Sunday Bulletin*:

. . . One is tempted to speculate a bit on Miss Carne's recent misfortunes. Police and prosecutors know they can get a lot of publicity by busting prominent people. The people shouldn't be *too* prominent, though, because they have powerful friends and remarkable lawyers who make the locals look like fools. . . . But a performer who is having trouble is a good mark.

After the trial Fred J. Cartolano ran for judge in Hamilton County with a campaign slogan borrowed from the American Express commercials: "Do you know me?" he asked in radio ads and handbills. "I prosecuted *Judy Carne* and *Larry Flynt!*"

Cartolano's campaign was so effective, he defeated a judge who had been on the bench for over twenty years.

Officer Doug Hensley, who found the alleged "traces" of heroin, was not so lucky. A year later he was pressured into resigning from the police force or else face criminal charges for tampering with evidence. He had allegedly planted drugs while working on a case.

My fate was even more dramatic. Only six days after my acquittal, I broke my neck in—of all places—the town of New Hope, Pennsylvania.

12. Reincarnation

Philadelphia *Journal,* June 17, 1978:

JUDY CARNE BREAKS NECK IN BUCKS WRECK

Judy Carne suffered a broken neck when a station wagon driven by her husband, Robert Bergmann, skidded off Rt. 232, Windy Bush Road, and slammed into a utility pole.

"You know kids with their cars, the way they drive," Bergmann said. "Well, this clown tried to pass, and we went off the road."

Makefield Township police said the car plunged into a drainage ditch after hitting the utility pole. . . . Bergmann was charged with operating a motor vehicle without a license and with an expired expiration sticker.

"I'm not worried about that," said Bergmann. "The great thing is that Judy's alive."

My eyelids fluttered as I regained consciousness in the intensive care unit of Temple University Hospital. My life was actually flashing before my eyes, a montage of scenes from my past: . . . as a little girl, I'm dancing under the watchful gaze of Noreen Bush . . . then I'm older, singing on a stage . . . I see the HOLLYWOOD sign, lots of glitter, my wedding, Burt, all of these images racing by . . . and then I'm alone. Next I'm being congratulated, and my name is in huge letters on a billboard . . . but suddenly it's being torn down. Finally a judge appears, pounding his gavel.

Like slides on a rapid-fire carousel, the images came split seconds apart, the last of which was me, getting into a car . . . then I woke up.

There were clamps on either side of my skull, and I was hooked up to a life-support machine. The first face to emerge from the blur was that of Dr. William Buchheit, head of neurosurgery at the hospital, who looked at me through horn-rimmed glasses with a curious smile.

"I know I've broken my neck, Doctor, I heard the voices.

"Don't worry, Doctor. I'm going to live. Only the *good* die young."

I was soon visited by a woman with kindly eyes and a soothing voice. "Hello, Judy," she said softly, "you don't know me . . . I'm Henry Gibson's sister, Sally."

"Aahh . . . *Heeenry*?" I asked groggily. "Is he *here*?"

"No, he's in California, but I work here at the hospital. I just came to tell you that Henry and Lois are thinking of you, and that I'm going to visit you every day when you get out of intensive care."

I was in a fog but her words came through loud and clear. What a divine coincidence—Henry's *sister*!

On the fourth day I was taken off life support. There had been no creeping paralysis, and I realized then that I was going to recover.

The nurses gave me a mirror, and I saw my face for the first time since the accident. There were no scars, thank God, but I was astonished to see that my hair had turned *orange*. I had colored it auburn before the accident, but the shock of the accident turned it silver—mixing with the auburn to produce an orange hue.

I had bed sores on my back from lying in the same position for so long, but this was remedied by an ingenious machine resembling a dry cleaner's steam press. I was strapped in between the layers and then literally flipped over, like a pancake. The next thing I knew, I was facing the floor and the nurses were spreading talcum powder on my back—a wonderful feeling of relief.

After a week in intensive care, I was fitted with the steel halo. A team of surgeons attached the brace to my head with four screws that, without breaking the skin, actually *dug* into my skull. I was allowed no anesthesia during this procedure because the doctors had to judge the depth of the screws by the amount of pain I was in. A fraction of an inch too far could result in brain damage.

"We know how painful this is for you, Judy," they said. "If you want to scream, fine, but try not to, it'll just make it worse. We'll give you something for the pain very soon."

As each screw was slowly tightened, I grimaced and let tears express the pain. "Atta girl, Judy," the doctors kept saying as they attached the four steel rods of the halo to a plaster cast, aligning my head with my body. When it was over, I was finally given a shot for the pain and taken to my own room.

Suddenly there were magazines, newspapers, and television. Glorious, *color* television. I spoke to my worried parents in England and my dad said he would fly into Philadelphia the following week.

Henry Gibson's sister, Sally Miller, visited each day, bringing me home-cooked food and other presents, like an extra-large nightgown to fit over my steel cage. She helped me sort through sacks of mail from all over the world—well-wishing letters containing St. Christopher medals and crucifixes.

I was soon able to make it to the bathroom with the aid of a walker, and then, exactly two weeks after the accident, I took my first walk down the hospital corridor and visited with some of the other patients. My progress was so encouraging, the doctors consented to release me early, under Bergmann's care, who had by now convinced everyone—including me—that he was in total control. He had assured the hospital that he was my husband, and no one was doubting his version of the accident.

Fortunately he didn't get away with it. My dad arrived that night and set the record straight. He immediately assured Dr. Buchheit that Bergmann was no longer married to me. "I think it only fair to warn you, Doctor, if I see 'im, I shall kill 'im," Dad said vehemently. "If I were you, I wouldn't let 'im past the threshold of your hospital."

Dr. Buchheit was relieved to hear this, and gave the order to have Bergmann barred from the building.

Evening Bulletin, June 29, 1978:

IT'S BEEN JUDY CARNE'S *WORST* YEAR

"Have I got a headache!" says Judy Carne, raising her eyes toward screws in her forehead that attach the "halo" to her body. . . .

. . . Her physician, Dr. William Buchheit, comes in. He wants to give a testimonial. "What a patient," he says. "From the time she came here ten days ago, her attitude has been wonderful. You know what she said when I first saw her? 'I guess this is the ultimate "Sock it to me!"' ' She's been cheering up the people on the floor, especially the kid in the next room. You don't practice medicine in a big city without getting to know the signs of a person who's on drugs. Judy isn't."

. . . Miss Carne hopes that this is the final misfortune in what has been her "worst year to date. I think I'm being saved for something. Whether for my career, or for my soul."

Dad arranged for me to be flown home on the Concorde, which required the help of British Airways' medical teams in both New York and London. I was boarded ahead of time in a wheelchair and then settled into a front row seat, surrounded by four large pillows. As the other passengers boarded, they were shocked by the sight of this space-age Bride of Frankenstein.

I was warned that the halo was not likely to fit in the Concorde lavatory, so I tried to make it through the flight. After a delicious meal and plenty of wine, however, I just *had* to go, and called for the stewardesses. They helped me to the door of the loo, but it was obvious I was not going to fit with the halo. I was so desperate, I bent over, shuffled in backwards, and lifted my leg like a dog, to the amazement and amusement of the startled crew.

The British press was out in full force at Heathrow, so when my parents met me at the gate, I got up out of my wheelchair and did a few steps for the photographers. Then it was into an ambulance for the hour and a half ride home to Northampton.

London *Daily Express,* July 18, 1978:

"SOCK-IT-TO-ME" GIRL JUDY IS HOME AGAIN
WITH A HALO OF STEEL AND COURAGE

C is for courage—and Judy Carne. She flew into Britain yesterday, down on luck but rich in bravery. Eight years ago she was a star with a million dollars in the bank. Now Judy is back home—with a broken neck and almost penniless.

. . . But 38-year-old Judy, whose catch phrase was "Sock it to me!" is still socking it to everyone. . . . "I have been saved for something and I feel it is going to be great from here on in. . . . Somewhere inside there was something fighting for me. When you have been close to death it makes you realize what you are all about."

Waiting for me when I arrived at Carne Lodge was Nurse Pat Freshwater, a cheerful lady who helped me through every step of my convalescence. She constructed an igloo of pillows on my bed, which would be my nest for the months to come. Every day Nurse Pat came to wash me, feed me, and put antiseptic ointment around the screws, since an infection would result in brain damage.

Nurse Pat always had funny stories about her other patients. Once she arrived after visiting an eighty-eight-year-old man.

"I was washin' 'im, Judy, and all of a sudden, his willy stood right up in the air!"

"What did you do?"

"What else could I do? I threw a cold cloth over it and suggested a cup of tea!" I looked forward to Nurse Pat's visits because she always made me laugh.

Luckily, one of England's finest orthopedic surgeons, Dr. J. Scott Ferguson, was only a few miles away at Manfield Hospital. His very name had the sound of eminence, and his perfect manner, tailored suits and waistcoats made me swoon when he first walked into my bedroom. Instead of a doctor's bag, he carried a common mechanic's tool kit, from which he produced a spanner and screwdriver to tighten the screws in my skull. This had to be done once a week.

"While you're at it, Doctor, would you change my oil?" I joked.

The family physician, Dr. Hall, was seventy-six years old and retired, but he still treated long-standing private patients such as my parents, and me, whom he had brought into this world. He had ruddy cheeks and a healthy glow—the last of the old-school, country squire doctors—and although his eyesight was failing, his uncanny sense of touch more than compensated.

I had been advised to exercise my arms and legs, in preparation for having the body cast removed, so I started isometrics and yoga. I'd sit on the floor, take hold of each leg, and extend it up into the air. When Dr. Hall arrived one day to find me doing this, he was alarmed. "You mustn't do that, my dear," he said, squinting at my outstretched leg. "People who are *well* don't do that!"

July 30: Funny things people say to me in my cage:
"You do take that off at night to sleep, don't you?"
Others say "Keep your chin up, Judy." Silly sods, where *else* am I going to keep it?

Reincarnation

In the shop today Mum heard a mother tell her kid, "Look, that's Judy Carne's mummy, the one in the newspaper."

"You mean the one with the TV aerial on her head?" said the boy.

My parents encouraged our family and friends to visit as much as possible. Some of them would break down and cry at the sight of me, amazed that I was joking after what I'd been through.

My mother had been going to a local hairdresser named Jon Barratt, whom she brought to visit one day. His look and disposition reminded me of John Lennon, and he had a great sense of humor. He'd heard so much about me from Mum that he felt he knew me. I couldn't believe my luck; he was someone I could relate to, and he lived in an eighteenth-century cottage a mile up the road. He often stopped by on his way home from work with Shep, his faithful sheepdog, to give me a boost in confidence by trimming my hair around the halo and toning down the hideous orange color.

I was visited by the first patient to use a halo in England, back in 1956. He was a Midlands miner who told me that I would still feel the screws in my skull long after they'd been taken out. He also warned me that when the sixty-five-pound apparatus was removed from my ninety-five-pound body, I would have no sense of balance and would feel rather weightless at first.

I was X-rayed each month and shown the plates, which allowed me to watch the break slowly knit itself back together—a truly miraculous process. We had a betting pool among family and friends as to the exact day and time I would shed my halo. Dad won: on September twenty-fourth, at 11 A.M., Dr. Ferguson gently unscrewed the steel from my head and then his team of assistants removed my body cast with an electric saw. For the next three months I was to wear a cervical collar.

As predicted, I was bouncing off the walls as I left the hospital. My head felt like a buoy in the water. Dad wanted to tie a brick around my waist to keep me from flying away.

When I returned to Carne Lodge, my mother had a hot bath ready and waiting. It was my first in *five* months, a glorious feeling.

Later Jon cut my hair short, matching the growth from the bald spots in the back of my head where the screws had been, giving me a "Joan of Arc" look.

My first excursion alone wearing the soft collar was to see Stirling Moss, in London. I boarded a train feeling brave and bold, like a child visiting a big city for the first time.

Stirling was in typically fine humor. He was testing a new jeep for British Leyland and insisted I come along. We started to tear through the streets on another of Stirling's famous test drives, weaving in and out of the crowded London traffic. Fifteen years earlier, I had helped him recover from a near-fatal accident; now, he was doing the same for me. That jeep ride ended my fear of being driven in a car again.

For my first night out on the town Jon and I went to the opening of Diana Dors's act, in which she sang and told wonderfully outrageous stories about herself, many of which had been in her best-selling autobiography. After the show she told me how rewarding her book had been and encouraged me to write my own story.

In the spring of 1979 I turned forty, and loved every minute of it. My dad reminded me of something that Burt had always said: "Judy won't really come into her own until she's forty. . . ."

As it turned out, he was right. I had the good fortune to meet a wonderful personal manager named Jo Peters, a woman not much older than myself, who had been a singer in her early years before going into management. In Jo Peters I found someone trustworthy to a fault, who knew how to inspire the right kind of confidence in an artist. Her first piece of advice to me was, "Judy, I can't tell you the secret of success in this business, but I can tell you the secret of failure: trying to please all of the people all of the time." These words made an impression on me. All my life I'd been guilty of trying too hard to please everyone, without first considering what pleased *me.*

I started to work again, beginning with television game shows and radio comedies. I returned to the stage in a national tour of Noel Coward's *Blithe Spirit.* I portrayed Elvira, the mischievous ghost who comes back to haunt her husband, played by Henry McGee, a brilliant actor and longtime straight man for Benny Hill. We did sixteen weeks in as many towns, a demanding schedule that gave me renewed confidence in my endurance as an actress.

On Christmas Eve of 1980 my parents retired from their business. This gave my dad time to pursue his desire to settle the score with Bergmann.

Reincarnation

The car involved in the accident was owned by Bergmann's mother and fully insured, but the insurance company had failed to pay my medical expenses, which by now had added up to a small fortune and had come from my father's pocket. A lawyer advised me to sue for the money, and said I could also collect for lost earnings while I was disabled. The company demanded a trial, so in July I returned to Philadelphia with my dad to face Bergmann in court.

To this day I shall never understand why Bergmann forced yet another trial on me. Apparently the only way he could prevent me from collecting from the insurance company was by "defamation of character."

For one agonizing week I had to listen to my life described in lurid detail: every bust, every hospital stay—even my traffic violations. The worst part of it all was that my dad had to suffer through hearing these things, many of them for the first time.

"Were you not addicted to heroin when you entered Lomax State Hospital in 1976, Miss Carne?" asked Bergmann's lawyer.

"Yes . . . I was," I said softly, looking at my dad and starting to cry.

For his summation the lawyer really went in for the kill: "Ladies and gentlemen of the jury, whom are we to believe? Are we to believe the word of a former drug addict? Are we to believe this woman, who has been in jails all across the country?" He walked over and stood in front of an American flag. "Are we to believe this actress, a fallen star from a foreign country, who has come here to ask us for *money*? I think not, and I trust you will think the same."

Later, outside the courtroom, I told my dad how sorry I was that he'd had to hear all of that. "Joyce, that was the past," he said to me. "All that's over with—you've got to think about *now*."

He was so right. By now Bergmann's antics had become theatrical. Throughout the trial he sat next to a man in a clerical collar, to whom he frequently whispered.

Fortunately my attorney, Richard Malmed, was fully prepared and welcomed the opportunity to question Bergmann on the stand.

"What time of night was the accident, Mr. Bergmann?"

"Around ten."

"In your deposition you say you were driving on a dark country lane. Is that right?"

"That's correct."

"And you say this car came at you on that dark country lane?"

"That's right."

"And you claim to have seen the driver of that car that supposedly came at you on this dark country lane in the middle of the night?"

"Yes."

"You've given us a description—blond hair, gray T-shirt, plus the make and model of this mysterious car."

"That's right."

"That's commendable, under the circumstances, since his headlights during that split second must surely have blinded your eyes. . . ."

Bergmann persisted, but Malmed finally slammed the door on him by calling to the stand a policeman who testified that Bergmann had said right after the accident that the car had come from behind.

Thankfully, the jury saw through Bergmann's testimony and I was awarded a total of $95,000 in damages: $45,000 for lost wages, and $50,000 for "pain and suffering."

Finally I was able to reimburse my father for my legal and medical expenses. This was small change, however, compared to the heartache the trial must have given him.

During the trial my dad's health was not good. His skin had a gray pallor and he frequently complained of stomach pain. When we returned to Carne Lodge, Mum and I tried to convince him to see a specialist, but Dad was stubborn. It was late November when he finally agreed, after much pleading, to let me take him to an internist, who X-rayed him and promptly suggested exploratory surgery the following week.

After the operation Mum and I visited him in the hospital. The nurse told me that the surgeon wanted me to call him at home. She let me use her office to make the call. The doctor told me that the operation revealed cancer of the liver, and my dad was not expected to live more than three months.

I put the receiver down and felt as though I were in a trance. I just stood and stared at the wall while the nurse brought me a cup of tea. I mustn't break down, I said to myself, not yet. I had to tell my mother and I knew if I crumpled, so would she.

"Where have you been, then, Joyce," my dad asked in a croaky voice when I returned to the room.

256

Reincarnation

"I was just checking to see what medicines they're giving you, Dad," I said with a smile, acting like a character in my own play. "You know I'm just a frustrated nurse."

This act was convincing enough at the time. But when we got home later, my mum could tell something was wrong.

"He's going to die, isn't he, Joyce?" she asked. I didn't have to tell her; instead we just sobbed together, letting out our grief, knowing we could not do this again, since Dad would be coming home the next day.

Nurse Pat Freshwater was assigned to visit Dad each day, which pleased him. Having helped me through my rehabilitation, she was considered family.

It was the longest winter of my life. Mum and I had a schedule to follow, since twenty-four-hour nursing was needed. Dad would look out his bedroom window at the snow and sleet, and then smile. "I'm in the best place in this bleedin' weather, Joyce," he said. He really enjoyed missing the foul weather for a change.

One day in February Dad suddenly said, "I'm goin' to make it till April, Joyce. That's what I want. April is our month—your mum and I were married, and you were born. I'm not goin' till it's April. . . ."

It was the first time he'd mentioned death. I looked at Mum, who said, "Oh, Harold, we don't want to hear all that depressing talk, 'cause when you're better, you'll laugh when we remind you what you said." Our smiles couldn't hide the tears streaming down our faces.

By March first Dad was already on borrowed time. He was by now a frail shell, shrinking before our eyes, but he never lost his sense of humor. On March twenty-first, he had a smile on his face.

"You know what day it is today, don't you, Joyce?"

"No, what day is it?"

"The first day of spring . . . the day you got your first job."

"If that isn't a cue for a song, Dad, I don't know what is!"

March 21: I'm sitting next to Dad in bed, listening for his breathing. God, please let him make it until April. I'm looking out of the bedroom window at spring flowers trying to bloom, while here is my dad, trying to hang on until the first daffodil appears in the garden. . . .

In Dad's last weeks Dr. Hall asked me to start giving him injections of morphine. He knew I could do it, since he'd taught me how to give myself my vitamin B-12 shots, and so I was put in charge of the medicine.

One day Dr. Hall asked me how many morphine ampules were left, since he couldn't tell with his poor eyesight. For a split second I realized I could say four instead of six—but I told him there were six. As I watched my father fading before my eyes, I felt no desire to numb my senses with the drug. I wanted to be awake and aware during my last moments with him, and feeling the pain was essential. By avoiding the temptation, I also realized that my problem with the drug was over. I was no longer chained to its anchor.

Just after midnight on March thirty-first, I gave Dad an injection of morphine. He was in agony. Mum and I sat in chairs all night, just watching and waiting, in case he needed anything. At dawn Mum went to the kitchen to make us some tea.

Suddenly Dad lifted his arm, as if he wanted something. I sat next to him and cradled him in my arms. He shivered. Then came a long breath, like a sigh, and it was over. I closed his eyelids and kissed him. "You did it, Dad, you made it . . . it's April first."

It took Mum and me about a year to fully grasp it, and face up to life without him. One way in which I tried to cope was by writing. I took segments of my life and started piecing them together. As I wrote, I felt Dad looking over my shoulder, giving me approval and inspiration. I'll never forget one of the last things he said to me: "Joyce, you get just so many cards to play in life. Don't mess this one up!"

Not long after Dad died I read that Goldie Hawn had lost her father around the same time. I knew immediately how devastating it was for her, because Goldie and I had always talked about our dads—they were alike in many ways. When I heard in the spring of 1983 that "Laugh-In" was being rerun in America, and that there would be a reunion party for the cast in Hollywood, I looked forward to seeing her again.

I was nervous about returning to L.A., having left under such a cloud, but as soon as I heard Henry Gibson's voice on the phone, inviting me to stay with the family in Malibu, I knew I was safe.

Reincarnation

I arrived at Henry's house to find him puttering in his garden. His face appeared through the greenery and he greeted me with flowers in hand while Lois arrived with some grapefruits she'd just picked. They were the same as ever, except for three things—Charlie, Jonny, and Jimmy were all now college age. Thanks to the reruns, they would be seeing "Laugh-In" for the first time.

Henry and I were petrified about the party. We didn't know what to expect. As I walked into the crowded room at Chasen's on the night of the party, it was like a flashback. Television screens all around the room ran "Laugh-In" clips, and out of the crowd came Alan Sues, then Ruth Buzzi, then Dick Martin. Lily Tomlin was there, and Gary Owens, and Ann Elder. Everyone looked remarkably unchanged. We heard from Dick Martin that Dan Rowan sent his regards from Paris, where he lives on a barge.

As I made my way through the crowd, I finally came across George Schlatter, looking as mischievous as ever.

"Hey, Judes, I hear you're writing a book! Are you going to tell about the 'Sock it to me' when your boob popped out of that shrinking dress and went into fifty million homes?"

"You bet, George. I'm also going to tell 'em what C.F.G. really stands for! And do you remember the paint party?"

"*Do* I? You guys ruined a perfectly good cashmere sweater!"

We were all herded together for a group shot. As I smiled for the cameras, only fond memories remained and I felt blessed to have been part of the magic of "Laugh-In."

Later, as I passed one of the many television monitors, I caught sight of myself on the screen, standing between Dan and Dick, wearing a micro-miniskirt. It had been nearly fourteen years since I'd seen an episode of "Laugh-In," and suddenly there I stood, bracing myself for the inevitable onslaught as Dan Rowan offered a last-minute plea on my behalf.

Just this once, gang, let's spare our blameless moppet these unending indignities, to which, Judy, I must say, you have displayed amazing fortitude and endurance. You have held in there no matter what they've done to you and you've taken it all, with never a whimper. . . .

Dan, that's really sweet of you, but the audience is getting bored.
What did you say, Judy?
They're getting bored. You know, bored?
Board?
Yes! (A board hits head from behind.) *Cute, fellas, cute.*
Well, at least it wasn't water. (Two buckets hit from in front.) *Oh, I get it, it was all just a trap, wasn't it?* (Vertical exit—via the trap doors.)

I stood there, transfixed by the sight of it all after so many years. The sketch had an ironic similarity to the pattern of my own life, in which boredom has always led to trouble—and self-destruction. As far back as boarding school, I remember Noreen Bush warning me to be careful. She said I had a knack for "never seeing danger." Over the years I've come to realize how right she was. I'm just an accident looking for a place to happen.

Fortunately, I've always had the ability to laugh at myself in the face of disaster. Sometimes life's tragedies are the very things that help us survive.

I'm an aging Peter Pan, a dowager groupie with a great past ahead of me. And I'm still a clown, laughing on the outside *and*—at last—on the inside.

Index

A

B

Index

Index

Index

Index

Index